Consulting and Evaluation with Nonprofit and Community-Based Organizations

Consulting and Evaluation with Nonprofit and Community-Based Organizations

JUDAH J. VIOLA, PhD
National-Louis University
Chicago, Illinois

SUSAN DVORAK MCMAHON, PhD
DePaul University
Chicago, Illinois

JONES AND BARTLETT PUBLISHERS
Sudbury, Massachusetts
BOSTON   TORONTO   LONDON   SINGAPORE

World Headquarters

Jones and Bartlett Publishers
40 Tall Pine Drive
Sudbury, MA 01776
978-443-5000
info@jbpub.com
www.jbpub.com

Jones and Bartlett Publishers
Canada
6339 Ormindale Way
Mississauga, Ontario L5V 1J2
Canada

Jones and Bartlett Publishers
International
Barb House, Barb Mews
London W6 7PA
United Kingdom

Jones and Bartlett's books and products are available through most bookstores and online booksellers. To contact Jones and Bartlett Publishers directly, call 800-832-0034, fax 978-443-8000, or visit our website, www.jbpub.com.

Substantial discounts on bulk quantities of Jones and Bartlett's publications are available to corporations, professional associations, and other qualified organizations. For details and specific discount information, contact the special sales department at Jones and Bartlett via the above contact information or send an email to specialsales@jbpub.com.

Production Credits
Publisher: Michael Brown
Associate Editor: Megan R. Turner
Production Manager: Julie Champagne Bolduc
Production Assistant: Jessica Steele Newfell
Senior Marketing Manager: Sophie Fleck
Manufacturing and Inventory Control Supervisor: Amy Bacus
Composition: Shawn Girsberger
Cover Design: Scott Moden
Printing and Binding: Malloy, Inc.
Cover Printing: Malloy, Inc.

Library of Congress Cataloging-in-Publication Data
Consulting and evaluation with nonprofit and community-based organizations / edited by Judah J. Viola, Susan Dvorak McMahon.
    p. cm.
Includes bibliographical references and index.
ISBN 978-0-7637-5688-8 (pbk. : alk. paper)
1. Nonprofit organizations. 2. Business consultants. I. Viola, Judah J. II. McMahon, Susan Dvorak
HD2719.15.C66 2010
001—dc22
                        2009013419

6048
Printed in the United States of America
13 12 11 10 09   10 9 8 7 6 5 4 3 2 1

Dedicated to our families who have given tremendous support:

Alina Alexandrovna Sternberg Viola
Donna and James Viola

John, Emily, and Katie McMahon
Frank and Rita Dvorak

Contents

Preface

This resource book is designed to provide the information we have gathered, organized, and synthesized from experienced professionals and diverse written materials to assist early career consultants. For us, consulting work has been one way to stay connected with the schools and community-based organizations that help our communities thrive. Reflecting on our own experiences, reviewing the literature, and engaging in dialogue with practitioners who consult full time has given us an array of useful strategies, tips, and advice to help readers get started with consulting, build a practice, and do effective work. Chapters 1–7 of the text delve into the nuts and bolts of building a consulting business. Chapters 8–16 cover the in-depth processes involved in consultation, challenges and benefits you may encounter, and advice about the consulting cycle from start to finish. All contributing authors have substantial consultation experience and have taken different paths to achieve success.

The intended audience for this guidebook includes all people seeking guidance regarding consulting in the public sector. Specifically, this may include students and professionals with a background in the social sciences (e.g., psychology [community, clinical, applied social, and industrial organizational], sociology, social work, anthropology, policy analysis, evaluation, behavioral sciences), education, nonprofit management, urban planning, public health, human services, and public service, as well as government or nonprofit employees and a host of other allied professions. Regardless of your background, we hope our focus on discussing and illustrating the processes with many examples will help you become an effective and successful consultant with community-based organizations. There are not a large number of people doing this work; however, the consultants we have spoken with (more than 50) have found an untapped market that stretches far beyond the amount of work they can provide.

Although there are written resources available to beginning consultants (see Appendix 1-1, Annotated Bibliography), there are few guides that incorporate the range of information needed to begin a consulting practice or start one's own consulting business. Prior to this book's publication, the information needed to start a sound consulting practice was spread across numerous government agencies (e.g., IRS, secretary of state, department of labor, chamber of commerce), private Web sites (e.g., private law or accounting firms offering services or advice), and books. There are books that are helpful for general business information ("how to" books about starting a business or working for oneself), texts that focus on the theory and practice of consulting/evaluation, and texts that focus on research methods. None of these written sources, however, are tailored to the specific niche of social science consultants desiring collaborative work with the nonprofit/public sector. We believe this book will help walk you through the steps of starting and building a consulting practice with nonprofit organizations, as well as provide you with the advice, examples, and tools to be successful.

Acknowledgments

We would like to thank the numerous experts who contributed to this book; without your input, this book would not have been possible. We appreciate the time and generosity from busy consultants who provided expertise through participating in interviews, completing surveys, and providing suggestions for less experienced consultants. It takes courage to reflect upon and share mistakes so that others may learn from them. Your shared experiences and thoughtful advice added richness and depth to the guidance we provide in the first section of this book (Chapters 1–7).

We also want to express gratitude to the 20 contributing authors who wrote Chapters 8–16. It was a pleasure to work with each of you, and readers will benefit from your perspectives, tools, and experiences. You provide examples, detail, and context to the work and demonstrate how a consultant can put the contents of this book into action to achieve a successful consulting career.

In addition we would like to thank those who served as readers and informal advisors while this book was in its various forms: Jean Haley, Bradley Olson, India Viola, Ronald Crouch, Natalya Gnedko, Katie McDonald, Nora Murphy, and Peter Hubbard all gave substantial suggestions that improved the book. Finally, thanks to our publishing team at Jones and Bartlett: Cathleen Sether, Jeremy Spiegel, Megan Turner, Lisa Gordon, Amy Flagg, Julie Bolduc, and Kimberly Potvin.

Introduction

Potential careers for professionals in the nonprofit sector and the social sciences are diverse and often untraditional. As community psychologists, we aim to use our training in the social sciences to help organizations evaluate and improve upon the services they provide to build safer, more connected, and healthier communities. We juggle multiple roles in an academic setting, including research, teaching, and service, and we also enjoy opportunities to connect with community-based organizations in consulting roles. Working as consultants with nonprofits, social service providers, schools, churches, and/or government agencies can be fulfilling for those with aspirations to become agents of social change. However, few classes or textbooks guide potential consultants through the process of forming a sound practice with the proper foundation to succeed, both in being true to their values and achieving financial solvency.

The purpose of this guidebook is to share findings from our investigation of what it takes to get started, be successful, and thrive in the consulting world. In addition, we hope to use the wisdom of today's professionals to make it easier for beginning consultants to avoid unnecessary setbacks and face the necessary challenges with our eyes open. Learning from others' mistakes and successes may help us better serve the community as we become tomorrow's consultants. However, before we go any further, it is important to understand what we mean by consulting.

CONSULTING: A WORKING DEFINITION

Consulting is a vague term often used but not always easily understood. Broadly stated, it involves using your expertise (in this case, your experience and understanding of experimental methods, statistics, and/or topical knowledge) to help clients (at times referred to as *community partners*) achieve their goals. Geoffrey Bellman, author of *Consultant's Calling* (1990), described it as helping clients narrow the gap between what they now have and what they want or need. Peter Block (2000) distinguishes consulting from management by describing a consultant as a person in a position to influence an organization but who has no direct power to implement changes, whereas a manager has direct responsibility over the actions of other employees or organizational decision-making.

Consultants are often topical specialists, but the title of *consultant* does not identify the background of a professional as is connoted by the title *accountant* or *lawyer*. In contrast, internal consultants are permanent employees of a company and may conduct evaluation or research projects for different departments within the agency. For the purposes of this book, we are focused on the necessary steps to get started as an independent *external* consultant hired on a project-by-project basis.

While much of the thought processes and career preparation discussed here will be relevant for internal consulting as well, independent external consulting will remain the central focus of the text. We use the term "independent" to emphasize the lack of institutional structure behind the work. In other words, we are not referring to consultants who are employed to consult as part of a university, think tank, or large business, even though some of the ideas presented are likely to be useful to consultants across a wide range of settings.

Becoming an independent external consultant is as simple as declaring yourself one. There is no certification or accreditation required, and no board review (this may change, as there is an effort to create licensure requirements within some disciplines). However, according to Carol Lukas (1998), consultants who primarily focus on working with nonprofits (as opposed to profit-driven companies) tend to have a sense of mission about their work and are deeply committed to benefiting the community. Therefore, when working with or collaborating with nonprofits, one of the consultant's main tasks is to try to add value and build capacity within the organizations with which they partner. For example, a typical service might be teaming with employees at a community clinic to write a grant to expand services for parenting classes for young expectant mothers and fathers. The consultant may also aid in designing and/or carrying out process or outcome evaluations of the parenting classes.

The reasons that nonprofits hire consultants can vary. They may want to bring in someone with expertise that they lack on staff (for example, data analysis). They may want someone with experience to build capacity among their own staff (for example, evaluation). At other times even if they have capacity to conduct a project in-house they may choose to bring in an external consultant to provide some new fresh ideas or a more objective perspective that might hold more credibility with board members or funders.

The role of the consultant can vary, such as helping organizations evaluate existing services, develop new services, build infrastructure, adapt to organizational change, or gain funding. Consultants may work on issues such as food security, affordable housing, job training, education, disability services, substance abuse treatment and prevention, public health, immigrant advocacy services, or domestic violence. These are just a few examples of the variety of possibilities, and, if any of them sound compelling to you, then starting out as a consultant may be the right move for you.

Many independent consultants serve as independent contractors for other consultants or companies or subcontract portions of their projects out to others. Some find it useful to distinguish between contracting and consulting work. Alan Weiss (2004) does this as a starting point for his views on value-based fees. Contracting is based on prevailing wage/salary rates and the evaluative process of whether to "hire out" a project or do it in-house. Consulting is the professional skill that marries breadth of experience with specificity of expertise that is virtually impossible to find, or even cultivate, in-house.

HOW THIS BOOK CAME TO BE

Judah Viola: During the fall of 2003, while in the thick of my doctoral studies in community psychology, I was thinking hard about my potential career choices. I knew that my options included academic research, teaching college courses, or "applied work." I also knew that one of the activities of an applied community psychologist or "practitioner" involves consultation with community institutions, nonprofit organizations, and government agencies. In fact, I had already done some statistical analyses for a local counseling center and teamed up with another graduate student to evaluate a school-based prevention program. However, I did not have a clear understanding of the processes involved in becoming a "bona-fide consultant." So, one reason for starting this process was self-serving because researching this topic has allowed me to learn more about one of my career options. Over the past six years I have continued to learn from experienced professionals and to use my skills gained as a community psychologist to build my client base and maintain a steady part-time consulting practice.

Susan Dvorak McMahon: When Judah proposed his idea to write a guidebook on consulting, I thought it was a creative and interesting project that would provide a needed resource, especially for students and those new to the consulting world. Because I teach a graduate course in program evaluation and have engaged in several consulting and evaluation projects with schools and nonprofit organizations, I was excited about this project. It was a pleasure to guide Judah through the process of conceptualizing the guidebook, gathering information, analyzing data, and writing. Next, as we continued to work toward publishing the book, I moved from a supervisory role to a collaborative partner role. We decided to build upon Judah's initial efforts of illustrating the detailed practical aspects of building a consulting practice (which became the first part of the book) to include case studies, projects, and stories from experts from a variety of settings doing different types of consulting work (which became the second part of the book). We are pleased to have so many experts represented in this text, and we hope it provides a useful guide to you as you engage in consulting and evaluation work.

OVERVIEW

The first section of this book consists of seven chapters devoted to describing the nuts and bolts of starting and building a consulting practice. These chapters are based upon a review of books and Web sites, surveys of 30 professional consultants, and in-depth interviews of 15 expert consultants, conducted by Judah Viola. In Chapter 1, we discuss reasons why you should be a consultant as well as some of the challenges you may face. In Chapter 2, we discuss the resources, personal characteristics, knowledge, and skills you will need to be successful and how to prepare yourself to be an effective consultant. In Chapter 3, we elaborate on when to start an independent consulting business and the pros and cons of beginning at different points in your career. In Chapter 4, we describe decisions related to what kind of business you might want to build, such as different organizational structures, services, and strategic planning. Chapter 5 illustrates the necessary steps to make your business official, and Chapter 6, co-written with Shaunti Knauth and Courtney Cowgill, relates to marketing and networking. Finally, in Chapter 7, we discuss issues related to running your business, such as setting a pricing strategy and submitting proposals. Now, we would like to tell you a little more about the surveys and interviews that provided the basis for the first part of the book.

Surveys and Interviews

Participants for both the interviews and surveys were identified through an Internet search of Web sites for consulting companies, professional societies (e.g., e-mail discussion lists for the Society for Community Research and Action, the American Evaluation Association, and the Society for Consulting Psychology), and advice from professors and colleagues.

Thirty professional consultants from 19 states responded to the survey, with information about their work, contracting methods, and perspectives on consulting. Sixty-three percent of respondents described their consulting work as being full time, and 36% of them described their work as part time. They reported that their company's annual budgets ranged from under $100,000 to several million dollars. Their level of experience ranged from four to thirty-eight years. The rates they charged ranged from sliding scales as low as $25 (not including pro-bono work) to $275 an hour, and daily rates reported ranged from $500 to $2500. The surveys provided many of the useful tips and strategies found within this book.

Semi-structured (40–80 minute) interviews were conducted with 15 consultants who serve primarily nonprofit or governmental organizations. The key informant interviews allowed in-depth responses to questions about the expert's career progression, reasons for getting started in consulting, descriptions of recent projects, common challenges, the level of commitment required to build and sustain their consulting businesses, and advice for people entering the field. The interviews were audiotaped and transcribed, and summaries were presented to the interviewees as a means to "member check" or verify the accuracy of facts as well as interpretations.

The key informant interview sample consisted of eight men and seven women. They ranged in experience with their consulting practices from four to thirty-eight years, and are based in nine states across the United States. Interviewees consisted of two professors who consult as sole proprietors on a part-time basis, three full-time sole proprietors, one graduate student, one member of a partnership, one member of a nonprofit foundation, three proprietors of limited liability companies, and four owners of subchapter-S corporations (explanations of each business structure are included in Chapter 4).

In summary, the surveys provided an overview of a broad sample of consultants and their practices, while the interviews provided more in-depth qualitative information about every facet of starting out in consulting. Throughout Chapters 1–7, interview and survey responses are paraphrased and quoted.

The second section of this book (Chapters 8–16) includes a diverse array of informative contributions that illustrate the processes involved in consultation, challenges and benefits you may encounter, and advice from start to finish of the consultation cycle. All contributing authors are experts with substantial consultation experience who have taken different paths to achieve success. It has been a pleasure to review these contributions and we trust that you will benefit from their stories and words of wisdom as you refer to the chapters that are most relevant to your work. The contributing authors provide many specific examples from their work, and have graciously shared tools they use, which can be found in appendices at the end of each chapter. In the following pages, we briefly highlight each of their contributions to give you an overview of the issues, dilemmas, and advice that are discussed in each chapter.

Dale Rose and Elna Hall illustrate challenges that arise during the initial phases of a project, with particular emphasis on managing client relationships, in *A Client-Centered Approach to Winning and Losing Deals: What to Do If You Get the Project (And What to Do If You Don't)*. They provide concrete and useful strategies to turn lost deals into future wins, align project work with your values and professional vision, and create action plans for difficult situations. They outline reasons to begin planning the work when you land the job, rather than jumping right in, and give helpful tips regarding the contracting process. Rose and Hall also help you think through challenging situations, such as what to do if a project doesn't fit perfectly with your expertise or interests, is too big, or doesn't meet your financial standards.

Kathleen Dowell takes you through an entire project, step-by-step, using a real example from her own experience in *From Start to Finish: A Typical Evaluation Project*. Dowell describes getting the contract, planning the evaluation, collecting the data, reporting the results, and recapping lessons learned. Dowell's participatory approach highlights the creation of an advisory board, development of a logic model, and a multipronged approach that utilizes both qualitative and quantitative methods in assessing context, implementation, and outcomes. She provides many helpful tools, including an elaborate logic model of a large project, a table illustrating the connections among evaluation questions, methods, data sources, timelines, and several instruments that were used in the study (e.g., surveys, focus group questions, interview guides). Dowell also includes the executive summary of her report for this project as an example for your reference. Finally, she illustrates lessons learned at multiple stages of the process.

Gary Harper, Maureen Blaha, and Carlos Samaniego collaborated to write a chapter from both the consultant's and the community-based organization's perspectives in *Developing and Maintaining Long-Term Consulting Relationships*. They discuss benefits and challenges of long-term consulting relationships and the developmental stages of researching, selecting, and beginning relationships with clients/consultants. In addition, they describe essential elements in maintaining mutually beneficial consulting relationships, such as relationship building, responsiveness, resource allocation, remaining focused, and re-evaluating.

Doug Cellar, Gary Harper, and Leah Neubauer discuss the evolution and creation of a consulting center, from generating ideas to developing and submitting a proposal, gaining approval, establishing an advisory committee, and marketing in *Consulting with Small Community-Based Nonprofit Organizations: Insights and Understandings.* Cellar and colleagues describe the benefits and challenges of working within a university-based setting and provide a glimpse into graduate student experiences with consulting. They describe the passion of small nonprofit organizations, developing partnerships, streams of funding, boards of directors, project scope, new areas, and planning for the future. Cellar and colleagues highlight personal experiences, finding balance in doing work that you are really interested in and remaining dispassionate enough to provide an external perspective to your clients.

As a consultant, you can specialize in specific types of work and use particular theoretical models to guide your work. In *Capacity Building with Faith-Based and Community Organizations: Lessons Learned from the Compassion Kansas Initiative,* Sarah Jolley, Scott Wituk, Tara Gregory, Maaskelah Thomas, and Greg Meissen describe a large-scale project using a capacity-building framework. They describe the framework, working with small nonprofit organizations, steps and strategies to assist faith-based community organizations, and lessons learned. They include helpful tips in getting funding through grants, contracts, foundations, and workshops. They describe a statewide initiative in which they enhanced knowledge, provided training and technical assistance, assisted organizations in seeking funding, and examined outcomes. Jolley and colleagues provide example tools that will assist you with organizing and tracking tasks, such as the memorandum of agreement, meeting agreement form, organizational capacity assessment survey, organizational assessment profile, and technical assistance form. While their chapter is built upon their experiences working with small faith-based organizations, the tools and advice provided translate well to working with a variety of community organizations or nonprofits.

Pennie Foster-Fishman and Kevin Ford use a different theoretical perspective to guide their consulting work that they describe in *Improving Service Delivery and Effectiveness: Taking an Organizational Learning Approach to Consulting.* They discuss ways in which organizations change and develop to improve organizational effectiveness through iterative cycles of data collection, knowledge sharing, and collective action. Foster-Fishman and Ford also provide a case study, based on their consultation experiences, to illustrate how to drive change using an organizational learning frame. They describe a series of steps and strategies in the context of this case study, including identifying problems, building team readiness, creating a vision of opportunities, developing strategies to overcome obstacles, planning group action, and building an active, vibrant membership. Tips for consultants focus on systems thinking, participatory processes, and leadership development.

Jon Miles and Steve Howe take yet a different tack in *Consulting in Public Policy Settings*, as they found a niche in public policy consulting. They provide a map that may help you navigate through policy work. They describe the roles of advocacy and nongovernmental organizations that aim to influence public policy and how the consultant's role differs depending on government level, function, and process. Miles and Howe guide you through political challenges and illustrate how issues such as timing and communication often play a more crucial role in policy consulting than the types of consulting described in the rest of the book. They share numerous examples from their work to illustrate their points and lessons they have learned.

Andrea Solarz discusses her approach to grant writing and offers knowledge, skills, and experiences that facilitate success in *Grant Writing for Consultants 101*. She describes the process of writing a grant proposal, from getting the job, mapping out the idea, and understanding what the funder wants to actually writing the grant. She highlights networks, knowledge, critical thinking, communication skills, and collaboration as important determinants that have contributed to her success as a grant writer.

In *The Path to Independent Consulting*, Dawn Hanson Smart describes her personal experiences in consulting from her graduate school years—through working with small nonprofits and government agencies and part-time consulting—to her current position as a full-time consultant working within a small firm. Smart speaks thoughtfully about her decision-making processes during each job transition, how her personal characteristics and work style contribute to the types of choices she made, and lessons she learned along the way with regard to consulting. Reading her chapter will help you in the self-assessment process and encourage you to think about what opportunities might be available and realistic for you.

Consultants use theoretical frameworks to guide their work, specialize in different niches, and take a variety of career paths, so there are a range of experiences to learn from and many options to create your own style, tools, and path to success. Although each chapter brings unique insights, there are also similar themes across chapters, such as the importance of building relationships, contracting, and setting clear goals and expectations. We encourage you to read about a variety of theories and guidelines, review the resources and tools provided, try strategies that fit with your style, and create your own niche as you begin or continue to develop your consulting practice with nonprofits.

About the Authors

Judah Viola, PhD, manages an independent consulting practice/sole proprietorship that specializes in needs assessment, program development, program evaluation, strategic planning, community building, and collaborative community research. Recent clients have included public school systems, museum and art institutions, social service agencies, and community development organizations. Dr. Viola also holds the positions of assistant professor of psychology and codirector of the community psychology PhD program at National-Louis University in Chicago, Illinois, where he teaches undergraduate and graduate courses in psychology, program evaluation, and consulting. He earned his BA in history and psychology from the University of Wisconsin–Madison and his MA and PhD in community psychology from DePaul University.

Susan Dvorak McMahon, PhD, is a professor in clinical and community psychology at DePaul University where she teaches program evaluation, community psychology, and thesis/dissertation seminars. Dr. McMahon is currently director of DePaul's doctoral program in community psychology and chair of the University Institutional Review Board. She is also chair of the Society for Community Research and Action's (Division 27 of APA) Council of Education Programs. Dr. McMahon often integrates consultation and evaluation with her research, and most of her work has focused on assisting the Chicago public school system to better serve at-risk urban youth. Areas of interest include risk and protective factors at multiple levels, inclusive and effective educational approaches that contribute to positive learning environments, and violence prevention. Dr. McMahon has written more than 40 publications and given more than 100 presentations. Her research has been featured in a variety of media outlets, including network television and a documentary. Dr. McMahon received her BS from the University of Iowa and her MA and PhD from DePaul University.

Contributors

Maureen Blaha has worked on behalf of youth and families her entire professional career as a teacher, an advocate, and a leader. As the executive director of the National Runaway Switchboard (NRS), she leads a team of more than 150 staff and volunteers who work to keep America's runaway and at-risk youth safe and off the streets. Prior to NRS, Blaha served America's youth in various organizations and capacities including the Children's Home and Aid Society of Illinois and the Massachusetts Office for Children. She also is the cocreator of the *Great American Wagon Pull: Families Pulling Together to Prevent Child Abuse* and has served as a member of the (Illinois) Governor's Healthy Families Task Force, the National Family Support Roundtable Leadership Council, and the Illinois Missing Children's Task Force. She received a bachelor's degree in education from Northern Illinois University.

Doug Cellar, PhD, received his doctorate in industrial/organizational psychology from the University of Akron and is currently on the faculty at DePaul University. Dr. Cellar's primary area of research has been in the area of work motivation. More recently he has been studying the relationships between personality, motivation, social support, coping, well-being, and health outcomes for people living with chronic hepatitis C (HCV) and those co-infected with HCV and HIV. Dr. Cellar is also conducting action research with the Chicago Department of Public Health Viral Hepatitis Task Force. He began his career in consulting in 1978 and has worked with numerous organizations in the public and private sector. He has also worked with small nonprofit community-based organizations as codirector of the DePaul Center for Community and Organization Development.

Courtney Cowgill, MA, CPA, CMA, CIA, CFE, has worked as a finance professional for more than thirty years, filling roles that include chief financial officer, consultant, member of the Colorado Lottery Commission, and National President of the American Society of Women Accountants. She considers networking an integral part of all her roles, and she is frequently asked to be a public speaker on how to network. She can help just about anyone learn to connect, and she still finds time to ride horses with her husband at their home in Colorado.

Kathleen Dowell, PhD, is currently self-employed as a program evaluation consultant, working primarily with state and local government agencies, universities, foundations, and community-based nonprofit organizations. She focuses most of her work on issues that affect children and families, including youth development, child abuse prevention, adolescent pregnancy prevention, substance abuse treatment, education, and teacher and curricular improvement. Prior to becoming an independent evaluator, she worked for a large research consulting firm in Fairfax, Virginia, where she managed a large multi-site evaluation study. She has also held several research positions for the state of Maryland in the Governor's Office for Children, Youth, and Families. She has a BA in psychology from University of Maryland Baltimore County, an MA in clinical psychology from Loyola College, and a PhD in policy sciences from University of Maryland Baltimore County.

J. Kevin Ford, PhD, is a professor of psychology at Michigan State University. His major research interests involve improving training effectiveness through efforts to advance our understanding of training needs assessment, design, evaluation, and transfer. Dr. Ford also concentrates on building continuous learning and improvement orientations within organizations. He is an active consultant with private industry and the public sector on training, leadership, and organizational change issues. He is a Fellow of the American Psychological Association and the Society of Industrial and Organizational Psychology. He received his BS in psychology from the University of Maryland and his MA and PhD in psychology from The Ohio State University. Further information about Kevin and his research and consulting activities can be found at http://www.io.psy.msu.edu/jkf.

Pennie G. Foster-Fishman, PhD, is a professor in the Department of Psychology at Michigan State University. She received her PhD in organizational/community psychology from the University of Illinois at Chicago. Her research interests primarily emphasize systems change, particularly how organizational, interorganizational, and community systems can improve to better meet the needs of children, youth, and families. Toward this end, she has investigated human service delivery reform, multiple stakeholder collaboration, coalition development, community organizing, and resident empowerment as vehicles for systems change. She has also worked with a variety of public sector agencies, nonprofit, and community and state-wide coalitions, aiming to improve their organizational capacity and the efficacy of their programmatic efforts.

Tara D. Gregory, PhD, is a community and organizational researcher for the Center for Community Support and Research at Wichita State University. Dr. Gregory has 20 years of experience in consultation and research related to youth empowerment, leadership development, substance abuse prevention, organizational development, and community mobilization/development. She currently facilitates a statewide intervention research project focused on multi-site evaluation of organizational capacity building and youth leadership development in afterschool programs. Additionally, Dr. Gregory acts as a consultant to a coalition of high school-aged youth who work to promote the positive contributions of youth in communities and build the capacity of other youth empowerment programs across the state. Dr. Gregory has a PhD in community psychology from Wichita State University.

Elna Moore Hall, PhD, is an independent human capital consultant specializing in leadership, succession management, and human resources best practices. For more than a decade she has worked with a wide variety of clients to align their people strategy with their business objectives. She consults with Fortune 500 and nonprofit organizations across such industries as telecommunications, financial services, technology, and aviation. She served for several years in organization development management roles at Motorola and as a senior talent and organization consultant with Hewitt Associates. Her research has appeared in the *Journal of Business and Psychology* and *Performance in Practice*, a journal of the American Society for Training and Development.

Gary W. Harper, PhD, MPH, is a professor in the Department of Psychology, director of the Master of Public Health program, and co-director of the Center for Community and Organization Development at DePaul University. Dr. Harper has more than 20 years of experience conducting community-based research and consultation projects with non-profit agencies that provide health promotion services to adolescents, with a primary focus on HIV/AIDS-related organizations. His consultation work has been conducted with local, national, and international agencies and organizations throughout the United States and in Kenya. The majority of Dr. Harper's consultation work has been focused on the development and evaluation of youth-oriented prevention programs that promote the health and well-being of adolescents, with a focus on runaway/homeless youth, urban youth of color, gay/bisexual youth, and youth living with HIV. Dr. Harper has published extensively on community-university evaluation and research partnerships and coedited *Empowerment and Participatory Evaluation in Community Intervention: Multiple Benefits.*

Steven Howe, PhD, is professor and head of psychology at the University of Cincinnati. He joined the faculty in 1993 as an associate professor after having spent 13 years doing grant and contract research at the UC Institute for Policy Research. Dr. Howe is a community and social psychologist specializing in policy research and evaluation. He also does program planning with nonprofits and governments and teaches statistics at the undergraduate and graduate levels. His enduring interest has been the causes and consequences of urban poverty. In the area of housing, Dr. Howe was a member of the Ohio Housing Research Group, which studied the impact of suburbanization on central city decline. He has prepared numerous policy studies for the city of Cincinnati on housing planning, neighborhood development, and barriers to fair housing. At the state level, Dr. Howe has provided research support to efforts to expand Medicaid coverage to the working poor and to persons with disability through Medicaid Buy-In. He has also conducted evaluation research on behalf of the Ohio Department of Job and Family Services and the Ohio Rehabilitation Services Commission. He is currently consulting with the Southwest Ohio Workforce Investment Board.

Sarah Jolley is a research associate at the Center for Community Support and Research, Wichita State University. Sarah has more than 5 years of experience designing, facilitating, and researching capacity building for nonprofits and other faith-based and community organizations. She has also been involved in the development and implementation of several mini-grant processes and has experience with various research-related activities, including surveys, focus groups, and grant writing. In addition to her work at the Center for Community Support and Research, Sarah is a student in the community psychology doctoral program at Wichita State University and anticipates receiving her PhD in 2010.

Shaunti Knauth, PhD, is the associate director of university assessment at National-Louis University in Chicago, Illinois. She has worked in educational evaluation and research for over a decade, always with the goal of building collaboration and knowledge among stakeholders. Her consulting clients have included universities, foundations, and educational associations. Shaunti completed her doctorate in education at the University of Chicago.

Greg Meissen, PhD, is the director of the Center for Community Support and Research and professor of psychology at Wichita State University. Dr. Meissen has been at Wichita State University since 1980 where he has served in a number of roles, including helping found and being the first director of the doctoral program in community psychology. In 1985, he brought the newly founded Self-Help Network to Wichita State University, where it has grown into the nationally recognized Center for Community Support and Research. He was the inaugural recipient of the WSU Award for Community Research and has received the Wichita State University Alumni Recognition Faculty Award. Dr. Meissen has received federal, state, and foundation grants from the Administration for Children and Families, National Institute of Mental Health, Center for Mental Health Services Research, the Kansas Health Foundation, and many others. He has published research articles in such outlets as the *New England Journal of Medicine*, *American Journal of Community Psychology*, *Psychiatric Services*, and the *Journal of Applied Behavioral Science* and has made more than 200 presentations at international, national, and regional scientific and professional conferences.

Jonathan C. Miles, PhD, is the director of Searchlight Consulting, LLC. He works on policy issues pertaining to child health and well-being with a focus on the promotion of mental health and prevention of mental disorders. Dr. Miles has authored or coauthored reports and articles on many topics, including prevention of school violence and bullying; risk and protective factors for Latino infants and families; the beneficial effects of fathers' and mothers' post-divorce parenting on children's mental health; and a meta-analysis of adolescent substance use among lesbian, gay, and bisexual youth. Dr. Miles has worked as a Society for Research in Child Development (SRCD) congressional fellow in the office of Senator Tom Harkin, where he advised the senator on health and early childhood education issues and developed policies to improve the health and well-being of children and families. Dr. Miles also worked as an SRCD Executive Branch Fellow at the Administration for Children and Families in the Office of Planning, Research, and Evaluation, where he helped evaluate the Head Start program. Dr. Miles received his PhD from Arizona State University in clinical psychology.

Leah C. Neubauer, MA, is associate director, Adolescent Community Health Research Group, and program manager, Master of Public Health Program, DePaul University. Ms. Neubauer has more than 10 years of experience in research, practice, and consultation related to domestic and international HIV/AIDS prevention, women's health, organizational development, financial budgeting, curriculum development, and evaluation. Ms. Neubauer currently leads the evaluation efforts of a CDC-funded "Waiting Room Intervention" in Chicago Department of Public Health Specialty (STD) clinics. Ms. Neubauer leads federally funded capacity building efforts in Kenya, and as the executive director of the *Rafiki Collaborative* leads efforts that assist in the development, adaptation, implementation, and evaluation of programs and services for communities impacted by HIV and AIDS. Ms. Neubauer serves as an ongoing consultant to several community-based organizations throughout the state of Illinois. Ms. Neubauer has a master's degree in interdisciplinary studies, with emphasis on multicultural/organizational communication and community psychology from DePaul University.

Dale S. Rose, PhD, is president of 3D Group, a Berkeley, California firm dedicated to helping organizations of all sizes enhance individual and organizational effectiveness through assessment-based interventions. Dr. Rose works with national and local nonprofits as well as major corporations to identify and develop leaders of all levels. He has previously published on topics related to human resources best practices, leadership assessment, and program evaluation as well as authored numerous commercial assessments of leadership ability and employee effectiveness. He received his doctoral degree in industrial and organizational psychology from DePaul University with a minor in organizational effectiveness technologies.

Carlos Samaniego is a prevention counselor for the YMSM (young men who have sex with men) Program at Project VIDA in Chicago. Mr. Samaniego was a participant in Project VIDA's Young Men's Program in 1998 where he learned about HIV/AIDS, domestic violence, sexually transmitted infections, and coming out issues. After being an active participant and volunteer in the program, he was hired by Project VIDA to work with the community at varying levels to address issues faced by gay, bisexual, transgender, questioning (LGBTQ) youth. Currently, Mr. Samaniego is the prevention counselor at Project VIDA who works with young men under the age of 25 who identify as LGBTQ or who do not identify at all but have sex with men, in order to assist them with creating the changes needed to prevent HIV. He also coordinates the agency's gay pride events/activities and other functions in order to make the community aware of the many different services at Project VIDA, while also handling fundraisers and events that acquire funds for the agency. In addition, Mr. Samaniego has been involved as a partner in National Latino/a Lesbian and Gay Organization's Avanzando and Horizontes programs providing technical assistance to community-based organizations in the Midwest.

Dawn Hanson Smart, MS, is senior associate with Clegg & Associates in Seattle, Washington. Her work spans more than 20 years of evaluation, planning, and facilitation experience with nonprofit, government, and philanthropic organizations in a broad spectrum of fields. Ms. Smart is a primary partner in The Evaluation Forum, a collaboration created to build internal evaluation capacity in community agencies and their funders through publications, training, technical assistance, and coaching. She is one of six consultants in the country available to provide training for United Ways and their funded agencies. She also is a member of the training team available through NeighborWorks America to provide training and coaching for community development organizations using its Success Measures evaluation system. Ms. Smart has collaborated on three evaluation publications and published articles in evaluation and planning journals. She received a BA from Antioch College and an MS from the University of Washington in Seattle.

Andrea L. Solarz, PhD, has worked as a consultant for behavioral health policy, research, and action since 1998. Much of her consulting work involves writing grant proposals on such topics as education research, HIV/AIDS prevention, adolescent health, and violence prevention. Previously, she held several public policy and analyst positions in Washington, DC, including the American Psychological Association and the Institute of Medicine. Currently, she is working part-time as director of research initiatives for the National Academy of Education. She received her PhD in ecological/community psychology from Michigan State University. Dr. Solarz is a Fellow of the American Psychological Association and the American Educational Research Association, and a past president of the Society for Community Research and Action, Division 27 (Community Psychology) of the American Psychological Association.

Maaskelah Thomas, PhD, is community development coordinator at the Center for Community Support and Research at Wichita State University. Dr. Thomas has worked for more than 20 years with community-serving organizations and agencies building, developing, and sustaining partnerships to leverage resources between community agencies, organizations, businesses, schools and colleges, civic groups, and citizens. Throughout her career, Dr. Thomas has assisted in building the capacity of communities through facilitating civic involvement and lifelong learning opportunities that have empowered individuals, families, and neighborhoods. Dr. Thomas holds a PhD in human and organizational development from Fielding Graduate University. A scholar–practitioner, Dr. Thomas' research interests focus on capacity building and strengthening for culturally based human service organizations.

Scott Wituk, PhD, is research coordinator at the Center for Community Support and Research at Wichita State University. Dr. Wituk has more than 10 years of experience conducting research with community coalitions, nonprofits, self-help groups, faith-based organizations, and community movements. Dr. Wituk has an extensive background in mixed methodologies, conducting research studies using qualitative and quantitative methods to better understand community leadership, afterschool programs, mental health consumer-run organizations, nonprofits, and self-help groups. He has worked with a variety of community populations, including mental health consumers, youth, people with developmental disabilities, and community leaders. He has published more than 25 peer-reviewed research articles and book chapters on these topics.

Chapter 1

Before You Begin

Judah Viola and Susan D. McMahon

WHY SHOULD YOU BE A CONSULTANT? (FIVE REASONS)

There are many interesting reasons why people choose a consulting career. One of the appeals of consulting is that it allows people to learn about a variety of topics and populations. One day you could be conducting research on access to health care, and another day you could be learning about employment barriers for immigrants. This variety keeps the work interesting and challenging. Yet, there are many other factors that draw people to consulting. Elaine Biech in her 1998 book, *The Business of Consulting*, wrote,

> I have always said it was because I am a lousy employee. I do not like to be told what to do; I like to march to the toot of my own saxophone; I like to take risks; I want to work during the hours I choose, not on someone else's time clock; I want to express my creativity; and I prefer to control my own destiny. (pg. 7)

When we asked today's professionals why they became consultants, they each had lengthy, multifaceted reasons for choosing consulting for their current career. In this chapter, we present five themes that emerged from fifteen interviews as the most important reasons for becoming a consultant and sticking with it. See if they sound convincing to you.

1. Seeing the Impact of Your Work

There are few better professional rewards for consultants than observing organizations they've partnered with thrive during and after their collaborations. Consulting work feels worthwhile when you have a role in the

1

improvement of organizations or their programs in the real world. Michael Morris, a professor and part-time independent consultant, explained that the draw of consulting for him comes from the opportunity to have a positive influence in a context outside of academics. He explained that consulting provides an opportunity to interact with people from a variety of organizations whose work he finds inherently interesting. He sees his consulting work as a way of contributing to the betterment of society. While progress is not always visible or quick, consultants across the board cite being able to make a difference as a key reason for getting into and remaining in the field.

2. Broadening and Enhancing Your Professional Life

In addition to being intellectually stimulating, consulting with a variety of organizations requires that you learn continuously. The work is too contextually based to just bring the same solutions to each new situation. Several consultants shared that consulting work forces them to look into and even develop expertise on topics they would not otherwise consider. While the job can be frustrating at times, it keeps your professional life from stagnating. In addition, it offers you a chance to grow and help others (students and clients) develop professionally. Morris finds that the practical experiences serve as valuable teaching resources, giving him greater credibility teaching courses in consulting because he has a wealth of examples to draw upon when answering students' questions.

3. The Flexibility to Work Wherever You Choose

A unique characteristic of consulting is that it offers you the opportunity to work on site with clients, from your own home, in an office, or in transit. Maryann Durland, who holds the full-time position of president for a small consulting company, made a choice to be available to take care of her children and did not want to relocate the family for work. Due to this priority of spending time at home and the limited number of desirable academic positions available in the area, Maryann found that starting a consulting business was the best route for her. Now Maryann "loves life" being the boss, taking charge of work and life at home, feeling free to determine when, where, and how to go about getting the job done. Patricia Kelly, MPP, also the president of a small company, knew that she wanted to work from home; the office environment was not as conducive for her to complete her best work. She explained that she loves people but needs to unwind and replenish herself in her own space. Among consultants living in big cities, their choice to work from home means saving both the time and aggravation of having to fight rush hour traffic. About 60% of the consultants we heard from started consulting from home. Then, depending on how this option fit their lifestyle and workload, some chose to rent office space at various points during their careers.

4. Working for Yourself

Several key informants brought up a variety of benefits associated with working for themselves above and beyond working at home. They cited everything from choosing which projects to take on, to determining their hours and how much to bill. Consultants appreciate their ability to set their own work hours to fit their unique and complex lives.

Melanie Hwalek had envisioned from the outset that she could carve out a career as a full-time evaluation consultant. She finds the work freeing and challenging. Hwalek noted that she has found that stability and independent security increased for her with time, and she believes it is ultimately better to work for yourself than work for someone else (e.g., "you know you won't be fired tomorrow"). According to another full-time consultant, Michael Wyland, he and his business partner were not enjoying their positions and felt underutilized, so they decided to create a private consulting company. Several consultants reported liking the personal empowerment and control they have over basic decisions compared to when they were working for others. Even if you will be working long hours, there is a psychological and real advantage to being independent, making your own decisions, and setting your own schedule. There are other advantages as well, such as not needing to get permission or complete paperwork to order needed tools or supplies, or more importantly having the ultimate say over which projects to end up pursuing or passing on.

5. Clear Indicators of Success

As people with an appreciation for evidence-based decision-making, informants discussed the benefits of clear markers of successful consulting. Andrea Solarz, PhD, who works for herself, explained that another nice thing she appreciates about consulting is that you are not taken for granted. "If people want to utilize your services again, then you are probably doing okay," she says. Every time a new client calls who has been referred from a recent client can be seen as an affirmation that the work you are doing is appreciated and has been found to be useful. In addition, some of the recommendations you offer clients can be implemented immediately and tested in the real world. This quickness and clarity is favored by many when compared to the pace of progress in other work environments.

For further inspiration and to learn about additional benefits of becoming a consultant we suggest several of our favorite well-written and accessible books on the topic of consulting in our annotated bibliography (see Appendix 1-1), as well as recommended reading from the many experts we spoke with in preparing this book (Appendix 1-2).

MAKE A COMMITMENT

In order to benefit from the full range of opportunities of working as a consultant, you will need to start the organizational setup of your independent consulting practice. Starting your own consulting company requires a tremendous commitment! This task shares many similarities to the commitment required in enrolling in graduate school, or starting any other sort of small business. In school, you make a monetary and time commitment to complete the required tasks for classes once you have registered for them. After reading through the syllabi, you have a short time in which to decide whether you have chosen appropriate courses or whether you are in over your head. If you are starting a small company, once you file your papers with the state, you have already committed money and time to the process. Therefore, it is wise to be certain that you have done the necessary research before filing government paperwork, to make sure you are in it for the long haul (or at least the short haul). This is not to say that if you lose interest or get a great job offer that you cannot "get out" unscathed. Good business plans include an exit strategy (see the "Strategic Planning/Business Planning" section in Chapter 4). You need to be honest about what you're getting yourself into. It is important to consider the hours and the amount of work needed to run a business that is productive financially as well as programmatically.

THE MANY CHALLENGES AHEAD

Some people are "classic entrepreneurs," who like the idea of starting a business and seeing it grow. Others are not that interested in business per se, but are looking for a chance to work for themselves and are dedicated to the actual work of consulting. If you are reading this book, you are probably already a focused and disciplined worker. People who are hard workers but not natural entrepreneurs may need to adjust to the ambiguity and flexibility of consulting, and leave behind the security and certainty of a regular paycheck (Edwards & Edwards, 1996). Ambiguity and flexibility can be perceived as challenges as well as benefits—in other words, two sides of the same coin. These characteristics allow consultants freedom to define their time and work in ways that are meaningful and convenient for them, yet they also lead to challenges with time, work flow, balance, and money. Thus, the very same factors that lead people to choose independent consulting as a career (e.g., continual learning, flexibility, working for yourself) also lead to challenges inherent in the work.

Although consultants cited several benefits of the work, nobody said consulting was easy. Some of the most commonly discussed challenges of the consulting lifestyle included hard and, at times, exhausting work, managing time to meet client needs, inconsistent work (too much or too little), balancing work and personal life, lack of institutional financial support and benefits, isolation, and ensuring organizational utilization of the work. Furthermore, consultants often feel pressure to be perfect, because your next job may well depend upon the satisfaction of your current and past clients.

Challenges of Time and Effort

Starting your consulting practice will no doubt take a lot of time and effort. This can vary drastically depending on how quickly you would like to get "up and running." All of the paperwork could be filed and registered within less than 6 months' time, or you could stretch the process out to take a year. On average, those full-time consultants surveyed and interviewed reported that they worked 65 hours per week while getting the business up and running, and about 50–80 work hours per week during the first 3 years once the business was already going. Most of them work fewer hours now than when they started. Not one consultant said that the amount of time they put in over the years has increased since they began as full-time consultants. Among part-timers who do consulting on top of their full-time jobs, the amount of time they put in ranges from 1 to 50 hours per week. Regardless of full-time or part-time status, 80% of respondents said that they carry between 2 and 5 clients at a time. The bottom line is that you need to be invested in the work, and need to perform well in order to gain a reputation that will lead to more clients and additional projects in the future.

Time management is also difficult once you have committed to a project because it is hard to predict when you may have to devote added time to a given project. You can get a phone call at any time and have to spend several hours trying to solve an unexpected problem. Informants expressed how the job can be frustrating when clients do not appreciate the amount of time it takes to conduct a quality project (e.g., evaluation).

Below are descriptions of four key informants' time and effort commitments when they began their practices, and how this has changed over time. You'll notice that while the amount of time they put in at the start did vary quite a bit, each professional was able to reduce their workload over time:

1. Dale Rose, the president and founder of a consulting firm, described his level of involvement in his consulting business during graduate school as "fanatical." He now takes a more balanced approach to the work, trying to leave the office by 6:00 pm rather than 10:00 pm. He still regularly works overtime, however, to deliver products as promised, and admits that on at least one occasion he has had to use his sleeping bag and toothbrush at work.

2. Maryann Durland says that she now works 45 hours per week on average (but this is a variable estimate; some weeks she works up to 80 hours). At any given time, Durland's company maintains approximately 20 clients.

3. Michael Wyland and his business partner started out with each of them working about 60 hours a week. Now (12 years later) they work closer to 40–45 hours each, and see this as the result of multiple factors including their age, family, and a shift in their priorities.

4. Yet another informant said that initially she worked 80–100 hours per week to get her business up and running. Three years later, she is averaging 55 hours per week of work (30–40 spent on projects, and an additional 20 hours looking for new projects and taking care of the business end of her practice).

Not only do consultants work long hours, but the work is also hard. For example, although Bellman (1990) gives consulting the highest praise, he also writes, "... and it exhausts me.... I need time to restore myself. I need the time off to re-create myself, to regain perspective, and to rest—physically, mentally, emotionally, and spiritually. The work consumes me at every level" (pg. 11). Without exception, every consultant interviewed said that the work is intellectually and emotionally challenging, and plain old hard work. One experienced informant put it bluntly, "Make sure you understand that for many years you'll be working your ass off. For several years, I was always working—holidays, weekends, and late at night. If you've got a family, your partner is going to have to do more because you won't be able to pull your share." (Patricia Kelly)

TIP

Coping with Stress: When projects do not go smoothly, or deadlines approach, the stress can mount. To handle the stress, several key informants emphasized the importance of scheduling in downtime to recharge and stay on top of their game. When you're not swamped, take advantage of the downtime to better cope during busy periods. Summer is generally busier than winter. Therefore, taking time off in the winter may work better than summer vacations.

Challenges with Work Flow

Consulting involves continually contracting to do new, time-limited jobs, and because of this, the work is not always consistent enough to provide a steady income. While at times you may be inundated with more projects than you could possibly complete in several years, at other times there may be droughts (e.g., due to hard economic times, budget cuts, or funding cycles). Keeping the work flowing evenly over time was the most commonly cited struggle for full-time consultants.

Informants explained that contracts often cluster seasonally causing the workload to fluctuate between "unbearably busy" and "unbearably slow." This can create a catch-22 in which you need to be able to commit enough time to each project to do a stellar job, but if you turn down a project because you are too busy, you risk losing that client for the future. Key informants repeatedly warned that, especially in the beginning, you should not expect to gain your primary income from consulting.

TIP

Work Flow Concerns: Consider seasonal patterns, short-term and long-term planning, and workload issues as you make decisions about which jobs to take when opportunities arise and when to seek new projects.

Challenges of Work-Home-Family Balance

The day-to-day operations of running the business (e.g., bookkeeping) are also time-consuming and challenging, often making it hard to separate life from work. For many consultants, work is life and life is work. Distinguishing between work time and family time requires even more discipline if you are going to try to work from home. In addition, books, files, and office equipment or supplies can quickly invade and take over more living space than you'd like if you are not careful.

For some, the distractions at home are hard to overcome. Cleaning, laundry, the garage, and even the refrigerator can be difficult distractions to avoid (not to mention children, other family members, or the television). Keeping work from overwhelming their lives is also a concern for full- and part-timers working at home or in an office. In fact, one of the most commonly cited challenges was keeping the number of hours spent on their consulting projects to a manageable level so that it is possible to handle all other commitments.

TIP

Balancing Concerns: If you are going to try to work from home, Patricia Kelly suggests cordoning off part of your living space just for the office. In addition, you may want to set aside specific hours for working at home (similar to those who work outside of the home), try to minimize distractions during this time, and refrain from household responsibilities so you accomplish the tasks you set out to complete.

Money Challenges

Just over half of the survey respondents reported that they invested their own money to get their practices started (ranging from $200–$30,000 during the first year). However, most of them stated that only a minimal initial investment was required. There are not a lot of start-up or operational costs in running a small consulting practice, but this does not mean that money is not an important issue. While there were few costs associated with equipment or resources for doing business, it is still crucial to have some savings to get through periods when there is a lull in paid projects. In addition, personal costs, such as health insurance or mortgage payments, were mentioned repeatedly as serious challenges.

The lack of external support in the form of an organization, a salary, a role, a direction—all of this has to be made up for internally. When you are working for yourself you have to pay for your own health benefits, which is often much more expensive than the group rates large employers are able to obtain. Paid sick leave is nonexistent, so this can be an added challenge if your health is a concern. If you want to set aside money for retirement, you have to do this yourself, which can be time consuming (in terms of added paperwork) and costly. Andrew White, a full-time student, and self-employed consultant admitted,

> The financial aspects of consulting represented an unforeseen challenge. Since I am working in the community with small nonprofits, I cannot charge as much as I would like and sometimes need. On top of that, getting paid in a reasonable amount of time has been a challenge as well. I'm making less money than I expected.

Another challenge expressed by several informants surrounds deciding how to bill clients, and deciding what rates to charge. Estimating how long work activities will take gets easier over time, and it is always difficult to find out what others charge. Market rates for consulting work are hard to pin down, and because each project can bring unexpected challenges, estimating the amount of time and fees required should be on the generous side.

If you're not weary of entering the profession yet, and you've decided on a general rate to charge, you still have to go through the hassle of collecting money from clients. Most key informants shared experiences of having to wait months to get paid for their services. Specifically, school systems and universities (whose funding comes from several government sources) were singled out as being particularly slow to pay. While large institutions such as schools are often slow to pay, they tend to be more reliable than smaller organizations with smaller budgets. Therefore, there may not be a perfect type of organization to target to increase your chances of getting paid on time.

Having back-up savings is helpful, as there is always a delay (at least 30 days) in payment once an invoice is submitted. For example, within any quarter of the year it is not uncommon to complete projects and supply clients with invoices only to have to wait until the next quarter to be able to deposit the checks. Even if all of your clients are good about paying on time, banks often withhold deposits for a designated period of time until the organization's check is cleared. The delay in checks clearing can be as long as 5 business days depending on your bank's policy, and whether the check is local or from out of state. Also, consultants who subcontract small parts of their projects to colleagues are expected to pay their subcontractors once their work is completed, which may be before getting paid by the client. Lastly, monthly or quarterly taxes may need to be paid before payments are received from clients. Having some reserves to handle these lag times provides security and peace of mind to you and those with whom you contract.

TIP

Living with Uncertain Income: When asked about money, some consultants said things like, "Make sure you save up some money first," or "Don't dive in without a backup." "Your partner or spouse may need to be the primary breadwinner for a couple years." As a general guideline, some suggested that you ought to have enough money to support yourself for 3 months if you are jumping into full-time consulting.

The Challenge of Isolation

Loneliness is a concern for many independent consultants. The first few weeks away from the busyness and politics of a bustling workplace may feel like a refreshing getaway. However, after a short period of time spent in the same room without seeing anyone, independent consultants may feel isolated. You may feel disconnected without coworkers to bounce ideas off of, and to provide informational and social support. While you may have ample opportunity to interact with clients during the early stages of a project, you are often expected to complete most of the report writing individually. Even if you are able to work collaboratively throughout all stages of the consulting process (e.g., using participatory action research methodology), you are still bound to spend many days between projects keeping up with paperwork on your own. Dawn Hanson Smart discusses her experience of isolation and loneliness in Chapter 16, "The Path to Independent Consulting," and these factors directly influenced her career decisions and progression.

TIP

Avoiding Loneliness: The most common piece of advice to combat this type of isolation is to foster relationships with other independent consultants with whom you share common interests and values. Networking is important for several reasons. For example, you will likely depend upon your professional network to increase your awareness of particular projects, and to refer you to clients when they are too busy or do not have the expertise to take on a project themselves. Your professional network can also serve a useful resource for you to turn to when looking for technical guidance, advice on how to proceed with a project, or for more general social support. For an extended discussion of the benefits of networking, see Chapter 6, "Finding Work." Try to arrange lunch at least once a week with a colleague or potential client. You may also consider establishing a partnership or small firm to work together on projects, either building a niche in a particular area, or broadening your expertise through adding people with different strengths to your consulting team.

Stakeholder "Buy-in" and Utilization Challenges

One of the most significant challenges of consulting work is to balance the desires of different stakeholders in collaborative projects. One of the most frustrating experiences occurs when the client does not implement or use recommendations from your final reports. Lack of utilization can happen for a variety of reasons, including budgetary restraints, diminished client or key stakeholder buy-in, political impediments, organizational inertia, or poor presentation of potential action steps on the part of the consultant. In other words, after spending several months of long days and late nights working for and with an organization, you may realize that the organization, which appeared motivated and ready for change when the project began, no longer has the resources nor commitment to implement your recommendations. When the organizations you work with are in transition or having financial difficulties, other more pressing needs take precedence. Staff turnover may also make it difficult to find a champion for your project within the organization. Regardless of the cause, failing to maintain client ownership or implement recommendations is more common than professionals in the field would like, and this has been a motivator for some former consultants to change career paths. Chapter 8, "A Client-Centered Approach to Winning and Losing New Business: What to Do If You Get the Project (And What to Do If You Don't)," discusses the concern of staff turnover and provides advice about how to handle such challenges.

TIP

> Attain and Maintain Buy-in and Utilization Focus: Think about utilization and buy-in from the beginning, and try to involve your client in all aspects of the project. Pose potential scenarios of different outcomes to help the client think through possibilities and invest in the process from the beginning (see Patton, 2008 for further detail on utilization-focused approaches).

CONCLUSION

The challenges mentioned above are real, and they only make up a portion of the difficulties you are likely to encounter along the way. Nonetheless, for students and professionals in the social sciences who have no desire to work in the private sector, consulting can be an ideal primary or supplemental career route. While everyone interviewed said they worked hard, they also said that they find the work rewarding. Carol Lukas, the president of a national nonprofit and veteran consultant explained, "When your values, goals, and practice are all aligned, you have fun." Most of the jobs we hear about these days aren't described as both fulfilling and fun. In his book, *How to Become a Successful Consultant in Your Own Field*, Hubert

Bermont (1997) has a simple and straightforward answer to the question of whether the life of an independent professional or freelancer is as great as it is cracked up to be. He writes, "Yes. Even greater" (pg. 25).

The more you are prepared for the challenges, the better you can anticipate and plan for them, so they become small bumps in the road, rather than detours or closed roads. Further, for many, the benefits of consulting with nonprofit organizations outweigh the challenges. Successful consultant and author Alan Weiss (2004) puts it strongly, ". . . don't believe anything you hear about this being an onerous and difficult profession. It is actually one of the best in the world, provided you have the resources, the focus, the talents, and the passion for it" (pg. 2). Consulting with nonprofit organizations creates many opportunities to guide your career, develop professionally, and make meaningful contributions to society. Geoffrey Bellman (1990) states, "[the work] is a most significant contributor to my growth; it gives me the opportunity to contribute to others. I continue to believe that it is good for the world. I cannot think of anything I would rather do" (pg. 11).

APPENDIX 1-1: Annotated Bibliography

Bellman, G.M. (1990). *The Consultant's Calling: Bringing Who You Are to What You Do.* **San Francisco, CA: Jossey-Bass Publishers.**
Bellman discusses consulting as a career from a person-oriented perspective as opposed to a business-oriented perspective. He covers less of the pragmatic details and more of the overall thought process (e.g., balancing work and life) involved in deciding to go into consulting full time. The book covers the role of the consultant in the world, and the author's philosophy of the field.

Bermont, H. (1995). *How to Become a Successful Consultant in Your Own Field, 3rd ed.* **Rocklin, CA: Prima Publishing.**
Bermont tells the story of his own consulting business and includes sections on how to get your first assignment, how to operate your business, rules for setting fees, advice on avoiding contracts, and several case examples.

Block, P. (1999). *Flawless Consulting, 2nd ed.* **San Francisco, CA: Jossey-Bass Publishers.**
This book is more about doing the work of consulting than getting started. However, we included it in this list because it was recommended by several survey respondents and key consultants. It uses case studies and personal examples to illustrate Block's ideas about the best ways to interact with clients. He breaks down the consulting relationship into five phases and walks you through potential problems that may arise during each phase and how to overcome or avoid them.

Edwards, S. & Edwards, P. (1996). *Secrets of Self-Employment: Surviving and Thriving on the Ups and Downs of Being Your Own Boss.* **New York: Penguin Putnam Inc.**
The authors of this book are like cheerleaders, encouraging you to go for it. Their intent appears to be to help you build confidence and motivation, and overcome self-doubt. It also has ideas for assessing your personal weaknesses and building on your strengths.

Greenbaum, T. (1990). *The Consultant's Manual: A Complete Guide to Building a Successful Consulting Practice.* **New York: John Wiley and Sons.**
This manual focuses on marketing your services (e.g., developing a brochure), writing a business plan, managing finances, and business growth. This book may be useful for those of you with less experience or talent in producing marketing materials.

Illinois Department of Commerce and Community Affairs (DCCA). *Starting a Business in Illinois Handbook.* **Retrieved June 1, 2008, from http://www.illinoisbiz.biz/bus/pdf/SBIRrev1201.pdf.**
As would be expected, the information in this government source is dry and specific to Illinois, however, there are likely similar guides in each state and the information should be reliable because it is coming from up-to-date, official sources.

Illinois Department of Commerce and Economic Opportunity (DCEO). *Step-by-Step Guide to Starting a Business in Illinois.* **Retrieved June 1, 2008, from http://illinoisbiz.biz/bus/step_by_step.html.**
Again, dry, specific to Illinois, but informative and likely there are similar guides in each state, and the information should be reliable because it is coming from an up-to-date, official source.

Kishel, G. & Kishel, P. (1996). *How to Start and Run a Successful Consulting Business.* **New York: John Wiley & Sons.**
This book addresses issues involved with setting up the business, determining fees, and maintaining good client relations in order to get future referrals. They also discuss what insurance you should have.

Lukas, C.A. (1998). *Consulting with Nonprofits: A Practitioner's Guide— The Art, Craft, and Business of Helping Nonprofit Organizations and Community Groups Get the Results They Want.* **St. Paul, MN: Amherst H. Wilder Foundation.**
This is an excellent and comprehensive guide for the practicing consultant. It discusses what is unique about consulting with nonprofits, how to handle ethical dilemmas, and lays out the fundamentals of good practice. The guide also includes sample consulting proposals, worksheets for budgeting, and strategies for developing your marketing plan, evaluating your work, and working with clients. This guide also includes an extensive list of informational resources.

Patton, M.Q. (2008). *Utilization-Focused Evaluation, 4th ed.* **Thousand Oaks, CA: Sage Publications.**
While it is not about starting a consulting company or working specifically with nonprofits, this is nonetheless a must read. Program evaluation is probably the most common type of consulting that many of us do, and all consultants want their recommendations utilized. This is one of the few textbooks we have found to be a joy to read. Utilization-focused evaluation covers a vast array of topics, and clearly illustrates ways to produce first-rate evaluations that will actually be used.

Shiffman, S. (1988). *The Consultant's Handbook: How to Start and Develop Your Own Practice.* **Boston, MA: Bob Adams, Inc.**
We have used this handbook less than the others listed above, however it does discuss finding clients, writing proposals, determining what prices to charge, managing finances, and also includes sample proposals.

Weltman, B. (2000). *The Complete Idiot's Guide to Starting a Home-Based Business, 2nd ed.* **Indianapolis, IN: Alpha Books.**
This guide provides a good overview of all the things you'll need to consider when starting a business. It is written simply and clearly. However, it tends to tell you where to look for information rather than actually giving you answers. This allows the guide not to get out-of-date too quickly, or provide poor legal advice. While several chapters are irrelevant for consultants, this is likely the case for most books written to such a broad audience.

U.S. Department of Treasury, Internal Revenue Service. *Recommended Reading for Small Businesses.* **Retrieved August 1, 2008, from http://www .irs.gov/businesses/small/article/0,,id=99083,00.html.**
This reading list provides just what its title implies—a list of essential readings for small businesses. The list conveniently includes links so you can read or print most of the publications without much navigation from this page.

APPENDIX 1-2: Additional Recommended Reading

The books below supplement those listed in Appendix 1-1 or those referenced in the text of this book. Each book has been specifically recommended by consultants who responded to our survey but were not cited in the text of this book.

Adams, B. & Kintler, D. (1998). *Streetwise Independent Consulting: Your Comprehensive Guide to Building Your Own Consulting Business.* Holbrook, MA: Adams Media Corp.

Allen, D. (2001). *Getting Things Done: The Art of Stress-Free Productivity.* New York: Penguin.

Beckwith, H. (1997). *Selling the Invisible: A Field Guide to Modern Marketing.* New York: Warner Books, Inc.

Fisher, D., Rooke, D., & Torbert, B. (2003). *Personal and Organizational Transformations: Through Action Inquiry, 4th ed.* Boston: Edge\Work Press Publisher.

Gedge, J. (1998). *A Legal Road Map for Consultants.* Medford, OR: Oasis Press.

Godin, S. (2001). *The Bootstrapper's Bible.* Online document, retrieved from Do You Zoom, Inc.

Green, D. (2002). *Fight Your Fear and Win: 7 Skills for Performing Your Best Under Pressure—at Work, in Sports, on Stage.* New York: Broadway Books.

Hancock, W.A. (1991). *Small Business Legal Advisor, 2nd ed.* New York: McGraw-Hill.

Herman, R.D. (1994). *Jossey-Bass Handbook for NonProfit Leadership & Management.* San Francisco: Jossey-Bass Publishers.

Howe, J.T., Mosher, M.P., McDonough, J.M., Mulack, D.G., Mills, E.M., Vanden Berk, K.M., & Walton, W.S. (2001). *Not-for-Profit Corporations.* Illinois Institute for Continuing Legal Education.

Mancuso, A. (2002). *How to Form a Nonprofit Corporation, 5th ed.* Berkeley, CA: Nolo Press.

Shenson, H., Nicholas, T., & Franklin P. (1997). *Complete Guide to Consulting Success: A Step-by-Step Guide to Building a Successful Consulting Practice Complete with Agreements and Forms, 3rd ed.* Chicago: Dearborn Trade Publishing.

Sitarz, D. (2002). *Simplified Small Business Accounting Simplified.* Lanham, MD: National Book Network.

Warda, M. (2003). *How to Form a Limited Liability Company, 2nd ed.* Naperville, IL: Sphinx Publishers Inc.

Weiss, A. (1997). *Million Dollar Consulting, New and Updated Edition: The Professional's Guide to Growing a Practice.* New York: McGraw-Hill.

Chapter 2

Preparing for Success

Judah Viola and Susan D. McMahon

WHAT YOU'LL NEED TO START

Internal Resources

Hearing that you need to "get experience" is a common, yet vague and un-helpful recommendation. Actually, there is much more to consider when contemplating a consulting career. There are specific internal resources that contribute to successful consulting. According to the experts, much of what is needed can be learned. However, a few informants felt that some important qualities can best be attributed to personality or innate talent. In other words, everyone may not be suited for a career in consult-ing. Edwards and Edwards (1996), authors of *Secrets of Self-Employment,* insist that, ". . . you can make it on your own if you have a strong desire and willingness to become a goal-directed, self-motivated person." If this is the case, then graduate school may be an excellent preparation for self-employment, because to successfully complete a graduate degree, you need to be goal-directed and self-motivated. In speaking with key informants about the prerequisite skills necessary to be an effective consultant, they consistently mentioned "people skills" or "social skills" as most important. For the purpose of gaining some clarity on what this really means, we'll consider these general terms to be comprised of several specific compo-nents, such as personal characteristics, knowledge, and skills/abilities.

Personal Characteristics

What type of person does it take to be a successful consultant with com-munity-based organizations? When describing what is needed to succeed as a consultant, nine personal characteristics were cited consistently. It is arguable whether these traits are learned or innate. Moreover, these characteristics were described by some informants as essential prerequisites and by others as the natural result of gaining experience.

- Authenticity
- Self-confidence
- Patience
- Flexibility
- Tolerance for ambiguity (and financial insecurity)
- Empathy
- Desire for continual learning
- Orientation toward service
- Interest in proving yourself time and again

Authenticity is a highly valued personal characteristic and helps to build trust with your collaborators/clients, which is one of the most important ingredients of successful consulting. Another commonly shared sentiment among informants was the need for the consultant to exude confidence in his or her ability to get the job done right. Organizations are looking to you as the expert, so they want to be assured that you know what you are doing. Nonprofits are not always well-oiled machines, and if they were, they would have little need for your assistance. Patience, flexibility, tolerance for ambiguity and financial insecurity are also frequently cited as necessary for consulting work. These personal characteristics make the challenges we discussed in Chapter 1, "Before You Begin," more manageable. In addition, internal self-motivation and fortitude are essential characteristics of a successful consultant who must often wade through projects that have been delayed due to circumstances beyond his or her control.

Furthermore, empathizing with clients and stakeholders is paramount when it comes to evaluating programs, providing useful advice, or finding workable solutions to organizational problems. Those who desire to continue learning and improving their many essential skills are going to become more effective consultants than those who try to apply what they already know well to each new situation they encounter. A service orientation is useful for helping you relate to collaborating organizations and individuals. Lastly, thick skin and persistence are essential. With every new client, you will have to prove your worth. This can seem like a daunting and tiring process at times, but it is also a challenge you must face with fortitude if you want to maintain success in the field.

Knowledge

What do you need to know in order to be a successful consultant with nonprofits?

> Knowledge . . . is the foundation on which abilities and skills are built. [It] refers to an organized body of [information], usually of a factual or procedural nature, which, if applied, makes adequate job performance possible. . . . Possession of knowledge does not ensure that it will be used. (pg. 65, Goldstein & Ford, 2002)

The knowledge you'll need prior to starting your practice falls within three categories: (1) "pure" consultancy, such as how to build and maintain relationships with clients; (2) topical or specialized knowledge; and (3) business operations. None of this should be surprising, considering you'll be running a business in addition to providing consulting services.

What you may find surprising, however, is that specialized knowledge was less emphasized and the least varied among the list of internal resources that key informants shared with me. Specific knowledge concerning human and organizational development was often cited. In addition, it is expected that you will either enter each new job with a greater understanding of the task at hand, or quickly gain knowledge about the unique strengths, challenges, and histories of the population and context within which you are working. More importantly, regardless of your specialty or consulting niche, you must develop a strong grasp of various key research methodologies. Qualitative and quantitative research design and appropriate technical knowledge (i.e., data analysis and analysis software) are fundamental. Even if you will not be conducting randomized trials or using an experimental design on a regular basis, in order to adapt the appropriate methods for the real world, you will need to understand and respond knowledgably to your clients' evaluation or research questions. More commonly, you will need to assist clients in articulating questions to ask of data based upon the client's implicit or explicit goals and objectives.

Action-research, or action inquiry, is a specific type of research that many consultants find useful. In comparison to traditional research, which is aimed largely at gaining information, action-research uses applied inquiry strategies involving cycles of data collection, evaluation, and reflection focused on generating genuine and sustained improvements in the quality of an organization (or program) and its performance (Lewin, 1958; Torbert & Cook-Greuter, 2004).

Some degree of expertise will also be required on collaborative and participatory models of research and evaluation, which involve clients and other key stakeholders taking an active role, to varying degrees, in determining the nature (i.e., questions asked) and the process (i.e., data collection, analysis, and write-up) of the project. In Chapter 9, "From Start to Finish: A Typical Evaluation Project," Kathleen Dowell describes in detail her involvement in an evaluation consulting project that utilized a participatory approach. For more information on participatory research methods, a good resource is the International Institute for Sustainable Development (2008). In addition to making your work participatory and collaborative, you should be mindful of how to help your clients use the evaluation effectively. Patton (2008) gives excellent guidance in his book, *Utilization-Focused Evaluation*. During every step of the process, from initial planning to implementation and presentation of findings, you need take action to maximize the likelihood that your deliverables are useful to your clients.

Basic knowledge of operating a business is also very helpful, and sometimes, essential. For example, some understanding of budgeting will be necessary to translate project tasks into the actual numbers of days and hours needed to complete them, as well as the costs associated with each task. Even if you do not expect to file your own tax returns or maintain quarterly or annual reports, knowledge of basic bookkeeping and accounting principles, such as accounts payable, accounts receivable, and invoicing, are necessary for making sure you get paid, keeping track of your available cash flow, and reporting your earnings or losses to the government (i.e., income taxes). Basic business knowledge can also help you efficiently learn about the organizations you consult with. While personality traits such as authenticity and knowledge of research methods and business basics are essential, they are not sufficient to keep you afloat as a consultant. You must also know how to put those personal characteristics and knowledge together to work for you and your clients. Knowledge in action can be described in terms of skills or abilities.

Abilities and Skills

Abilities and skills usually refer to the cognitive capabilities necessary to perform a job function, requiring the application of some knowledge base, and the capability to perform job operations with ease and precision (adapted from Goldstein & Ford, 2002). Most of the abilities and skills that informants and survey respondents listed as crucial to successful consultants fit in three broad categories: (1) interpersonal communication, (2) strategic thinking, and (3) organization.

Communication

Within interpersonal communication, the ability to quickly establish rapport and build trust is highly valued and can increase the likelihood of an effective and efficient collaboration. The most successful consultants have superior listening, reflecting, negotiating, dialogue facilitation, and conflict resolution skills. Being able to translate people's questions or desires into concrete tasks and ideas is important as well, as is the ability to communicate across disciplines, cultures, and styles. When consulting with nonprofits, it is not uncommon to interact with a varied set of stakeholders who straddle language, culture, and socioeconomic status.

Part of communicating across cultures effectively requires the ability to communicate technical information in layperson terms. But more concretely, it is the ability to interact with various people at many levels of corporate, academic, or community positions. Lastly, formal communication, such as business writing, and presentation and networking skills are essential, as most work is generated via word-of-mouth. You need to be able to think on your feet and sell yourself at times. But you also need to know when to step back and ensure that your partners take ownership and are recognized for their roles and accomplishments. The ability to move fluidly between working in isolation to interacting with large groups of people must be learned quickly on the job.

Strategic Thinking

Favorable cognitive abilities for problem solving included analytic and strategic thinking, as well as organizational diagnostics. Several informants spoke of intangible talents such as an ability to quickly size up the power dynamics and politics that exist within an organization. Consultants enjoy the new challenges and unique nature of each organization with which they collaborate. However, the individuality of each project necessitates thinking on one's feet because projects tend to change much more quickly in the public service sector than they do in university or laboratory environments.

Good consultants also have the ability to focus on when and what the client needs while acknowledging internal and external barriers to success. Being aware of the range of interests involved in a project can be helpful, but at times consultants also need to be able to tune out issues that are beyond their control, or are outside the scope of the contracted work. Furthermore, attending to both the processes as well as the outcomes of programs is important when you value building capacity within the organizations you choose to work with. Often, clients get caught up focusing on outcomes, when they could benefit from reassessing their assumptions and processes they employ to try and attain their goals.

Organization

In order to stay in business, it is necessary to begin new projects before completing others. Therefore, the ability to manage multiple projects effectively, as well as meeting stated deadlines, is a required internal resource. This ability stems from being organized and thoughtful about your own planning processes, so you are able to follow through with plans and don't waste a client's time. In addition, keeping track of your hours, records, and invoicing requires strong organizational skills. While you cannot always plan for the unexpected, running a well-organized project will reduce the frequency of having to work late into the night to meet deadlines, and help you conserve resources so you can step up when unavoidable stresses arise.

Self-Evaluation

How do your capabilities and development needs compare with the core competencies listed above? Don't worry—nobody has *all* of these traits, especially prior to beginning the work. However, it may be wise for you

Checklist 2-1: General Traits and Skills Needed to Thrive in Consulting

☐ I am comfortable speaking with people across disciplines and at all levels of an organization.

☐ I have the authenticity, self-confidence, and patience to build trust in others.

☐ I have excellent oral and written communication skills.

☐ I have the ability to say "No" when it is in my best interest, even if it will disappoint someone.

☐ I have the self-discipline, attention to detail, willingness to put in long hours, and drive to complete projects on time at the highest standards of quality and integrity.

☐ I have thick skin and a willingness to learn from my mistakes.

☐ I have an awareness of my weaknesses as well as my strengths.

☐ I have strong organizational skills.

☐ I have the flexibility and tolerance for ambiguity and financial insecurity to adjust project time lines as necessary.

☐ I have a desire for continual learning.

☐ I have an appreciation and openness to diversity of thought and culture.

☐ I have a service orientation and value base that suits me to working with nonprofit organizations.

☐ I have an interest in proving myself over and over again.

Adapted from E. Biech (1998). *The Business of Consulting: The Basics and Beyond.* San Francisco: John Wiley & Sons. Reprinted with permission.

to engage in some self-assessments to obtain a clear sense of where your strengths are and what you have to offer clients. Then, you might compare your strengths with several of the important qualities discussed throughout the chapter to assess your readiness for beginning a consulting practice. Which skills do you already hold, and which ones do you still need to develop? The Amherst H. Wilder Foundation has developed a worksheet for this purpose (see Lukas, 1998). Another set of quick activities you can use to see how suited you are for the profession is to complete Checklists 2-1 and 2-2. The first list includes general traits and skills needed to survive and thrive in the profession. This checklist is adapted from Biech (1998) to use as a self-check for the characteristics that are ideal for you to have as a consultant. The second checklist includes more specific skill sets for doing the work of consulting, and is adapted from a "Core Competencies" worksheet designed by Lukas (1998).

Checklist 2-2: Specific Skill Sets Required to Consult Effectively

☐ I have the ability to reflect and synthesize what clients tell me, and clearly articulate this back to them.

☐ I have the ability to quickly diffuse resistance and resolve conflict with clients without getting defensive.

☐ I have the ability to establish a safe, open learning environment in groups.

☐ I have an understanding of organizational systems and the interrelationships between parts of the system.

☐ I have the capacity to apply a variety of theoretical models of organizational behavior and performance to new settings.

☐ I have an understanding of the process and dynamics of collaboration and the ability to facilitate collaboration with clients even when it is not on their radar.

☐ I have an understanding of basic community organizing methods.

☐ I have an understanding of adult learning principles and the ability to use them when facilitating workshops, trainings, or conducting presentations or writing reports.

☐ I have the ability to design learning experiences to meet individual differences in learning and organizational styles.

☐ I have skills in using a variety of data collection and analysis methods.

☐ I have technological literacy and competence using current software packages as well as recording and presentation equipment.

☐ I have the ability to clarify and articulate the values and beliefs that guide my work.

Adapted from C.A. Lukas (1998). *Consulting with Nonprofits: A Practitioner's Guide—The Art, Craft, and Business of Helping Nonprofit Organizations and Community Groups Get the Results They Want.* St. Paul, MN: Amherst H. Wilder Foundation. Reprinted with permission.

If there are more than 3 out of the 12 items on Checklist 2 that you cannot honestly check off, you may not be ready yet to begin consulting independently. However, if you feel like you have a chance of developing the knowledge, skills, abilities, and personal characteristics listed above, then go ahead and read on. There are still many more ingredients needed for success.

External Resources

In addition to the necessary internal resources listed above, successful consultants were also quick to mention external resources that allow for success. An understanding partner, spouse, or family, as well as a community of other consultants, will most likely become your support system. A good network of professional colleagues and a strong, established reputation are necessary so that you can continue acquiring new clients. In order to be an effective resource that community organizations will seek out, you also need to be well-connected with colleagues whom you can refer jobs that you do not have the time or skills to complete. A good professional network is also crucial so that you can pull in needed expertise as required on the jobs that you do take on, or to just have someone to bounce ideas off of or commiserate with.

In addition, you need to have enough financial resources to rely on when you are getting started. Starting slowly, while maintaining your job, or making the transition by working part-time while building a network of clients, or having a cushion through the income of a significant other can all be potential options in the beginning. Space is another important external resource, and decisions about whether to rent office space or work from home should take into account your financial resources, workload, personal preferences, and home situation.

HOW TO PREPARE YOURSELF

Programs, Courses, Workshops, and Certificates

The most obvious place we turn to for building our knowledge is through formal consulting, evaluation, or social science programs or courses at colleges or universities. One foundational degree that prepares students to consult with nonprofits is community psychology. Community psychology focuses on understanding, preventing, and addressing psychological and social problems, and empowering individuals, organizations, and communities. Students in community psychology programs learn consulting and evaluation skills, as well as advanced skills in research methods. However, there are lots of degree options to pursue, and you should explore programs that provide a good fit with your interests. Given the cross-disciplinary nature of consulting, courses in consulting may be offered through a variety of departments, schools, and programs, including, but not limited to the following: applied psychology, clinical psychology, community psychology, applied social psychology, evaluation, education, social work, sociology, urban planning, public service, public health, policy analysis, business management, or nonprofit management.

You probably cannot make it through graduate school without completing courses in quantitative research methods, statistics, and diversity. These classes will provide a good base; however, you can position yourself best by taking some elective classes that are most relevant to consulting. For example, classes such as program evaluation, consultation, qualitative research methods, grant writing, community fieldwork/practicum, and small business accounting, will all provide you with knowledge and skills you can use as an independent consultant. Local community colleges typically offer affordable and effective courses in accounting and running a small business. Distance learning and Internet-based courses or webinars are also growing in popularity and respect.

Many professional organizations also offer courses, certificates, and continuing education credit workshops that are much shorter, less expensive, and more narrow in scope when compared to university-based courses. For example, the Evaluators' Institute offers 1- to 4-day courses, as well as certificate programs in research methodology and a variety of topics related to program evaluation (e.g., data analysis, report writing, policy analysis, etc.). They even offer a course on "How to Build a Successful Evaluation Practice." The American Society for Training and Development (ASTD) offers certificates for Professionals in Learning and Performance, such as a 2-day course in "Consulting Skills for Trainers." Other examples of training programs involve collaborations between government agencies, such as the Centers for Disease Control and Prevention (CDC), and professional organizations such as the American Evaluation Association (AEA), who sponsor joint summer institutes that offer over 50 different week-long courses on a variety of topics relevant to consulting with nonprofits and community organizations (e.g., community collaboration, survey design, interviewing techniques, project management, etc.)

You may also want to look into free or very inexpensive classes offered by your local Chamber of Commerce or Small Business Administration (SBA) office. The SBA is a federal agency that exists to help small businesses get started and survive. It is worth taking advantage of this valuable resource funded by your tax dollars.

Of course, there is also a plethora of related information available for free on the Internet. This information can serve as a great supplement to your existing knowledge base. However, when it comes to gaining skills, non-structured independent research and reading books on your own are inferior to taking classes or completing training programs that include guided practice and feedback, in addition to presenting new information.

Work Experience (Volunteer or Paid)

While much of the knowledge, abilities, and skills mentioned above can be developed at a university or in the workplace, many key informants mentioned the importance of having some guided, practical consulting experience. A common suggestion was to complete a few years of a formal or informal internship in a practice where you will be mentored. Having an understanding of the consulting cycle from beginning to end is helpful before you go out on your own or join a small firm. The more direct guidance you can receive, the better. Try to apprentice yourself to someone you judge to be solid in terms of ethics, competency, values, and philosophy.

Participating in real-world projects while under supervision is both challenging and safe. As you hone your observational and listening skills, you will learn how various nonprofits work. You will likely gain knowledge of the strengths and needs of multiple organizations and communities with which you work. Obtaining related work experience will also allow you to show your commitment to an issue or population of interest, and build trust through developing personal relationships and learning the desires of various stakeholders. In addition, it will allow you to build contacts and a network of potential future clients.

Finding a senior consultant who has the commitment and resources to mentor you may not be realistic for everyone. In general, it is a good idea to look specifically for jobs that provide you with a chance to build skills related to consulting, such as project management, interviewing, community organizing, report writing, presenting, and grant writing. In addition, if you are itching to be your own boss, another way to gain valuable relevant work experience is to volunteer (if funding isn't available) on a few projects with an experienced consultant you respect before trying to market yourself as an expert. This will allow you to build a base of experience, as well as a resume of completed projects.

Establishing Networking Relationships

Networking is about building relationships with people who share some of your goals and interests. Networking can be a great way to increase your knowledge. By interacting with various people, you will likely be exposed to a multiplicity of styles and opinions on the best ways to conduct research, evaluation, and development work. Start expanding your network early. An easy source from which to begin gaining knowledge, abilities, and skills for consulting are university professors who trust your skills and have an understanding of your strengths. Therefore, building a favorable reputation through working with numerous professors at your university is a good way to start creating a network.

While the mentorship model found in most doctoral programs is useful for specializing and learning how to become an academic or top-notch researcher, it is not necessarily set up to expose you to the multitude of relationships that members of the university community have with the outside world. Partnerships and collaborative projects between the university and businesses, government, and the local communities are on the rise. Try to learn about the work beyond that of your direct supervisors.

To summarize, consulting with nonprofits requires skills that are interdisciplinary. Take advantage of opportunities to learn from faculty outside of your specialty. Furthermore, expand your base by looking across disciplines to see the overlap and interrelatedness or contrasts of how different social sciences frame and/or attempt to solve similar problems. Most professors are more than happy to discuss their work and their discipline with interested graduate students. Since you are likely spending several years at one institution, your graduate school experience can be an opportunity to build your own capacity to do the work, as well as establish relationships with people who can be stable sources for work in the near and distant future (see Chapter 6, "Finding Work," for exercises to help you build your network).

Learn about Funders

One of the abilities that you likely already have is to digest information quickly. This is a good skill to hone in preparation for starting a consulting practice. Increasing your knowledge through the Internet and professional journals is a good habit to get into. It is also advisable to expand your knowledge base through learning the "ins and outs" of nonprofit and local government funding in your area.

Determine the "who," "what," "where," "why," "when," and "how" of the major funders in your area. What foundations are active? Learn about their missions, funding priorities, and funding cycles. You can call them and ask for annual reports and funding guidelines. This will be useful for understanding what they are looking for when you are working with an organization that they fund. In many areas, the United Way is a major funder of nonprofits. Find out how involved the United Way is in your area. Foundations, government agencies, and institutional funders are either potential clients themselves, or sources of funding for your clients. If you develop a relationship with a representative from a foundation or state funding agency, he or she can help you work through the grant process. In addition, sometimes funders hire consultants directly to do grant reviews or to help write Requests for Proposals (RFPs).

If you are able to build a reputation as a knowledgeable person in one or several substantive areas, you may be asked to help write an RFP, or review grant proposals. This can help you learn the perspective of funders , and may also provide ideas for ways to present your next grant proposal. Since many nonprofits are strapped for cash, coming to them with ideas about where they can get additional funding, or where the funding for an evaluation you are proposing may come from, will make you more desirable as a consultant.

CONCLUSION

Getting started in consulting may seem a more daunting process after considering all of the internal and external resources discussed in this chapter. However, we hope that our suggestions provide you with a pathway to accomplishing this task. We recommend that you start by conducting a self-evaluation and exploring your internal resources, then building your knowledge and abilities in areas where you see gaps in knowledge or ability through coursework, increasing your skills and confidence through relevant work experience, re-evaluate for consulting skill sets, and then return for more training to fill in gaps when necessary. We also suggest that you work to build relationships with colleagues and potential clients, and learn as much as you can about funders. However, this process can happen over an extended period of time and does not have to strictly follow our suggested order.

So what would all of this preparation look like in practice? Well, Geoffrey Bellman wrote in his book, *The Consultant's Calling*, that during the 7 years prior to beginning his consulting career, he wrote and published an article each year, co-led about 3 to 4 public workshops a year, presented papers once or twice a year at conferences, spoke to a few civic organizations, and attended at least one public workshop a year. Presenting and publishing were important for building his credibility as an expert, as well as developing his professional network, while leading public workshops and speaking with civic organizations were helpful in developing a positive reputation and relationships in the community. Lastly, attending workshops was beneficial for continued learning, as well as maintaining his network. These activities seemed to prepare him well for the career ahead of him. While the number and types of specific activities that are best for you to engage in will vary depending on your starting point, it will be helpful to keep in mind the various important domains raised in this chapter, and to consider your options as you prepare for success.

Chapter 3

When to Start a Consulting Practice

Judah Viola and Susan D. McMahon

START YOUR BUSINESS AT THE RIGHT TIME

"If I had it to do all over again, I'd still start my own business. It's worth the cut in pay just to have control over my life." (Patricia Kelly, The Kellidge Group)

"Go for it. It's great to be your own boss. You just have to learn to enjoy the free falls when no money is coming in or is in sight!" (Martha Henry, SPEC Associates)

It should come as no surprise that successful professional consultants are enthusiastic about the field and encourage others to follow suit (with eyes open to the challenges, of course). However, consensus does not exist among those attempting to answer the question of *when* is the best time to start consulting. Strong opinions abound as to the *right time* to start consulting or building an independent practice. Recommendations include beginning to build your practice and take on consulting projects while: a) you are a student, b) soon after graduating, c) after working in a private firm, d) after time in a nonprofit or public sector job, and/or e) after working under a seasoned independent consultant. While choosing the "correct" response to this multiple choice conundrum is something only you can answer, in this chapter, we describe some pros and cons that you may want to consider with regard to starting out as a consultant during each of these career phases.

WHILE IN SCHOOL

Starting while you are in school (most likely graduate school) may be the perfect time to begin gaining consulting experience. With no professional experience as a consultant, it can be difficult to land a job as a consultant at an existing firm. And, if you do get hired, you will likely have to start as a low-level employee. While this may be a useful means to learning the trade and working your way up the chain of command, after many years of school, you may not feel like spending several more years doing data entry or being under multiple layers of supervision. In addition, existing companies may not be open to your suggestions or ideas for change. And most likely, you will not have a say in what projects are accepted and who gets credit for the work. Starting as a consultant while still in school provides an opportunity to build your skills, resume, and network all at the same time.

As a student, you likely won't have time to commit to a full-time job. So, you might as well make your part-time job a consulting gig. If you start picking up part-time consulting projects as a student, you can build your experience and pick up some needed extra cash. You will have free access to what would otherwise be costly resources, such as university libraries, computers, and statistical software. You may be able to take advantage of advice from faculty or help from other students. You may even be able to have a consulting project serve more than one purpose. For example, you could gain valuable experience, earn money, *and* earn course credit for doing the work as a requirement for a fieldwork or service learning course, or independent study with faculty supervision. For two of the consultants I spoke with, working on a consulting project under faculty served as their graduate assistantships.

Although there are benefits to starting in the consulting business while in school, there are also cons to discuss. First and foremost is the time and effort given to your school obligation. It is hard enough for many students to complete their graduate degrees in a timely manner without moonlighting. If you are able to earn money doing consulting work, your coursework or school-related research may seem less pressing, and may get stretched out further. Keeping school as your priority can certainly be challenged by contractual deadlines. In addition, some of the expectations of clients may be different for you as a student than if you were further along in your career. For example, you may be asked to do more work for less money. Your rates generally should be lower than consultants with their PhDs, for example, or those who are published and known as specialists in the field, but you want to set boundaries and think carefully about agreeing to do things outside the scope of the project. In addition, clients may assume that you will be supervised by a faculty member or someone who has more seniority than you do. Other expectations might include an assumption that, because you are affiliated with a university, the consulting work you are doing is supported and or sanctioned by the institution that you attend. Any of these assumptions may or may not be true, but it is important to have a clear line of communication open between yourself and your clients to avoid unmet expectations.

JUST OUT OF SCHOOL

After you have graduated from school, you will have much more time to devote to this endeavor. You will already have some credentials to back up your opinions, and will no longer be seen as "just a student." However, you will likely need to begin paying off student loans soon, and thus feel pressure to earn a living. The pressure to earn enough money to support yourself, as well as pay back loans, can detract from some of the advantages of being a consultant, such as the freedom of choosing jobs that are consistent with your values, and the freedom to set your own hours. As with other fields, potential consultants may have difficulty getting hired without experience, or have difficulty gaining experience prior to getting hired. One potential fix to this problem is starting your own consulting business.

If you have been doing some consulting along the way, and feel confident in your ability to have enough work to pay the bills, then you may want to dive in headfirst and go full time. However, the majority of the key informants consulted for this book warned against taking the leap just after finishing school. The more experience you have before going out on your own in this field, the better prepared you will be to handle unforeseen challenges that arise within projects. Building up a steady client base takes time. It is safer to get a steady job with health benefits, and build up your experience, skills, and clientele before jumping to full-time independent consulting.

AFTER WORKING FOR A PRIVATE FIRM

Another ideal time to start consulting on your own is after getting some experience working for a private consulting firm. However, it may be difficult to find an enjoyable job at a private firm. But if you are dedicated to learning the craft, and flexible in terms of the work you are willing to do, there are likely to be some experienced consultants who are looking to hire young people interested in the field. In addition, you will be better prepared as a consultant and a businessperson if you have the chance to learn from others who are more experienced than you. In effect, taking this route allows you to learn from your own and others' mistakes without paying the consequences, such as losing contracts or letting down clients.

Gaining prior experience at a large firm will allow you to focus primarily on consulting and generating business because the firm will handle the contracting and administrative support. This is ideal for gaining pure technical skills and amassing experience. Smaller firms are more likely to need you to take on more tasks and responsibilities in a shorter period of time. Either setup can provide a good background for becoming an independent consultant. However, if your interests are in the nonprofit sector, there are fewer firms to choose from that do not work with corporate clients.

AFTER TIME IN A NONPROFIT OR PUBLIC SECTOR JOB

According to Carol Lukas, a consulting specialist and president of a nonprofit organization that does consulting, publishing, and research to strengthen the nonprofit sector, "You *cannot* come right out of school and start consulting. You need to build contacts, your reputation, and your business skills." In fact, these were the sentiments of several key informants. Many experienced independent consultants concurred that the absolute best way to prepare yourself is to start working within a nonprofit organization where you can build specialized skills and knowledge, and get to know people in the field.

Working in service delivery and/or management positions within a nonprofit can be useful preparation for a consultant. You can gain a better understanding of how decisions are made, how the organization is functional or dysfunctional, and hone in on key strengths and weaknesses. Furthermore, you can learn the cultural context of working within a nonprofit. Understanding the perspective of your future clients is invaluable. In fact, Carol Lukas suggested that working at multiple levels of a nonprofit is a necessary prerequisite for gaining credibility with clients and doing a good job as a consultant. Another advantage to working in the nonprofit arena prior to consulting is that when you meet with new clients, you can honestly tell them that you have been in their shoes, and know the types of issues with which they are struggling.

There are several advantages to starting out as a consultant after working for a government agency. You will build an understanding beyond your education in terms of how municipalities or federal agencies work. You will be ahead of the game in terms of knowing how to maneuver within the political landscape and navigate the bureaucracy. Any knowledge of the government's budget process, funding streams, and grants is helpful, as well.

AFTER WORKING WITH A SEASONED PROFESSIONAL

Several experienced consultants suggested taking a mentorship or an apprenticeship approach to the field. They recommended finding an expert who does the work you're interested in to gain experience. You need to be willing to do trivial work initially to learn from them, and work your way up to gain increasingly advanced skills and knowledge of consulting. There are several advantages of training under the tutelage of an experienced consultant. First, you do not have to reinvent the wheel. Second, if you work on a team with a tenured consultant and can be included in phone calls and meetings, you will get a deeper understanding of the work than you would in the same amount of time figuring it out on your own. Being an apprentice may allow you to work on multiple complex projects at one time, whereas, if you are working on your own, you would likely be able to take on fewer, less complex projects at any given time. In addition, before your name is established, you will have to spend a portion of your time generating business.

TIP

Three Tips for Gaining the Necessary Experience and Contacts

1. Work for a research or consulting firm for at least 2 years before venturing out on your own.
2. Work your way up within a nonprofit agency, making sure to perform a variety of jobs, and serving on different boards so you can say, "I've been there," to your future clients.
3. Find a consultant who will serve as a mentor for you or someone you can apprentice with to learn the ropes and build a reputation.

KEEPING IT ALL IN PERSPECTIVE

Choosing to be an independent consultant does not have to be a long-term decision. For example, Carol Lukas has noticed a cyclical process in which independent consultants tend to move back and forth between working alone, and forming groups or joining firms. They often go for a 4–5 year stretch independently, and then the urge to merge with others becomes so strong that they join some type of consulting group for 3–5 years. Then, as is common in the consulting crowd, they cannot stand to work in the system. They are constantly trying to change the system, and they prefer not to have an external authority over them. When being part of the "group" becomes intolerable, they go off and work independently again. Dawn Hanson Smart discusses how some of these types of cyclical dynamics influenced her career path in Chapter 16, "The Path to Independent Consulting."

Sometimes, individuals even end up in consulting when they hadn't planned on it. In fact, several informants said they had landed in the consulting business by accident—"Voluntary assistance turned into paid work," "I didn't plan on becoming a consultant," "We started with no business plan, because we didn't seek, or need, other people's money." So, there is some flexibility in the process, and even when you plan for certain things, other pathways can open up.

CONCLUSION

Many great consultants' backgrounds vary. Regardless of what job you held prior to consulting, it is clear from key informants and the literature on the topic that building up some credibility is crucial for success. In other words, the more experience you have, the better off you will be. Because most people believe that wisdom comes from years of experience, you and your clients will likely be more comfortable if you have been doing similar work for at least the past 5 years. Dale Rose, president of his own consulting firm, said, "Make sure you feel comfortable dealing with data and are not merely talking the talk." In a similar vein, Andrew White, an independent consultant, said, ". . . know the ins and outs of what you are doing. I know some other consultants who are really just 'face men'—they talk a good talk, but can't do the actual evaluation to save their life (they usually contract me to do their analyses). . ."

However, other successful consultants did start their practices right out of school (a few while they were advanced students). For example, Rose, whose training was in industrial organizational psychology, began doing contract work for a large company in his first year of graduate school. He also quickly gained a reputation among students in his graduate program for having a facility with statistics. He was not without experience, though, having completed several internships along the way, and even working as an internal evaluator for a few years while simultaneously building his consulting business. Rose and the others whose first consulting jobs happened during graduate school all had some supervised consulting experience before trying to venture out on their own. It appears that the perfect time in one's career to start a consulting practice is unique to the individual, his or her personality, skill sets, interests, and opportunities that arise. Whether you start consulting while in school, just out of school, after working for a private or public firm or seasoned professional, the common thread for success is obtaining some experience and mentoring prior to consulting on your own.

Chapter 4

What Kind of Business to Build

Judah Viola and Susan D. McMahon

ORGANIZATIONAL STRUCTURES

Regardless of what business structure you choose, if you are going to start your own business, it will likely be a (very) small business. According to Kishel and Kishel (1996), more than 50% of consulting firms are one-person operations, and of those that have employees, 25% are made up of between 2 and 10 people. There are many important considerations to make when trying to decide how to form your business, because your business structure affects how much you pay in taxes, the extent you can be held liable if sued, and how you can raise money if you want to grow. Most consultants usually make this decision based upon the vision that they have for their business (e.g., Is it expected to grow quickly? Is there risk for legal troubles?), or their personal circumstances (e.g., Do you have assets that you'd like to protect?). The time it takes to start up different entities, the amount of paperwork involved, and the way you will be taxed are all common factors that influence this decision. Many consultants without much of a business background often trust experts, such as accountants or lawyers, to guide them through these decisions.

The short descriptions in this section are meant to be a broad overview to introduce some of the possible business entities that one could work in or start up as a consultant. The descriptions are not complete, and they are definitely *not* meant as legal advice. Four primary business entities are described from the most simple to the most complex, as well as some pros and cons of each.

1. Sole proprietorship
2. Partnership (general, limited, and limited liability)
3. Limited liability companies
4. Corporations (for profit and not-for-profit)

Sole Proprietorship

Sole proprietorship is the simplest business structure. It basically means that you work for yourself. There is only one owner or boss of the practice, but you are allowed to hire employees or subcontract out business to other individuals or businesses. Therefore, depending on the demands of the current project and your personal preferences, you can choose to work alone, or as a member of a team. You have flexibility to work for many different organizations or companies throughout the year, but you need to keep track of extra paperwork and file income taxes for your consulting practice together with any other personal income you may earn. Your clients are different than employers in that they do not withhold taxes or provide any fringe benefits (i.e., worker's compensation insurance, health insurance, pension, or deferred tax savings plans such as a 401(k), etc.). Thus, the onus is on you to set aside an amount from the payments you receive from clients, and use it to pay taxes. An additional added cost is "self-employment tax," which refers to having to pay both halves of Social Security and Medicare (over 15% of adjusted gross income). Typically, an employer contributes to that tax (an employer covers one half and the employee covers the other half). However, as a sole proprietor your taxes are relatively simple to file because they are completed using your Social Security number, and your personal income is not separated from the business income. Clients are responsible for sending you 1099 forms (instead of W-2 forms that employers provide), and if you pay any independent contractors, you'll need to complete a 1099 form for each contractor, as well as a 1096 form for the IRS. The highest number of respondents in our consultant survey (57%) reported that they have sole proprietorships. Sole proprietors can use their own name (e.g., Jane Smith Consulting), or use assumed names for their business (e.g., Superior Consulting). However, if you do not want to use your own name for the business, you need to apply with your secretary of state's office to register the name, and to make sure that no one else is already using the same name.

A major concern with sole proprietorships is that there is no legal or economic separation between you and the business. As the sole proprietor, you are liable for any business-related expenses or debts, and you are also vulnerable to be sued personally for a business-related problem. For example, if you are unable to complete a project that you had contracted to do, the

Table 4-1 Sole Proprietorship

Advantages	Disadvantages
1. You are the boss.	1. You have unlimited liability.
2. It is easy to get the business started.	2. It is harder to raise money.
3. You keep all of the profits.	3. You often do all of the work, from
4. Your income from business is taxed as personal income.	working with clients, to marketing, and bookkeeping.
5. You can hire help as needed.	4. Your growth is limited, and the business ends when you stop.
6. You can close up shop whenever you want or need to.	

client may be able to sue you for monetary damages. In other words, as a sole proprietor, your business-related errors or misfortunes could have a negative impact on your personal or family wealth (such as savings and/or property). In the worst-case scenario, if you are sued, you could lose your savings, house, or have to declare bankruptcy.

The most common reason that key informants cite for deciding to work as sole proprietors is that forming a more complex business structure is not worth the money, time, or effort involved. Record keeping for sole proprietorships is kept to a minimum, and government regulation is also relatively nonexistent. Furthermore, many believe the likelihood of being sued is so small that it is not worth the extra time and money to avoid this risk. Furthermore, for those who do consider a lawsuit to be a realistic risk, they can offset this risk by carrying business insurance (types of insurance are discussed at the end of Chapter 5, "Getting Official (Actions)"); this provides many sole proprietors with peace of mind.

Many consultants start as sole proprietors while their practice is small, part time, or just getting off the ground. Then, when they decide to go full time or expand by hiring full-time staff, or moving out of the house and into an office, they can choose to incorporate.

Different paperwork is involved for each type of business. Besides the sole proprietorship, each business type has a unique form you must complete through the secretary of state's office, and each type of business is associated with individual Internal Revenue Service forms. Tax information is available on the Internal Revenue Service's (IRS) Web site.

General Partnerships and Limited Partnerships

General partnerships (GP) and limited partnerships (LP) are another business form that you can choose to create. Similar to sole proprietors, partnerships are not separate legal entities. Therefore, like sole proprietorships, the business income is reported on each partner's personal income tax forms. However, if you choose any type of partnership, you will need to obtain a Federal Employer Identification Number (FEIN), and file a partnership tax return even though you pay no separate federal tax. Regardless of the type of partnership established, a partnership agreement is used to spell out how power and money are divided among the partners, and how the partnership can be dissolved when necessary.

In general partnerships, all partners usually have equal shares in the business, equal say in how the business is run, and are equally liable for business debt or legal suits. The upside of this is that you: 1) do not have sole responsibility for the business, 2) can accomplish more work than you could on your own, 3) can split up undesired tasks, and 4) can focus on your strengths. However, the downside is that you may not always agree on how to run the partnership, and one partner may have to pay for another partner's mistakes or poor judgment. Only one of the key informants we interviewed was a member of a general partnership.

In contrast to general partnerships, limited partnerships have only one managing general partner and several "limited" partners who invest money but are not liable for more than the amount of money they invested. This is a good way to bring in capital, and to limit the number of people who are responsible for running the business. Limited partnerships are unequal partnerships in that the managing partner and the limited partners differ in their amount of influence on running the business. In some cases, senior partners will take on junior partners in their business, and then, over time, the roles and responsibilities of the junior partners will become more equal.

A registered limited liability partnership (LLP) is a more recent form of business in which the partners are not liable for most of the firm's debts (you'll need to check with an attorney about the exceptions to this). This business form is growing, but still constitutes a small percentage of consultants. From speaking with a few LLP members who did choose this form, all said that their decision resulted from their lawyer's recommendation.

If you are looking for some of the benefits of creating a partnership but want to avoid the negative aspects of partnerships, other options exist. As mentioned above, being a sole proprietor does not mean that you have to work on projects alone. In addition, some of the interviewed consultants have loose affiliations with colleagues, and they decide whether or not to team up on a project-by-project basis. Informal associations of independent consultants can also market services together and have a common brochure, and list each other on their Web sites while maintaining their own business

Table 4-2 Partnerships (Both General and Limited)

Advantages	Disadvantages
1. You can benefit from a greater knowledge base and broader expertise.	1. There are more egos to manage.
2. Partners will have a larger network to draw upon and attain business.	2. Contrasting opinions can pose added challenges.
3. There is the potential for more diversity of thought.	3. Team consulting often increases the cost for the client.
4. Partnerships are easy to initiate.	4. Partners have unlimited liability.
5. You can likely raise more money than on your own.	5. Profits must be shared amongst the partners.
6. Partners pay only personal income tax.	6. Partners may disagree on how to run the business.
7. Good employees can be groomed to become partners.	7. The business ends when the partners stop working.
8. It may be more fun to work with others rather than working alone.	

entities. We've included a section in Chapter 7, "Running Your Business," that discusses when team consulting is and is not most appropriate.

Limited Liability Company

A limited liability company (LLC) is also considered a "newer" type of business entity, and legally, it fits somewhere in between the partnership or sole proprietorship and the corporation. Like owners of partnerships or sole proprietorships, LLC owners pay taxes on their share of profits, or deduct their share of business losses on their personal tax returns. Also similar to sole proprietors, LLC members are considered self-employed business owners. They must make their own contributions to Social Security and Medicare directly to the IRS. However, LLC owners also have the unique option of instead electing to have their LLC taxed like a corporation. This may reduce taxes for LLC owners who will regularly need to retain a significant amount of profits in the company.

Like a corporation, all LLC owners are protected from personal liability for business debts and claims. If the business owes money or faces a lawsuit, only the assets of the business itself are at risk, as long as the business owners did not do something illegal. You can be the sole owner of your LLC in all states except Massachusetts. However, some states, including California, prohibit professionals such as accountants, doctors, and other licensed health care workers from forming LLCs. You'll need to check with

Table 4-3 Limited Liability Company (LLC)

Advantages	Disadvantages
1. An LLC is easy and inexpensive to set up.	1. Not everyone is eligible to create an LLC.
2. LLCs have no board of directors to tell you what to do.	2. LLCs have no board of directors to provide guidance or oversight.
3. You will have no stock to sell and keep track of.	3. Because there is no stock, it may be harder to raise money for an LLC than a corporation.
4. Owners have limited liability.	
5. LLC allow for flexibility in the number of owners.	4. You may have to pay self-employment tax.
6. You can decide how you want to be taxed.	5. LLCs may have to pay a yearly state "franchise tax."

a lawyer or state-regulating agency to determine whether this will affect your own possible choices.

Creating an LLC will take more work than forming a partnership, but is still easier than creating a corporation. To form an LLC, you are required to file articles of organization and an operating agreement. For a list of tasks you need to complete to form an LLC, see Appendix 4-1. Maintaining an LLC may also be more expensive than partnerships or sole proprietorships. Some states charge an annual fee that is not income-related. The fees differ from state to state, but range from about $100–$900 per year. You can find out whether your state charges a separate LLC tax or fee at the Web site of your state's secretary of state, department of corporations, or department of revenue or tax.

For-Profit Corporation

The for-profit corporation (Corp. or Inc.) is the most complex business entity, but it is also the safest in terms of personal legal liability, and is best positioned to attract investors for raising capital. For-profit corporations must issue stock, have a board of directors, and an executive committee. Typically, for-profit corporations are expected to eventually turn a profit and benefit the shareholders. For-profit corporations are taxed differently than other forms. The corporate entity must pay a corporate income tax and replacement tax, as well as a franchise tax each year based on their paid-in capital and a corporate personal property text replacement income tax. Of course, people who are paid by the corporation must also pay individual income taxes on the same earnings.

Table 4-4 Corporations

Advantages	Disadvantages
1. Stockholders have limited liability.	1. Corporations are taxed twice.
2. Corporations can raise the most money.	2. Corporations must pay capital stock tax.
3. The business continues even when you stop working for it.	3. Starting a corporation is expensive.
	4. Corporations require more paperwork.
4. Ownership is transferable.	5. Corporations are more closely regulated by the government than other business entities.

Besides tax differences, corporation owners enjoy limited liability, and for-profit corporations also have additional powers such as buying and selling other corporations or filing lawsuits. Two common types of corporations that consultants run are S corporations and C corporations. None of the consultants interviewed or surveyed for this book ran C corporations. Because of taxation issues, C corporations are usually reserved for larger businesses. Subchapter S corporations (for smaller corporations) provide owners and employees with liability protection, but allow the advantage of being taxed as an individual from the federal government. However, it is important to note that some states recognize the distinction between a subchapter S corporation and other corporations while some do not. Again, you'll need to check with your state's taxing agency, or a lawyer or accountant in your area for details.

Not-For-Profit Corporation

Not-for-profit corporations (nonprofits) are different from for-profit companies in that their purpose for existing is to provide charity, education, scientific knowledge, or arts, as opposed to making money for their stockholders. However, nonprofits can take in more money than they spend. In other words, your nonprofit can make a profit. Income can be used for operating expenses, including salaries for officers and staff.

Forming a nonprofit corporation is similar to creating a regular corporation, except that nonprofits may or may not be tax exempt (501(c)(3) status). Incorporating as a nonprofit does not guarantee that you will not have to pay taxes. You must take extra steps to apply for tax-exempt status with the IRS and your state's tax division. Whether or not a nonprofit's income is taxable depends on whether the activities are related to the nonprofit's purpose. All nonprofits must have a board of directors, bylaws, and an executive committee. Employees, executives, and board members all have limited liability. However, a board member may be held personally liable for unpaid taxes and penalties for failure to file returns, or failure to withhold and pay payroll taxes. Nonprofits are required to submit their financial statements and other information—including the salaries of directors, officers, and other key employees—to the IRS. The IRS and the nonprofits themselves are required to disclose this information to anyone who asks. Nonprofits must allow public inspection of these records during regular business hours at their principal offices. (See Appendix 4-2 for steps required to form a nonprofit.)

TIP

Researching Potential Clients and Funders: If you want to find out information about a potential client or funder that is a nonprofit, you may be able to find their annual reports online. If not, you can send a request to the IRS. The request should include the name of the organization, the year and the type of return requested, and should be submitted in writing to:

Commissioner of Internal Revenue
Attn: Freedom of Information Reading Room
1111 Constitution Avenue, NW
Washington, DC 20224

WHAT SERVICES WILL YOU PROVIDE?

Building capacity within organizations with which you work is a value in community psychology. In other words, (you are trying to) enable organizations to do more and work yourself out of a job. If you teach organizations to improve their planning, implementation, and evaluation skills, you can work toward increasingly advanced improvements, or move on to assist other organizations. There are many ways to build capacity within an organization. Jolley, Wituk, Gregory, Thomas, and Meissen discuss some methods for capacity building within organizations in Chapter 12, "Capacity Building with Faith-Based and Community Organizations: Lessons Learned from the Compassion Kansas Initiative."

The roles available to a consultant at times seem boundless, but often fit the broad categories of planner, researcher, advocate, advisor, or evaluator. You can help create a vision for the neighborhood, design a program, train a board of directors, or develop a fundraising strategy. Consultants also build capacity by providing structure throughout a planning process (e.g., strategic planning, operational planning, business planning, marketing planning, financial planning, fundraising planning, or crisis planning).

Many nonprofit service providers or government agencies are too busy to stop their day-to-day work and look at how others around the country are attempting to solve similar problems or provide similar services. You can do research and bring "promising-practice" ideas back to the organization. You can help gather information about changing trends in the needs of the populations they are trying to serve, or how current trends in public policy decisions are affecting the population they serve. Assessments of supervisory practices, training programs, or service provisions are also common tasks carried out by independent consultants.

Of the consultants we surveyed, 96% said they provided program evaluation services. However, the vast majority also said they had either fallen into or carved out a niche within the field of consulting for the public sector. These 13 niches are described as follows:

1. Grant writing: assisting or even taking the lead in writing foundation or government grants to fund new or existing programs, staff positions, or services. For more information on grant writing for community-based organizations, see Chapter 15, "Grant Writing for Consultants 101," by independent consultant, Andrea Solarz.

2. Asset mapping/needs assessments: helping organizations or communities determine the strengths or assets that they should be taking advantage of, and identifying specific challenges or needs that may exist.

3. Program development: activities directly related to either the establishment of a new program or service(s), or the improvement, expansion, or integration of an existing program or service(s).

4. Strategic planning: aiding an organization to envision its future and develop strategies, goals, objectives, and action plans to achieve success in the future.

5. Logic modeling: clearly determining the goals, objectives, inputs, and rationale for expected outcomes for a particular program or set of services (for a sample logic model, see Chapter 9, "From Start to Finish: A Typical Evaluation Project," by Kathleen Dowell).

6. Evaluation training: building capacity within organizations by training them how to systematically collect information to answer questions they have about the process or outcomes of their organization.

7. Process evaluations: focus on how programs are implemented and operate. They identify the procedures undertaken and the decisions made in developing the program. A process evaluation describes how the program operates, the services it delivers, and the functions it

carries out. By documenting the program's development and operation, it allows for an assessment of the reasons for successful or unsuccessful performance, and provides information for replication.

8. Outcome/impact/summative evaluations: the systematic collection of information to assess the impact of a program, present conclusions about the merit or worth of a program, and make recommendations about the program's future direction or improvement.

9. Policy research or topical area research: providing background information or helping to establish expectations and planning based on current or proposed public or organizational policies (for more information on policy consulting, see Chapter 14, "Consulting in Public Policy Settings," by Jon Miles and Steven Howe).

10. Advocacy: including speaking or writing on behalf of an organization or community to government officials, funders, or other groups that could impact the health or success of the client.

11. Data analysis: systematically applying statistical and logical techniques to describe, summarize, and compare data.

12. Report writing: often encompasses annual/quarterly reports, white papers, literature reviews, requests for proposals, or research reports.

13. Leadership training/executive coaching: helping to transform management and executives into better leaders, listeners, and learners.

As demonstrated by the list above, there are a variety of niches that consultants can choose, depending on one's interests, training, and expertise. Developing a niche helps you to become known for specific skill sets that can help you establish a client base and reputation in the field. In Chapter 11, "Consulting with Small Community-Based Nonprofit Organizations: Insights and Understandings," Cellar, Harper, and Neubaur discuss the importance of developing a niche.

PART TIME VERSUS FULL TIME

Consulting can be a big commitment, so it may be a good idea to try it first on a part-time basis to see if you like the work. Not everyone is cut out for a full-time consulting career. Even if you feel like this is your life's calling, unless you are fortunate enough to have clients already lined up, it can be very difficult for the first few years to maintain a steady stream of contracts. The literature emphasizes that part-time consulting allows one to build a client base years before actually moving into full-time, external consulting. Established full-time consultants often subcontract to graduate students and recent graduates (this saves them time and money). In addition, many consultants would like to find someone currently in or straight out of graduate school who sincerely wants to learn about the business. Conventional wisdom on this question of part time vs full time indicates that you should take it slow, and build up to full time as your project offers, experience, skills, and desire increase over time.

WORKING FROM A HOME OFFICE VERSUS OFFICE AWAY FROM HOME

Available resources, the size of your business, and your working style will influence your choice to work from home or in an office. About half of the informants for this study reported that they run their practice out of a home office. There are pros and cons to both options of renting office space versus working from home.

Office space costs money but offers a place to see clients. However, most clients will be just as pleased or happier if you meet with them in their offices. This will also allow you to learn a little bit about them through your observational skills on site. You can meet more people and be recognized when you return. To offset the high cost of renting office space, you may want to consider sharing space with one or more independent small business people. For instance, clinical psychologists who are at the beginning stages of private practices often share office space while they build up their clientele. Working in an office also allows you to keep work and personal life separate.

On the other hand, working from home gives you a lot of flexibility, costs less, and may allow you to be more comfortable. You don't have to waste any time or money commuting to and from an office. You don't need to get dressed up, and you can easily step outside for fresh air whenever you like. You can walk the dog, take your kids to swim practice, or do other tasks at a moment's notice. Depending on how separate and dedicated your home office is, you may be able to write off some of your expenses. However, all of the possible distractions while working from home will require a higher level of self-discipline, and home is often a more difficult space in which to keep your work and personal/family time separate. Your time is likely to be more interrupted, and you may risk getting less done or working longer hours to compensate for interruptions. Depending on your situation, working from home may or may not be worth it.

When considering working from home, you also need to see whether your city or county planning department has set up any zoning laws that restrict you from conducting business from your home. While residential zoning in most municipalities allow for small nonpolluting home businesses, there are enough exceptions that it is something worth looking into. You can get a copy of your local ordinances either through a link on your city's Web page, or from your city or county clerk's office, the city attorney's office, or your public library.

TIP

Mailing Address: If you decide to run your practice out of your home, it is a good idea to obtain a post office box as a business address, as this is perceived as more professional than using your home address.

TIP

Liability Concerns: If you decide to run your practice from an office, you need to look into general liability insurance that will cover any injuries that may take place on the premises.

TIP

Increase Professionalism: Spend a little extra money for a higher quality printer and copier. To keep your documents looking professional, clean your copier glass often with glass cleaner to avoid picking up dust or dirt specks from the glass on copies for clients.

You need to think through your options carefully regarding where you choose to focus on your work. If you have employees or partners, you need to take into account your own preferences, as well as the working styles of others, in order to make the best decisions for your business. Figuring out what other questions you need to answer when considering starting a business can be done by going through the process of creating a strategic plan or business plan.

STRATEGIC PLANNING/BUSINESS PLANNING

Only 22% of survey respondents reported that they completed a formal strategic planning process or business plan. However, over half of them said that it would have been useful, and they recommend that someone getting started in consulting go through this process. A strategic or business plan involves getting your vision for your consulting practice on paper. The more detail you can include, the better. If you are having trouble writing out a clear vision, this is a sign that you have more thinking and research to do before you start. One way to begin the process is to write a mission statement for your practice. Next, write down your answers to the following nine questions. These correspond to different sections of a traditional business plan document.

1. What type of practice will I run? (Business Description)
2. Will I work out of my home or an office? (Business Description)
3. Will I have partners or go it alone? (Personnel Description)
4. How much time will I devote to my work? (Personnel Description)
5. What services will I provide at the start? (Product or Services Description)
6. Who will my clients be? (Marketing Plan)
7. Will I consult locally, nationally, and/or internationally? (Marketing Plan)
8. What will be the economic costs of doing business? (Operation Costs)
9. What if a partner or owner wants out? (Exit Strategy)

Once you've answered these questions, then you need to set goals and measurable objectives for the practice. Develop and write out your plan for achieving your objectives, including a time line and means to achieve success. Thus, your written plan will help you think through the process at the start, but it can also be used as a tool in the future to measure success. See Appendix 4-3 for more details about the structure of a traditional business plan, and what information goes in each section.

CONCLUSION

The decision to start a business is significant. Deciding when to start the business and what type of business is dependent on your personal goals and capacity. For example, only you know whether it is better for you to start out on your own or with a partner. However, in most cases it is not necessary to incorporate until your business is more established. Operating a sole proprietorship is a lot simpler, and until the business is actually making sufficient money, the extra record keeping and fees may not be worth the potential tax savings, liability protections, or air of professionalism that may come with forming a company. On the other hand, some clients may shy away from hiring a sole proprietor, and prefer an official and established incorporated company. In addition, as a sole proprietor, your personal assets are at stake (to pay debts or lawsuits), and for some, it is not worth risking property or savings for this new business, no matter how slim the chances seem of being sued or going into debt.

Consulting offers a lot of flexibility in terms of developing a niche that fits with your interests, guiding the decision-making process for your business, and working from home if you choose. Take some time to figure out the best type of company to form, and engage in some strategic planning. Consider the services you want to provide, marketing, operating requirements, and finances, so you can be well-prepared on your journey to becoming a successful consultant.

APPENDIX 4-1 Five Steps to Forming a Limited Liability Company

1. Choose an available business name that complies with your state's LLC rules.
2. File formal paperwork, usually called "articles of organization," and pay the filing fee (ranging from $100 to $900, depending on the state).
3. Create an LLC operating agreement, which sets out the rights and responsibilities of the LLC members.
4. Publish a notice of your intent to form an LLC (if required by your state).
5. Obtain licenses and permits required for your business.

See www.nolo.com for details on each step.

APPENDIX 4-2 How to Form a Nonprofit Corporation and Receive a 501(c)(3) Tax Exemption

1. Choose an available business name that meets the requirements of state law.
2. File formal paperwork, usually called "articles of incorporation," and pay a small filing fee (typically under $100).
3. Apply for your federal and state tax exemptions.
4. Create corporate "bylaws," which set out the operating rules for your nonprofit corporation.
5. Appoint the initial directors. (In some states, you must choose your initial directors before you file your articles, because you must list their names in the document.)
6. Hold the first meeting of the board of directors.
7. Obtain licenses and permits required for your corporation.

See www.nolo.com for details on each step.

For more information on forming a nonprofit, The Community Tool Box has great information on bylaws and standard operating procedures at http://ctb.ku.edu/tools/en/sub_section_main_1098.htm.

Also, the Ohio State University Information Extension provides a useful fact sheet on the topic of bylaws and standard operating procedures, which can be found at http://ohioline.osu.edu/cd-fact/co-bl.html.

APPENDIX 4-3 Writing a Business Plan

The following recommendations for the core elements of a business plan are adapted from recommendations from the Small Business Administration (SBA), a government agency devoted to helping small businesses get started.

Cover Sheet:

Include company name and address, business contact information, including phone, fax, email, Web site, names of owner(s), and the date.

Purpose:

Usually a one-page statement about why you wrote the plan. Consultants often write the plan to raise money, and if this is the case, be specific about how much is needed and why.

Table of Contents:

List the elements of the plan.

1. Executive Summary

This section is a short abstract of the entire plan. Try to include only a sentence or two summarizing each section of the plan. It should include who you are, what you want, and what the reader should do (i.e., hire you, refer you to their clients, loan you money, etc.), and why. The executive summary is usually written after the rest of the plan is completed.

2. Business Description

Include the who, what, where, when and why, of the business.

Also include the resources of the business (in our case, the experience, knowledge, skills, and abilities of the consultant(s)).

3. Product or Services Description

Describe the services you will provide. Describe what final products you can provide for clients.

Services and products may include:

1. A written report with suggestions for better service delivery, or efficiency
2. An evaluation portion of a grant proposal, or an entire grant proposal
3. A needs/assets assessment

4. A program development or evaluation report
5. A portion of the organization's annual report
6. Evaluation/research instruments

Describe the core of the business. Be specific, yet concise. Include your areas of interest and/or expertise. Even if you expect to work within a niche, don't limit yourself too much in your description.

4. Marketing Plan

Describe how you stand out from the competition and why you will succeed. Take some time to think about this. The opinions of friends and colleagues may be helpful. Describe the market for consulting services in the geographic and topic areas you choose to work within. Find out information about the size of the existing market. You can do this by answering a few simple questions. For example:

- What major foundations provide funding to social service agencies in your area?
- What foundations provide funding for new education initiatives, theater, arts, and public radio and television in the area?
- What price will you charge? How does this compare to others?
- What are the operating budgets of the nonprofit social service providers incorporated locally?
- How many consulting companies in your area already provide similar services to those you are planning to offer?

Some of this information is available through the Internet or yellow page searches. You can also find out from funders who they have hired in the past few years. University professors in the area and members of the local affiliate to your professional associations will also have lots of information about the market.

Within the marketing plan you also want to include a brief explanation of how you expect to get contracts.

5. Operating Requirements

List your general overhead or nondirect costs. Overhead is usually divided into two types: business-related expenses and client-related expenses.

Business-related expenses may include:

- Rent and utilities (e.g., gas, water, and electric)
- Office equipment, furniture, and services (e.g., phone, fax, printer, photocopier, desk, file cabinets, paper, Internet service)

- Travel costs (for commuting, site visits, and professional development).
- Yearly cost of professional support services (e.g., an accountant, lawyer)
- Any tools that you use (e.g., computer hardware and software)
- Health insurance and other insurance you carry

Business-related expenses are billed indirectly to the client through consulting fees. Client-related expenses, on the other hand, are billed directly to the client in addition to consulting fees, and will vary depending on the particular project.

6. Personnel

List the people who will be directly involved in doing the work of the business. Include bio-sketches with background and expertise of personnel. Strong words can be powerful. Check out how existing firms that do what you want to do describe themselves on their Web sites. What about their descriptions do you find appealing? Would you hire them? How can you be competitive?

7. Financial Data

This section is usually aimed at impressing potential investors so they are confident they will recoup their investments. However, even if you are not trying to raise start-up money, it is still useful to include a financial section. This section should include projections of what doing business will cost, and how you can make it worthwhile. According to the *Idiot's Guide to Starting a Home-Based Business*, the financial data that are essential for a brand new business plan include: (1) projected start-up costs; (2) projected income statement; (3) statement of expected profit and loss; (4) projected monthly cash flow statement; and (5) personal financial statement(s). Lukas (1998) also provides useful worksheets on this topic.

8. Exit Strategy

In this section, you need to consider the "what if" scenarios, and write down a plausible answer to the following questions: What will you or your partners do if you get a great job offer as the result of the work you have done? What happens if you decide to move away, or if one of you burns out? What about an unexpected illness or injury? Who will be responsible? Will the business cease to exist? How will money, assets, or clients be divided up among the investors?

9. Supporting Documents/Appendices

Examples of past work and testimonials from past employers/clients/professors can strengthen your business plan. It is nice to have your work speak for itself, or have other people speak for you. The *Idiot's Guide* also states that including the personal tax returns of all owners for the past 3 years is necessary if you are trying to get a loan. Resumes and curriculum vitaes are also recommended. On the Small Business Administration's (SBA) Web site, there is computer software that walks you through the steps of how to write a business plan. Some of the forms can be completed online for free, while others can be purchased. For more information, see: http://www.sba .gov/smallbusinessplanner/plan/writeabusinessplan/index.html.

Chapter 5

Getting Official (Actions)

Judah Viola and Susan D. McMahon

STEPS TO TAKE

Once you have decided to become a consultant—prepared by building your internal and external resources, determined what type of business structure to form, and written your detailed business plan with time-oriented goals— it is now time to take action. While many consultants start getting official while working on consulting projects, ideally you can get the paperwork out of the way first. This chapter will discuss many of the mundane steps you'll need to take to get official, while avoiding legal or financial trouble before you begin.

Business Name and Logo

After you have created your strategic plan, it is time to create a name for the business. Many books on writing business plans or starting up a small business discuss branding and name creation (e.g., Barrow, Barrow, & Brown, 2008; Elias & Stim, 2007). This process can be as simple or complicated as you want to make it. In general, you want your business name to differentiate you from others, as well as be descriptive so that your name will be associated with the services you provide, or at least an image you want to create. Of course, you also want your name to be memorable. Once you have found a name you like, you need to look up whether there are any other businesses already using this name within the state you reside. In most states, there are Web sites that provide this information, and they are typically run by the secretary of state's office.

If you choose a name for your business that is different from your own name or you add a label such as "and Associates" to your business, you are required by law in most states to notarize, register, and publish a "fictitious business name statement" (the names for this document vary by state, but the process is largely the same). Regardless of the name you choose, once you discern whether it is unique, you should register your name with your secretary of state's office (registration usually lasts for 5 years). This will help ensure that someone else does not use your business name. Once you register the name of your business, you will be eligible to open a bank account in the name of the business. Banks typically require that you show proof of business name registration, as well as an Employer Identification Number (EIN), which you can obtain through the Internal Revenue Service (IRS) Web site.

You may also want to create a logo, slogan, or tag line for your business. Logos, slogans, or tag lines are less crucial for small consulting businesses that will not do much advertising. Nonetheless, they help establish your brand identity and make you more memorable to both potential clients and people who might refer business to you. Rather than hiring a design firm to create a logo for you, there are Web sites that allow you to hold an online "contest" for your logo (or business cards or Web sites, for that matter). The Institute of Management Consultants USA, in a recent "Consultant's Tip of the Day" explained,

> . . .You specify who you are, what kind of image you want, including preferred colors, shapes, backgrounds (only if you want), and how much of a "prize" you are offering for the design. Within a week, some of the 15,000 designers connected to the service will create a range of logos you can select from. You can also see what designs you find appealing by using the search feature, and then refining your "contest" request. Most recent contests are in the $200–$400 range.

Copyrights and Trademarks

Once you start writing reports for clients, you'll want to understand the distinction between a few basic types of intellectual property protections. A copyright is a form of protection provided to the authors of "original works of authorship," both published and unpublished. For the purposes of consultants, copyrights are most often used to protect your writing from being duplicated or sold by someone else.

According to the Illinois Secretary of State's Web site, a trademark is a word, name, symbol, or device used to identify and distinguish the goods or a unique product of a person, from those manufactured and sold by others, and to indicate the source of the goods. The purpose of a trademark is to protect words, phrases, and logos used in federally regulated commerce, which identify you as the source of the goods or services. Basically, if you create a logo or slogan for your business, a trademark will help you prevent others from using the same logo or slogan.

The process of registering a copyright and trademark are entirely different. The filing fee for a copyright is small (approximately $30), but can add up if you produce many reports, surveys, or other products you want to protect. Obtaining registration is relatively easy, requiring a short registration application. For a trademark, the filing fee is more substantial, and the time to obtain registration is longer. The Illinois Secretary of State's Web site and similar sites for other states provide comprehensive information on registering a business, trademark, name, or symbol.

Licenses and Permits

It is important to receive information from your State Department of Revenue to find out permit requirements for running a business in your area. Most states' revenue offices either provide business registration kits on their Web site, or will send them to you upon request. These kits will explain whether or not you need any licenses or permits to conduct business within their jurisdiction. For example, if you are trained as a psychologist, social worker, or counselor but will not be working as a clinician or therapist, obtaining a license is typically not required. However, if you have been trained as a clinician and hold the appropriate credentials, from a marketing perspective, it could be to your advantage to keep your license up-to-date, because you are not allowed to market yourself as a psychologist or therapist without holding a license in the state in which you are working.

Become a Certified Woman-Owned or Minority-Owned Business

Once you are an official business entity and have taken care of any basic licenses or permits needed to conduct business, you may be eligible to be listed as an official small business enterprise, woman-owned, or minority-owned business. Similar designations include:

- Women's Business Enterprise (WBE)
- Historically Underutilized Business (HUB)
- Disadvantaged Business Enterprise (DBE)
- Small Business Enterprise (SBE)
- Emerging Small Business Enterprise (ESBE)

- Small Disadvantaged Business (SDB), with or without 8(a) certification
- Minority-Owned Business Enterprise (MOBE)

The benefits of such distinctions include:

- putting certification on marketing materials
- listings on Web sites
- eligibility for technical assistance/business support, such as training, and access to loans or bonds
- preference for local, state, or federal contracts or foundation grants

Typically, the requirements for certification include that the business be at least 51% owned, as well as have the daily operations overseen by a woman or an Asian Pacific American, Hispanic American, Native American, African American, and/or American woman who is a U.S. citizen. Furthermore, the business must operate in the state or local principality that is offering the certification. In addition to government certifications, there are private entities (e.g., The Women's Business Enterprise National Council) that provide such distinctions/designations/certifications, each with similar yet independent requirements, fees, and time lines.

For many of the certifications, financial records from the business are required in the application, and for the Small Disadvantaged Business and 8(a) certifications, your personal financial information is requited (i.e., income tax returns and W-2 or 1099 forms). The 8(a) certification is a business development program. You are required to work with a mentoring firm that will oversee and assist with your business planning. If you are not interested in oversight or being mentored, then this certification is not for you. (For more information on the 8(a) certification, see the SBA's Web site.) While at first glance these programs may seem to be tailored to manufacturers or retailers, if you look a little further you will find that there are categories of business that choose to get these certifications that fit within the "Professional, Scientific, and Technical Services" area. The type of business structure you set up may be relevant, as not-for-profit companies do not qualify for any of these certifications. Some certifications do accept sole proprietorships and others do not.

Getting on Vendor Lists

School districts and government offices sometimes have preferred vendor lists that allow members to receive Requests for Proposals (RFPs) or other notices about potential projects. Often, becoming a preferred vendor is just a matter of submitting the appropriate paperwork that can be found online, or by contacting an office directly. For example, "Fedvendor" is a federal government vendor directory that lists consultants and other vendors, as well as postings for RFPs. These Web sites typically provide a profile of each vendor with information about the services you provide, your credentials/certifications, and your contact information. Some vendor directories even allow you to provide a link to your own Web site.

ACCOUNTING ISSUES

Since clients do not withhold taxes from your payments, you need to take care of withholding taxes for yourself or your business on a quarterly basis. To learn more about this and register with the federal government, contact the Internal Revenue Service at 1-800-829-3676, and request:

- Your Business Tax Kit (YBTK) for either a sole proprietorship, part-nership, or corporation
- A Tax Guide for Small Business (Publication 334)
- Employer's Tax Guide (Publication 15)

Depending upon what type of business entity your practice falls under, you will file your taxes differently. No matter what form you choose, it is advisable to employ an accountant (at least for the first filing). Accountants can help you design a system that is tailored to your specific needs. Among other things, they can help with budgeting, forecasting, preparing financial statements, obtaining loans, and preparing tax returns.

Surprisingly, only 40% of respondents to our consultant survey reported that they used an accountant when they first began consulting. However, many of those who didn't seek an accountant in the beginning said they wished they had done so. Now, 90% of the full-time respondents reported they use accountant services to file their taxes. Overwhelmingly, they said this was a worthwhile expense. We suggest you meet with a few accountants before you select one you'll work with. Your relationship with your accountant will remain important as long as you are in business. You want to make sure you are working with someone you trust, and you feel can give you the attention and expert advice that you will need. Many great consultants are not naturally savvy with bookkeeping, and may not be interested in keeping up with changing tax regulations.

Many informants also recommended getting QuickBooks, Peachtree, Quicken, or a similar type of accounting/bookkeeping software as a means to keep financial records organized. In addition to being a good business practice, keeping good records and being organized when it comes to your receivables and payables will reduce the amount of time you or your accountant will need to spend in order to complete your taxes, and thus, will save you money.

LEGAL ISSUES

Many consultants we've spoken to periodically use lawyers, but not everyone believes they are necessary, especially in the early stages of your business. As lawyer fees can add up quickly, there is not really a consensus on how worthwhile their services are for consultants to community based organizations. Here are some of the reasons why you may want to use a lawyer. The first thing that a lawyer can help you with is choosing the type of business organization that best suits your needs and objectives. An attorney can help you protect your assets, and advise you about local, state, and federal regulations that may affect your business. They will be familiar with all of the risks and regulations associated with each business structure, and can advise you on what will be the safest or lowest cost form of business you can build in your location, while still meeting the needs of your clientele. At different phases of business planning, your lawyer can assist with a variety of questions. For example, when you are getting started, you may want to ask a lawyer about personal and company liability issues. An attorney is also useful when it comes to filing paperwork in order to obtain licenses, permits, or getting incorporated. They can help you draft or review articles of incorporation, business bylaws, or partnership agreements. When you are in the contracting phase with a client, you may want to ask about intellectual property issues, such as who owns the data, reports, and publications. A lawyer can prepare or inspect contracts, resolve tax questions, assist in obtaining financing, and help when dealing with financial institutions, or governmental bodies. For instance:

- You or the business may face collection problems with clients.
- You or the business may become involved in disputes with creditors.
- You or the business may have disputes with present or former employees.
- You may want to expand or restructure your business in the future.

Then again, there are many tasks that a lawyer would gladly do for you at his or her hourly rate, which you could easily and safely complete on your own. The following is a list of tasks that you can accomplish yourself with self-help resources rather than paying a lawyer:

- Research and reserve a trademark or trade name for your business.

- File a fictitious business name statement if you will do business under a different name.
- Apply for and reserve a domain name for your Web site.
- Apply for your business Employer Identification Number (EIN).
- Apply for the required business licenses and permits.
- Lease commercial space.
- Complete the necessary IRS paperwork for hiring new employees.

One of the nice things about taking care of your own legal tasks is that if you educate yourself about basic legal issues, you can take care of a lot of the legal legwork yourself, and only involve your attorney when you have a specific question. For example, many consultants like to create their own contracts, and then ask their lawyer to look them over to make sure there aren't missing pieces or legal issues, as opposed to asking a lawyer to write contracts for them. This "legal coach" arrangement can be one of the most cost-effective ways to use legal services.

If you do decide to hire a lawyer, there are several ways to find one. The most highly recommended option is to get a referral from a colleague who knows and has worked with the lawyer personally. Another decent option is to look into area law schools. Many of them offer discounted services or clinics for small businesses, nonprofits, or those who primarily work with nonprofits. The state bar association can also provide you with names of reputable lawyers in your area.

BANKING

Our advice for banking is rather simple. Establish a separate bank account for your business, whether it's a sole proprietorship or a corporation. Opening checking and savings accounts for the business is inexpensive, makes bookkeeping easier, and is more professional than using your personal accounts. Once you are a bit more established, do not hesitate to get a business credit card, but make sure you pay off your balance on a monthly basis to avoid high rates of interest. A business credit card will help you separate your personal/business expenses, track your overhead costs, and establish a track record if you want to get a loan in the future. Business loans are not recommended for the novice consultant for a few reasons. First, initial start-up and operating costs are low, and second, landing additional contracts is not guaranteed, and business tends to be more inconsistent when you are starting out. The experts in the field suggest waiting until business is booming to spring for the nice office equipment.

INSURANCE

Health insurance may be the thing that you have the most difficulty affording at first—it was the one most commonly raised concern during interviews. Health insurance is very costly for individuals, and maintaining other jobs with health benefits is a common reason why people choose to keep their consulting practices as part-time or side occupations. Choosing the proper health insurance is a very personal decision, and the costs and benefits of different options should be weighed carefully.

There are three main types of business-related insurance you will want to consider obtaining. The first is called business liability insurance, which is important for protecting against injury at your offices or on the surrounding premises (i.e., stairs, walkway, etc.). The second relevant business insurance is called errors and omissions insurance (E&O). Business-related mistakes are covered by E&O insurance. Most of the consultants interviewed stressed the importance of insurance; however, some of them explained that they do not carry these types of insurance due to cost (especially if they work out of their homes and already have homeowner's or renter's insurance). The third type of business insurance is only relevant for consultants who hire employees. By law, if you have employees, you will need to pay for workers' compensation insurance to cover wages in the case of employee absence due to injury on the job. Having to provide benefits such as workers' compensation insurance is cited as one reason why some consultants prefer subcontracting work instead of hiring employees. Accountants or lawyers can advice you about the legal implications of subcontracting, and when this is and is not a valid option.

One way to find business insurance or professional insurance at a reduced rate is to look for opportunities to purchase the insurance through a chamber of commerce or trade association. For example, if your work is within the fields of either psychological evaluation or educational research, you can look for insurance through your professional organizations such as the American Psychological Association (APA), the American Evaluation Association (AEA), or the American Educational Research Association (AERA). Specifically, through AEA, two types of insurance are currently available:

1. Professional liability/errors and omissions insurance is for evaluators and consultants whose services include assessing, evaluating, and/or advising on organizational structure, systems and procedures, employee relations, human resources, and/or other management-related issues. This insurance can protect policy holders against money lost in lawsuits.

2. Business liability insurance covers financial obligations incurred through lawsuits, as well as the repair or replacement of a building and any equipment, stock, or furniture that are property of the business owner, with an option to get extra coverage for cars.

   Two other types of insurance you may want to consider are comprehensive insurance, which protects the business against robbery, theft, burglary, and a variety of other hazards; and personnel insurance, which is relevant if your company is a partnership, and covers you if one of the partners dies, is disabled, or for some other health-related reason cannot continue to work. In this case, the proceeds are paid directly to the consulting firm.

Chapter 6

Finding Work

Shaunti Knauth, Judah Viola, and Courtney Cowgill

MARKETING AND NETWORKING

The best thing you can do to find new projects is to provide useful and top-notch products for your current clients. In other words, do your work well. With quality work as your core strategy, however, there are other strategies you can and should use to build your consulting practice. In this chapter, we discuss marketing and networking. You'll find some overlap between these two topics. Both involve creating exchanges and building relationships, which are at the heart of building a consulting practice.

Marketing

Marketing is usually defined as actively selling your product. As the American Marketing Association puts it, "Marketing is the activity, set of institutions, and processes for creating, communicating, delivering, and exchanging offerings that have value for customers, clients, partners, and society at large" (AMA, 2008). The purpose is to create exchanges.

Most traditional components of marketing have not proven to apply particularly well in the small niche of consulting with nonprofits. Advertising, for example, is virtually nonexistent. Potential clients do not expect consultants to advertise, and they are typically not responsive to it. Cold calling potential clients is also not recommended. Even targeted mailings do not seem to be worthwhile. For example, when Andrew White was a motivated student attempting to build up his consulting practice, he gave traditional marketing a try. He sent a mailing out to all area hospitals and related agencies that he felt he could offer useful consulting services, but received absolutely no responses. He has since decided to join the rest of the consultants we spoke with and focus on gaining clients through word of mouth.

However, there are features of a marketing approach that are useful to building your consulting practice. The main one is developing *promotional materials* that are helpful when you do get the call to meet with a potential client. While most consultants in the nonprofit sector do not get clients through advertising, this does not mean you should not be prepared to showcase what you can do.

The first step in developing the materials is to spend some time defining for yourself, and what it is you have to offer. Before you can market your services, you must have something of value for potential clients. What are the knowledge, abilities, skills, and experience you offer to your clients? What are your unique strengths?

Promotional Materials

We recommend you compile these seven basic promotional materials:

1. Resume (two versions): Develop a top-notch resume and, curriculum vitae. Different clients prefer different formats. Some clients are used to scanning brief credentials, and want to see that you can convey your message in a concise manner, which is best illustrated in a resume. Others will be more interested in the credibility that comes with publications and professional presentations on the topic for which they seek your help, and this more extensive version of your resume is a curriculum vitae. Have your resume and curriculum vitae reviewed by experienced colleagues you trust.

2. Biographical sketch: A brief (two- or three-paragraph) narrative that focuses on your strengths, lists some of your clients or the industries you work in, and identifies your accomplishments. This document is listed as among the more useful marketing materials that consultants keep on hand and up-to-date.

3. Client lists: A list of satisfied clients that you can share with potential clients is a good tool to use with new clients who may not be familiar with your work. You might find it useful to have two versions of this document as well. The first can be a simple list of names and locations. The second, a more detailed list with more information about the client and a short description of the work (including the amount of money or time spent on the project), and successful outcomes of the project, such as how useful your training or research project was for them.

4. Business cards: These are often produced in sets of 500, so don't be shy about handing them out.

5. Brochures or service descriptions: A brochure can be a fancy, sophisticated marketing tool, or it can be a very simple one-page handout that highlights important information you want clients to know about you. If you are not ready to develop a brochure, it will be helpful to at least create a fact sheet that concisely explains the benefits of your services.

6. Web site: As we all spend more and more time on the Internet, having a Web presence becomes more important. The content of your basic Web site can be made up of the same promotional materials listed above, plus a mission statement. Look at other consultants' Web sites for ideas. However, if you don't have the time or skills to keep the site up-to-date, and you are not willing to pay for the service on a regular basis, do not set up the site. It is worse to have an old and poorly maintained site than no Web site at all.

7. Work product samples: It is always nice to have some examples of your work products to show clients. While every report, survey, interview protocol, strategic plan, grant, training manual, or presentation materials will be unique to each client, it can come in handy to show what some of your finished products have looked like in the past. Harper, Blaha, and Samaniego discuss materials they find useful from both a client and consultant perspective in Chapter 10, "Developing and Maintaining Long-Term Consulting Relationships."

Tactics That Don't Cost Money

It may be useful to examine other marketing approaches, such as those presented in *The Business of Consulting* (Biech, 1998), which includes 113 tactics for low-budget marketing. Biech's book is not tailored to folks working in the nonprofit or public sector, and some of the tactics are merely common sense. However, we've picked 10 items that we think are particularly useful. You'll find some overlap with other ideas in the section on networking that follows. Notice the importance of building relationships and exchanges.

1. Invite potential clients to a mini presentation to get an idea of your expertise and services.

2. Find reasons to call your current and past clients periodically.

3. Pass on your extra work to trusted colleagues. Sometimes the best way you can serve a client is to pass on a project that will require time and attention that you just don't have at the moment. While some clients may be turned off, or not think of you first in the future, your

reputation will be hurt more if you agree to take on a project for which you cannot deliver great services.

4. Help your clients or potential clients locate other consultants who can do work you are not qualified to do. Referrals of this sort will help you build trust with clients, and maintain reciprocal relationships with colleagues.

5. Share your expertise (e.g., advice, ideas, materials, instruments) freely with clients and other consultants. Remember why you do this work in the first place—to see your ideas in action, and building capacity of organizations whose work you value. Successful consultants argue that this makes business sense, because it allows you to be authentic with clients and doesn't turn every interaction into a business transaction.

TIP

Some consultants suggest being more careful about setting limits with regard to intellectual property, and mentioned having problems they called "creeping freebies." This occurs when consultants meet with clients or discuss projects, and share their ideas about methodology or how to move forward with a project prior to contracting. Then the potential client decides that they will take the ideas of the consultant, and attempt to complete the project internally and not compensate the consultant. While this is impossible to prevent completely, one way to reduce the likelihood is to discuss your plan as a suggestion in broad general terms, and then start discussing the scope of your role, and the client's budget for the project prior to sharing a more detailed plan.

---

6. Write letters to the editor of your local newspaper or professional journal. Letters can serve multiple purposes. They force you to think through an issue, and provide exposure to a wide range of potential clients, colleagues, and organizations. Letters to the editor are much less time-consuming, and often more widely read than published research studies in academic journals. Publications of any sort help you establish yourself as an authority on the given topic.

7. Write a book chapter or book. Similar to the reasons above, a book or chapter will force you to learn and organize your thoughts and experiences. A book or chapter can help you build your credibility and exposure. You can also give your book or chapter to existing or potential clients if you think it will address a concern they have, or demonstrate some of the knowledge or skill you bring to the table.

Feel free to contact us in a few years, and we'll let you know how this tactic worked for us!

8. Tactfully ask your clients to refer you to their colleagues if they are satisfied with your work. While this may happen naturally, a subtle reminder can help boost business.

9. Teach a course at a college or university, or lead a workshop for a professional society or community group. Much like writing forces you to dive in and think carefully about a topic, teaching forces you to learn or re-familiarize yourself with material in a deeper and more meaningful way than you have in the past.

10. Create a list of success stories you have had with past clients to share with potential clients. Being able to articulate the value you bring to an organization through narratives is a powerful tool. While clients may be impressed by who you have worked with or how much you have published, those things will only get you on their radar. Hearing stories of concrete instances when your work has benefitted others can really help you win business.

Networking

Time and time again, we hear from the experts in this field that they survive and thrive on word-of-mouth business. Your first clients will likely be, or be referred from, people with whom you have already worked as an employee or student, or already have some existing relationship. All of the consultants interviewed said they already knew the person who got them their first consulting job prior to starting their practice (i.e., either their first client or the person who referred them to their first client). Your network is more likely to lead to consulting work than traditional marketing activities, or responding to official calls for proposals. We cannot stress enough how essential networking is to your consulting practice.

In this section, we begin by discussing how to think about networking as part of your everyday work, and the opportunities opened up by that perspective. Next, we describe two exercises that can help you get a clear view of your own network, and then practice successful networking approaches. We apply those approaches to further strategies for networking, and discuss how to overcome challenges to networking, and being comfortable with your own style.

Reframing Your View of Networking

A commonly held view of networking is that it is merely accumulating new connections that will get you work. Instead, we recommend thinking of networking as connecting further through your work with the people you already know. When viewed in this light, you are more likely to see opportunities such as:

- *Connecting your clients to others in their field*: An evaluation consultant had clients who wanted to become part of the national policy conversation around their work. The evaluator suggested and then organized a panel at a research conference, and arranged for her clients to serve as members on the panel. This brought both the client's and the evaluator's work to the attention of others in the field.
- *Bringing in other consultants and professionals*: There are many means beyond full partnership to bring others in your field onto a project. For example, you can budget in reasonable amounts to offer an honorarium for an external review of a report. This strengthens the work you submit to clients, and connects you with professionals in your field.

To turn this view into a definition of networking: Networking is the process of forming linkages, making connections, expanding resources and bringing people and ideas together in a reciprocal manner for mutual benefit. Three components are inherent in this definition: trust and reliability, generosity, and continual building. The following exercises will help you experience the value of these components.

Getting Some Practice: Two Exercises

These two exercises will clarify existing connections in your network, and help you practice building your network. The first one, the circle exercise, gives you a clear picture of who is currently in your network. This exercise should take about 1 to 2 hours to complete; it's best done with a partner, or in a class session. The second exercise, networking with a purpose, gives you practice in working with your network to build information. This can be done over the course of several days.

Exercise 1

The Circle—Getting a Clear Picture of Your Current Network

We suggest you work with at least one partner. Start with a sheet of blank paper and put a stick figure in the middle—that's you. Draw a circle around the figure, and label it family/housemates. Now think of how you spend the largest amount of time besides home time—it may be with friends, at school, at work, or working on a hobby. Draw another circle around the

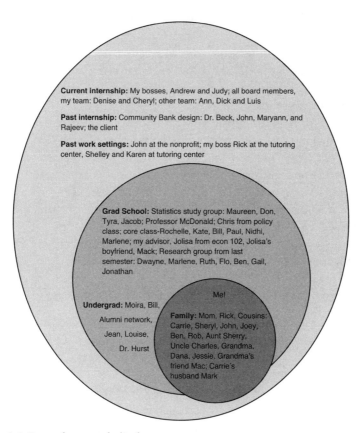

Current internship: My bosses, Andrew and Judy; all board members, my team: Denise and Cheryl; other team: Ann, Dick and Luis

Past internship: Community Bank design: Dr. Beck, John, Maryann, and Rajeev; the client

Past work settings: John at the nonprofit; my boss Rick at the tutoring center, Shelley and Karen at tutoring center

Grad School: Statistics study group: Maureen, Don, Tyra, Jacob; Professor McDonald; Chris from policy class; core class-Rochelle, Kate, Bill, Paul, Nidhi, Marlene; my advisor, Jolisa from econ 102, Jolisa's boyfriend, Mack; Research group from last semester: Dwayne, Marlene, Ruth, Flo, Ben, Gail, Jonathan

Me!

Undergrad: Moira, Bill, Alumni network, Jean, Louise, Dr. Hurst

Family: Mom, Rick, Cousins: Carrie, Sheryl, John, Joey, Ben, Rob, Aunt Sherry, Uncle Charles, Grandma, Dana, Jessie, Grandma's friend Mac; Carrie's husband Mark

Figure 6-1 Example network display

first, and label it according to where you spend the most time. Think of where you spend the next greatest amount of time, draw another circle, and give it that name. Keep going until you feel that you've accounted for the majority of the spheres where you spend your time. Don't forget transit time, volunteer time, hobby time, or children's activities if you're a parent. Though this exercise is about networking, don't hesitate to put down any kind of "alone time"—the point is to get an accurate picture.

Now look at each of the circles, and see if they could be subdivided into "past/present" categories. For example, are there past workplaces, or past school settings, or past social groups? If you work or have worked in a large organization, consider whether a former department or job position within the agency could count as a "past" setting for you. Put labels in your circles that capture these categories. If your history is a long one, and you're trying to think of how far back to take this, at this point, more is better—list all you can remember.

If you're working with others, stop when everyone has had time to complete the steps above, and take a look at what everyone has done so far. Notice if there are any circles that someone else has that you may have forgotten, and add those.

Next, do a quick count of the number of people you know (not are close to, but know) in each circle, and write the number of each circles. Add up the numbers.

The picture and number show your current network. If you're working with a partner or a group, see how many in the group can provide an example of how a person in their network helped them out this month, or even this week.

If you listed names in each circle, instead of a number, you would be amazed at the size, depth, and breadth of your network. And that is the next step for this exercise: list all names behind the numbers in your circle. Though it may take some time, the result is worthwhile, and your list will be the basis for the next exercise.

Exercise 2

Networking with a Purpose

Networking is often seen as a process of gathering connections, with the end result being a list of names. This next exercise lets you instead use the list you made in Exercise 1 as a starting point to expanding your resources and strengthening relationships. The key is to network with a purpose—get in touch with people you know to gain something you genuinely need. We suggest five steps to this process:

1. Define your need.
2. Identify resources in your current network.
3. Contact your network.
4. Snowball—grow your network.
5. Follow up.

We'll lead you through these five steps in the exercise that follows. Throughout the process, we think you'll find three principles that make it work: generosity, trust, and reliability.

There are two stages to the exercise. First, you'll do some networking that is specifically *not* about work or consulting. This gives you the opportunity to carry out and reflect on networking without the weight of having it connected to your professional growth. It also may give you a fresh view of connecting around useful information. Second, you'll network again, focused on work.

First Stage

- Step 1: Define your need. For this exercise, generate a specific, clear, and answerable question. Think of an informational question you genuinely need answered in your life within the next couple of weeks, a question that is NOT about your current or future professional life. It may be anything from suggestions for a good mechanic, to views on a particular course you're thinking about taking next semester, to possible better routes for your commute. We'll use asking for views on a course you're thinking of taking as an example as we go through the steps. Specify your question. For example, rather than just asking if someone liked the course, ask: What about this course was most useful to you? Would you recommend it?
- Step 2: Identify resources in your current network. Look at the network list you built in Exercise 1. Choose at least two people that you think might have the answer to your question, or whom you think can put you in touch with someone who has information. With your question specified, think of who could really answer it, and give you information that is genuinely useful to you. If, for example, a good friend took the course but you find you often have different views on your school experiences, ask someone else with whom you've found you tend to agree with on coursework, such as a former study group partner.
- Step 3: Contact your network. Take the time to ask the question specifically of the people you've identified. Over the next couple of days, have a conversation or send an e-mail that is specifically about your question. The main point here is to let the person know that this information is valuable to you.
- Step 4: Snowball/grow your network. If the original people you target don't have the full answer to your question, ask if they know who might have helpful information, and look at your network list to see who else you might ask. Contact additional people from your network list or those whom your existing network member recommended until you find the information you need.
- Step 5: Follow up. As soon as possible, follow up with each person you spoke with to provide them with an update since your conversation. This step is essential to your future success in networking. While thanking the people you talked to is essential, follow-up

should include more than thanks. The follow-up conversation should continue to build the exchange that is part of networking by letting people know how you used the information. If the outcome will be indefinite for quite a while, let them know the process is under way (e.g., "I'm still deciding what classes to take, though I'm leaning towards the one we talked about."). Do this step for everyone you ended up contacting, so that if someone gave you a name, you can let them know that you talked to their suggested contact. If you learned anything new that would be useful for others (e.g., you now have a list of good mechanics), report back this information, as well. Just as you asked the question specifically, make the time to let them know the outcome specifically, and share any additional knowledge you gained through the process.

Reflection on the Process and Outcome of Networking with a Purpose

Once you have the information you wanted to obtain, and have followed up with everyone you talked with to let them know the outcome, take time to reflect on the experience. One question to ask yourself is, "What felt different about searching for specific information, rather than merely having a social conversation?" We suggest three interrelated components to focus on during this networking activity process:

a) *Generosity*: Anyone willing to give time, help, or information, is being generous with their own time and thought; there is a real generosity inherent in networking.

b) *Trust/reliability*: Most people who complete this exercise talk first to people they trust at some level, whether it be the reliability of their information, or that they would take the time to answer the question. Starting with one's known network allows for relying on others with whom we have developed relationships.

c) *The importance of follow-up*: Letting someone know how their time and thought helped you acknowledges their generosity, and contributes to building and sustaining connections. Being specific about results in the follow-up process, rather than just saying "thanks," leads the members of your network to keep their mind on the question you raised, and lets them know their contribution was genuinely valuable to you.

A useful question to ask yourself at the end of this process is, "If you didn't follow up fully, how would you begin your next conversation if you wanted to approach that person for something else?" If you imagine this scenario, you may note that it is easier and feels more natural to start by acknowledging how much you appreciate the last time they were helpful to you. Your gratitude will sound, and will be, far more genuine if you express it sooner rather than later.

Second Stage

For the second stage of the exercise, you'll go through the five steps again, this time focusing on your professional development.

- Step 1: Define your need. Just as in the first stage, the question should be specific and something you genuinely need or want to know. As you network in your professional life, you'll find that having a purpose for contacting someone is likely to lead to a focused, comfortable conversation. If what you want to know right now is general (e.g., Should I go into consulting?), specify the question: What traits do you think are necessary to be a consultant? What do you wish someone had told you before you started consulting?
- Step 2: Identify resources in your current network. After the question is specified, look again at your network. Pick at least three people whom you will ask your question. One should be outside your work sphere—a family member or friend. If you do not see anyone in your network you think could offer the information you're looking for, asking for ideas about other sources is the next step to take. Remember how often information comes from various sources, and continue to turn to various spheres as your professional life develops. Reaching beyond your own work sphere can be particularly useful when considering sensitive questions about professional issues. For example, if you want to know how much consultants charge in your area, asking in your social network may help put you in touch with someone willing to discuss fees, but who might not have been as comfortable sharing this information if contacted professionally.

   If possible, move beyond your comfort zone and choose at least one of the three people as a "stretch"; someone who is very likely to have information that's useful to you, but whom you might not be in touch with regularly.
- Steps 3 and 4: Contact your network and snowball. Again, as in the first stage, keep asking your question of different people until you get the information you need, and whenever appropriate, also ask members of your network for suggestions for anyone else who might have answers to your question. It can be highly useful to find a contact in a particular organization or field in which you have a strong interest. Current networks are often rich resources

for finding the most appropriate contacts to help you gain much needed information. If, for example, you're interested in working for a consulting agency, your current network might know someone at one of the agencies who would be willing to give you an informational interview.

- Step 5: Follow up. As before, make sure to follow up with every person you spoke with. If your question is exploratory, you might find your follow-up sounds more like a traditional thank you (e.g., I appreciated your time, etc.), because you don't have a result to report back yet. Specify as much as you can, letting your informants know you talked to others, and where you are in the process.

Reflecting on Your Networking Experience

Was what you learned genuinely useful to you? If not, can you reframe your question and ask again, going to others in your network? This networking activity is a continual learning process. Think again about generosity, reliability, and follow-up. You may find that as you move further from your social circle, the generosity of others is more visible to you in the networking process. For example, you might be more conscious of taking up their time. This is partly because your relationships have less reciprocity and trust. Building up reciprocity and trust is achieved through the follow-up process, and looking for opportunities to help others.

Networking Strategies

Apply what you learned from the exercise outlined above, and incorporate generosity, reliability, and follow through into the networking strategies described below:

- Expanding your professional circle
- Connecting through your current work
- Mentors
- Connecting to colleagues
- Maintaining relationships with past clients

Tailor the strategies for your career stage—we give some suggestions throughout.

Expanding Your Professional Circle

Going through the networking process will help show how all your network circles—family, friends, and others—can provide meaningful connections to your work. However, focusing on expanding your professional circle is important. Take a look at the network circles that encompass your professional life. Before, you defined these circles according to where and how you currently spend your time. Now, think of how you can expand your professional circle.

Professional conferences: One way to ensure you meet others with shared interests is by attending professional conferences. Better yet, presenting at conferences helps you develop your resume and your reputation. Not all conferences are created equal. Find the ones where you feel most comfortable. Look for conferences that offer opportunities to interact informally with people who have more experience than you. Find people who are where you want to be in 5 years, and ask them about their story. Again, almost everyone in this field loves to talk about themselves and their work. Everyone we've spoken to is passionate about their work. They have told us that they enjoyed passing on their knowledge, and hope that others can learn from their experiences. We have been pleasantly surprised with the generosity of time and advice we've received from busy professionals.

Professional organizations: Another way to get linked up with other consultants and find out what they are doing is to join local professional organizations. These organizations can be built around the fact that everyone does independent consulting. For example, the Institute of Management Consultants USA (IMC USA) is often cited as a useful resource for independent consultants. Other organizations bring together professionals who work within a discipline or subject area in which you specialize or have an interest. For example, the Chicagoland Evaluation Association (CEA), a local affiliate of the American Evaluation Association, is made up of evaluators in the Chicago area. CEA provides a forum for professional evaluators in the area to network, exchange ideas and knowledge, and participate in professional development activities that promote excellence in the field of evaluation. Some of the members are internal evaluators, some are university based researchers, and others are independent consultants. Members' specialty areas vary from education, health care, and criminal justice to the environment. Joining and participating in the local chapter of a professional organization can be very valuable for an independent consultant. For example, Carol Lukas, president of Fieldstone Alliance, explained that the American Society for Training and Development (ASTD) was critical for her in building a professional network and establishing her reputation. She joined her local chapter by attending meetings and getting involved with a subgroup that worked with nonprofits. She ended up chairing the group, and was very involved for years. This became (and is still) her primary professional network. When she was freelancing as a consultant, 60–70% of her work came from referrals from professionals in her local ASTD chapter.

When you join an association, apply networking with a purpose—at meetings and using membership lists, search for and share specific information and opportunities, with generosity, reliability, and follow-up. Many avenues are available through universities, such as alumni groups, workshops related to your areas of expertise, and discussion groups. We strongly recommend making use of these.

Opportunities outside of your specialty: In expanding your professional circle, be willing to look outside your specialty. Consulting with nonprofits requires skills that are interdisciplinary. Take advantage of opportunities to learn from professionals outside of your specialty. Furthermore, expand your base by looking across disciplines to see the overlap and interrelatedness or contrasts of how different groups frame and/or attempt to solve similar problems. Most professionals and academics are more than happy to discuss their work and their discipline with people who are truly interested.

Community work: Getting involved with community activities can help you stay in touch with your neighbors, and can help fill a social void when you start your consulting practice that would otherwise be filled by coworkers. A common denominator in all of these community activities is that they all provide you with knowledge of existing issues, and the ability to build a reputation as someone who is a leader and a problem solver.

Connecting Through Your Current Work

As mentioned earlier, there are many opportunities for building your network by connecting with others through your current work. This can be true regardless of your career stage, whether you are currently in school, in your first job, or an established consultant. For example, if you are in school, look for opportunities through research papers, projects, and internships. Is there any professional source you can call as a resource for a research paper? Shaunti, while doing a paper in graduate school on a relatively new policy and its implications, identified authors of recent reports, and then called and asked for their views. This led to discussion on research that needed to be done—she later proposed and obtained summer work with one of the organizations to help them fill a research gap.

If you are currently working at a nonprofit or other work setting, consider ways in which you can bring in other consultants, others in the field, or even colleagues in other departments of your organization, when appropriate. For example, while working in the evaluation section of an education consulting firm, Shaunti built strong connections with colleagues on the program side of the organization; that is, those people offering direct services to clients. Some of the connections came naturally through projects she was involved in, while others came from asking for advice and expertise whenever possible. Her program network led to her first contract when she began consulting on her own.

The key here is to look for a genuine need to be addressed, whether it is for information, a review, comments, assistance, sharing the work of clients, or other help. In the example of the research paper above, the newness of the policy led to a genuine need for further information—the author was not calling about literature that could have easily been found through a literature search. The connection should always strengthen the work being done.

Mentoring

Being mentored can be a very helpful way to enter consulting. Effective mentoring is often done through having several mentors, rather than through a singular relationship. This allows access to an array of expert opinions, and builds several supportive relationships. It can also help mitigate what can become overdependence on a singular source of expert support. Developing your own network of mentors is something worth undertaking for any new consultant.

Finding an "information mentor" can be one way of building a relationship without the time commitment or need for a close match that working together might require. This type of mentoring can be developed through networking with a purpose, and can start by asking experienced consultants and professors for advice.

Connections to Colleagues

To start a consulting practice, one needs a network of associates, connections to people and places who will use your services, and a background of expertise to offer. Your colleagues from all workplaces will form the core of that network, and are one of your most important resources. To grow and maintain this network, do your work well, and build trust and reciprocal generosity. Stay connected when you leave a workplace. This is a part of your networking that does not always need a purposeful approach—check in, have lunch, keep in touch.

Working with other consultants: An effective yet challenging method of preparing yourself to work in consulting on your own, is to team up with established consultant(s) to gain experience. These consultants can act as mentors or guides for the present time, and can become referral sources in the future. Working with or for an established consultant is difficult because the right match is not always easy to find, but it may be a good way to start, providing you with experience and eventually referrals.

Maintaining Relationships with Past Clients

The length of time between a first meeting and an actual job can be quite variable. It can take any amount of time, from 1 month to over a year, from the day you first speak with an organization until the day you begin a project. Use this time for keeping in touch with old clients, going to lunch with friends, and getting plenty of rest and relaxation. Be patient while waiting for new clients. Keeping in touch with old clients may mean sending thank you letters and referral sources, or calling them to check in every few months. Several successful consultants we interviewed said they keep themselves in front of their clients by stopping by their offices when they are in the neighborhood, or sending them interesting articles or notes about recent news that is relevant to their organization.

EXHIBIT 6-1 Challenges to Networking

Courtney Cowgill, one of the authors of this chapter, works in the information technology world, yet her challenges, and those of many of her colleagues, will be familiar to those in the nonprofit world. Following is a speech that Courtney often gives at association meetings.

Excuses for Not Networking
My excuses for not networking seem very similar to the excuses that I use for not exercising and being out of shape. The Excuse: I am an Introvert.

> "Networking is embarrassing, painful. You want me to talk to someone I barely know? You want me to walk into a room of people/women/ men who I barely know, and start talking? You want me to drive to a meeting after a long day to talk to a bunch of people that I haven't met and probably won't remember?" *Yes—I do!*

How many of you have ever done the Myers Briggs? How many of you start with the letter "I" for introvert? Well, I do. But—I have become a trained extrovert. I don't have the money or luxury of being "shy." In fact, being shy and introverted is a luxury for the young and very rich. We are probably not either! Sometimes, I have to just take a deep breath and plunge in.

The Excuse: Not Enough Time
I don't have the time to network. My schedule is already packed.

You are right—building a network takes lots of time. It is much easier to say no! Yet, when you are saying no, you are ignoring your opportunities to help your friends, families, clients, coworkers, and clients. Participating in these groups (the same ones you drew in your circles) helps you form relationships, develop alliances, keep abreast of current issues and solutions, and represent the interests of your clients. Expanding your contacts makes you and your network a future benefit.

Where do I find the time to create and maintain a network? Well, that changes. When I was working full time, I used breakfasts. At school, it depended on my class schedules. But, regardless of where I find myself, I spend at least 5 hours a week networking. I also use Saturday mornings, and I can be home by 8:30—when the rest of the house is starting to wake up.

The Excuse: Cost

Yes . . . all these breakfasts can be expensive. But you can do it cheaply! Eating a bagel at LePeep with coffee can cost less than $4. And, every sixth breakfast is free! You can earn a free breakfast every other week on that plan! Now I even have a great network of LePeep employees, too!

You will not build a network if you are the last one to enter a meeting and the first one to leave. You must make a commitment to get involved, make a contribution, and spend the time needed to get to know people personally.

The Excuse: Fear of Rejection

Someone gave me this reason as an excuse for not networking, saying, "I don't have anything to offer. I don't have special information or contact to add to the network."

I agree—networking is an exchange of favors. But you cannot anticipate what another person wants or needs. You just don't know about what, or who you know, that may benefit another person!

Networking is the exchange of information for mutual benefit—it is not just the potential job contact or client. It is the referral of a doctor, babysitter, or attorney, or the suggestion of a solution. I have worried a lot about how I could pay back a rich or famous contact—until I realize that there is always time and/or a way. Sometimes having one of my contacts call another contact is enough benefit. Sometimes you can't return a favor for a year or more!

Have you heard of the concept that there are "only six degrees of separation between any two people"? Well, I have found this to be very true. I think that everyone is only six people (or fewer) from anyone in the world. The larger your network, the fewer links separate you from anyone else, and the more people you can be linked to.

What reasons do you have for not networking?

Places to Look for Projects and Support

Joining professional associations (e.g., American Evaluation Association, The Society for Community Research and Action) often open doors to multiple avenues to look for work. Many associations host electronic mail discussion lists as a way to communicate with others who have similar interests and or expertise, and are places to post questions or answers related to your work. Jobs are often posted on e-mail discussion lists before you see them in print. A formal Request for Proposal (RFP) is the most common way that federal and state agencies, as well as large foundations, solicit research and evaluation investigators. Topical RFPs are often distributed through e-mail discussion lists, as well. Otherwise, RFPs can be found on government and/or foundation Web sites.

However, Melanie Hwalek, President of SPEC Associates, says,

> In our practice, we seldom respond directly to RFPs for three reasons: 1) RFPs are often a poor way to solicit the most appropriate consultant 'fit' with the client and the client's needs; 2) RFPs are sometimes used in situations where the preferred consultant is already selected, but documentation of a selection process is required; and 3) RFPs often focus too closely on the cost of the work rather than the quality and value of the work. Clients focused on cost are less likely to be satisfied with the consulting experience, less likely to refer other clients, and less likely to add to the consultant's stock-in-trade—their body of work and their marketable professional reputation.

Many foundations keep consultant banks that you can add your information to by contacting them or posting your information directly via the Web. For example, the Rhode Island Foundation maintains a nonprofit consultant directory, and Works in Progress Inc., a Minnesota based nonprofit, also houses a consultant directory. Other consultant banks are kept by professional organizations or universities. For example, Western Michigan University has a directory of evaluators you can find online.

Sometimes getting on a foundation's referral list is as simple as going on their Web site, or calling them up and providing them with your resume and a list of past projects and clients. A simple Google search revealed almost 700 nonprofit consultant directories to choose from.

Politicians are often looking for volunteers in their districts to serve on committees or task forces to help inform them about problems and potential solutions. For folks who are even more highly motivated to be involved with local issues, serving on the PTA, school board, or even city council should be considered. Greenbaum (1990) makes many suggestions when it comes to consultants doing volunteer work in the community, and three seemed particularly relevant. First, only get involved with causes to which you have a personal commitment. Second, aspire to leadership positions. Merely being a "joiner" is much less effective than becoming a leader. Finally, when doing community work, keep a low profile about your consulting practice. It is always better to have someone ask you about what you do rather than to go around pushing yourself on others.

Other referral sources can be found at local universities:

- Professors (in and out of your discipline's department, school, or college).
- Alumni who do consulting work themselves.
- Community relations offices may be able to connect you with organizations looking for assistance.
- Service-learning offices where they send students can often use professional help, as well.
- Community research centers often have to turn away requests that do not fit into their focus areas.
- Grants office/office of sponsored programs and research—while they are geared toward assisting faculty and staff of the university, if you develop a relationship with the officers in these offices, they can provide you with a heads-up when new opportunities are available.
- Reference librarians are some of the most helpful people on Earth when it comes to looking for obscure information.

CONCLUSION

Some people are natural social butterflies and have a flare for marketing. However, for the rest of us, these are activities that require quite a bit of effort. Nonetheless, being able to clearly articulate the value you add for clients is an essential piece of maintaining a successful consulting practice. The exercises and resources discussed in this chapter can be applied to many disciplines, but are of particular importance to independent consultants. Simple marketing materials can help you communicate your strengths to potential clients and colleagues, and effective networking combined with quality work can provide you with a steady stream of community and non-profit partners.

Chapter 7

Running Your Business

Judah Viola and Susan D. McMahon

WHEN TO SUBMIT A PROPOSAL

Clients hire consultants to identify and/or solve stated or unstated problems in their organizations. Before you decide to submit a proposal for a consulting project, you should decide whether the probability of a successful collaboration outweighs the cost of putting together a first-rate proposal. This decision of whether or not to pursue a job should rest on essential information about the client and your ability to respond to the client's need. As adapted from Staggs (2004), here are nine steps to follow to ensure you make a thorough assessment of whether or not to pursue a project:

1. Determine whether your values and background coincide with the values and viewpoints of the client.
2. Determine whether the client is willing and able to take ownership and responsibility for his or her role in a collaborative process.
3. Determine whether the organization is in a position to benefit from advice by implementing change. Does the organization have the resources necessary for change?
4. Determine how the client would potentially benefit from your solution.
5. Consider whether you have the knowledge and skills to meet or exceed the client's expectations.
6. Assess contractual issues, such as who will have ownership and/or rights to the data or any other tools (e.g., measurement tools) that may be created during the contract.

7. Determine whether the working environment will be suitable for you.
8. Determine whether the client is willing and able to pay enough for you to meet your own financial obligations.
9. Consider how likely conducting this project will provide you with meaningful experience or future referrals in an area of interest to you.

Once you decide the project is a good fit with your interests and skills, you may then consider whether you have all of the appropriate skills, and whether the job will require one or more partners or subcontractors to complete it within the requested time frame.

WHETHER TO TEAM UP OR GO IT ALONE

Team consulting may be appropriate when:

1. The personal styles or technical backgrounds of partners/subcontractors are complimentary.
2. The nature of the project suggests the need for more than one person, or you are convinced that having more than one person carry out the tasks of the project would be more efficient than attempting to have one person complete the consultation. For example, if there is a short window of time in which to collect data in multiple locations, this would usually be completed more efficiently with multiple consultants or staff.
3. Training or development of one of the consultants is a goal. Team consulting is a way to mentor beginning consultants or enhance your own development (this can be done behind the scenes).

Team consulting may be inappropriate when:

1. The job is small, and a second consultant would add too much cost.
2. Adding a second consultant may put too much distance between the client and the consultant.
3. It is inefficient to subdivide required tasks.

DECIDING WHAT TO CHARGE

When deciding what to charge, the first step is to try to figure out what the marketplace will allow you to charge. Several key informants suggested that ideally, prices should depend on what the market will bear. You will need to estimate the number of hours a project will require to be completed, and also take into account the amount of money you need to earn. However, as a businessperson you *need* to pay attention to the marketplace in addition to how much time a task will take. As mentioned above, this is not an easy task because clients and competitors are seldom going to tell you what they have proposed to charge for a specific project. One reason why others are hesitant to share their pricing strategies, especially in open forums such as email discussion lists (which are great places to get advice on almost all other topics), is that they are advised by legal counsel not to do so, or prohibited by the rules of the group from discussing pricing. There is a fear among professional associations that they will be suspected of breaching the U.S. antitrust laws and be accused of price fixing. There is less fear about prosecution than expensive inquiries that will entail legal fees.

Email discussion list policies often state that users can discuss approaches to pricing, reasoning behind pricing, and thoughts about what works and what does not work in the decision-making process. However the discussion of "I charge this, what do you charge?" is off limits. While many new consultants are frustrated by these policies, other more experienced consultants sometimes support these rules for reasons other than risk aversion. They argue that the more important issue for the growth and success of a consultant's practice is not the dollar amount they charge, but the thinking behind the pricing—the value you believe you bring to the client. Learning what to consider in setting fees gets a consultant to determine whether: a) what you do is something you need to set the price for in your own way, or b) if it is simply a commodity and its price is determined by the market. If it is determined by the market to be merely a commodity, you don't need an email discussion list or message board on a Web site to tell you what it costs—you will learn this through communicating with clients over time.

We will give you some ideas about how to figure out what to charge and how to estimate what to charge clients for your services. Billing and contracting is contextually based. It is important to get as much information as possible from clients up front in order to understand what they need, and to identify the required steps in the project. Start by estimating the number of hours needed to complete the project.

COST AND LENGTH ESTIMATION

Many early career consultants create estimates by working backwards from an end date. This is not advisable because it does not produce an accurate assessment of the work required to complete a project. Try to utilize the information you have about what the project will entail, and use your best judgment based on past experience as to how long tasks will take. If you are heading into new territory, use your network of experts to get some estimates for specific tasks for which you are unfamiliar. Then add a cushion to account for delays that are not within your control (e.g., limited access to the client during a busy season). Finally, do not forget to add in your overhead costs of doing business, such as income taxes, insurance, unemployment taxes, workers' compensation, vacation time, professional services (e.g., lawyers and accountants, office space, office equipment, utilities, furniture, computer hardware and software, printer, photocopier, Internet and phone service, project supplies, time to keep records for taxes and billing, time for preparation, and professional development). Additionally, if this is your full-time work, you will need to consider the amount of money you need to earn in about 120 billable working days per year. Even if you are only taking 2–3 weeks of vacation per year, you still will only be able to complete about 120 billable week days after accounting for holidays, administrative and professional development/marketing days, and difficulties matching your availability with clients' availability (Biech, 1998).

Many of these costs can be projected for the year, and then assigned to each project depending on the percentage of time you believe the project will take. Experts suggest that approximately 60% of what you bill should cover overhead costs, and the rest should go toward salaries and profit (if your business is fortunate enough to turn a profit).

Elaine Biech (1998) offers the "3× rule" to determine how much to bill clients. The idea is that in order to bring in enough money to cover overhead, salaries, and generate a profit for the company, you will need to bill 3× your salary.

Once you have estimated the number of hours you think it will take to complete the project and any overhead costs, then ask yourself these five questions:

1. Does this price look reasonable on its face?
2. Is the client likely to pay this much?
3. Is this price close to competitors' prices?
4. How much do I/we want the contract?
5. Would it be useful for me/us to do this project regardless of earnings?

If your time line or price does not appear to be consistent with what the client is looking for, then you may need to reconsider the project scope (smaller scope = quicker delivery) and staffing (more people = quicker delivery) (Staggs and Shewe, 2004).

SETTING A PRICING STRATEGY

There are quite a few different ways you can choose to bill clients for your work. We will outline the advantages and disadvantages of several of the more common pricing strategies below.

Hourly Rates

Charging hourly is simple and safe. You get paid for your time. If the project takes longer than expected, your rate does not change. This is advantageous for small projects or projects that require you to work with clients directly because there is transparency. The client sees you doing the work and knows what they are paying for. If you are doing discreet tasks such as conducting trainings, interviews, or focus groups, at first glance charging hourly makes sense. However, you still need to build into your hourly rate the preparation time as well as overhead costs. While almost all the key informants for this study estimated the amount of time tasks would take when creating their proposals, and some calculated hourly rates they were hoping to earn, few consultants to nonprofits recommend charging clients hourly. When tasks take longer than either the client or you expect they should take, it can be difficult to keep clients happy and wanting to work with you again in the future. Nonprofit clients may also take umbrage with what they see as an exorbitant hourly rate when they do not consider your overhead costs or taxes, and assume the dollar value is equivalent to your earnings. When comparing their own salary to what looks like an inflated number, this can create resentment or reduce the likelihood of them hiring you. Also, for a consultant who is just starting out, it may be difficult to obtain a high hourly rate. When determining fees for her clients, the owner of an S corporation and a veteran consultant calculates an hourly rate of $135 for her services, $85 for Masters-level staff, and $50 for support staff.

Daily Rates

Charging daily rates is similar to the hourly rate in that you are guaranteed to be paid for your time. However, there is a little more wiggle room. You can determine how many hours a day that you actually work, and this will not change the rate. Thus, if the project is taking longer than expected, you can absorb some of the overruns along with the client. In addition, there is more incentive to get your work done quickly and efficiently as the time you save within a day is yours, and will not reduce your bottom line for the day.

When calculating daily fees as opposed to hourly fees, Bermont (1997) suggests charging seven times your hourly fee as opposed to eight. This gives the client one hour free, and guarantees you more hours of work. The most highly esteemed, experienced, and published consultants in the field charge up to $5,000 per day, which includes all expenses, including national or international travel. This type of rate gives you an idea of the potential and need in the field, although most consultants working with nonprofits do not earn this level of income.

Fixed Project Price

Most consulting projects will involve many tasks and more than one deliverable. Providing one fixed price for the entire project may be tempting because it provides you with an incentive to complete the project in a timely manner and allows for flexibility.

However, Requests for Proposals (RFPs) often have specific dollar amounts attached to them, along with a list of specific tasks the client would like accomplished. Some consultants warn against responding to RFPs at all because the cost is usually based on the budget of the organization or funder as opposed to the scope of the project. This inconsistency can create headaches. In addition, responding to RFPs is time consuming and can take a lot of work, and you often don't know your chances of landing the project. Furthermore, many consultants have had the experience of responding to an RFP only to find out later that the organization already knew the consultant they would hire before sending out the RFP, but sent it out to follow requirements of their board or their bylaws. Some have been on the other side when organizations have said they really wanted to hire them, but needed to put out a public RFP first so they could turn down a few bids. If you do choose to respond to RFPs, one challenge is to create a strong proposal without overextending yourself for the money available. You want to find out the price range prior to writing your proposal, even if it is not listed (i.e., you don't want to write a proposal that costs $75,000 if only $25,000 is available). You can often do this by contacting the organization that is putting out the RFP, and asking questions about the project. Understanding the context beyond the scope, time line, and budget that might be outlined on paper is crucial to appropriate estimations of time, expertise, people, and other resources required to complete the task at hand.

Deliverable

Several consultants interviewed said they prefer to use a set fee based on a detailed estimate of the amount of time and effort the project will take, as opposed to charging clients hourly. They recommend using an Excel spreadsheet to meticulously determine the costs and hours it will take to complete each task required for all aspects of the proposal. You can then provide the client with a summarized version with budget lines such as: "Instrument Development (x dollars)." Some consultants also find it helpful to provide information in the initial proposal about which sections of the proposal are flexible and which are not. When providing more detailed accounts of hours, clients are more likely to ask you to cut down on the length of time spent on specific tasks. This can lead to distrust or resentment, or even harm the quality of the project.

You can choose to make your fees all inclusive, or to separate out the charges for your work and for *other charges,* such as travel expenses, special services (e.g., food at events, translations, data entry, transcriptions, etc.) or materials (e.g., copies of surveys, reports, transcripts, data files, etc.). It may be helpful to separate the charges, so you can become better at estimating the actual expenses for each area, and from the client's perspective, they get a better idea of what services their dollars are covering.

TIP

Tip 1 for Negotiating Your Fee: When dealing with a client, Geoffrey Bellman, author of *The Consultant's Calling,* suggests using the statement, "I want x dollars a day for my services," as opposed to, "My fee is. . . ." This approach creates a starting point, which then allows for negotiation. But also try not to take the price negotiations personally. Your personal worth should not be on the line with every negotiation. Rather than determining your worth, you are determining what clients are willing to pay for your services at this point in time, taking into account a myriad of factors.

Once you have estimated your costs involved in completing a project, then you need to determine whether the project is worth x dollars to the client. If your estimated costs and your estimate of the project worth to the client are similar, you can comfortably move forward on the project. However, if you determine the worth to the client is higher than the amount you estimated based upon the number of hours you think it will take, then you can charge what it is worth to the client (in this case, the higher price). On the other hand, if the expected hourly costs will outweigh the benefit to the client, you may need to: (1) Work at a fraction of your break-even hourly rate, otherwise known as "buying the business." If you are a new consultant, this can help you build your experience and reputation, thereby earning a glowing reference for the future. However, you risk having to justify your new rates when you want to be adequately paid for your services, when this client and others may want the same great rate for the next project. (2) Explain to the client that you cannot do the project as budgeted and still make it cost effective. Then suggest either coming up with an altered project to meet their needs, or providing a reference of another consultant who may be more appropriate to carry out the project they are looking for.

Several informants emphasized that you do not need to reduce the number of hours you were planning to spend on any tasks to fit within the budget of the project, but rather, it is better to change the scope of what you are going to do for them. If you try to do the same job in less time, you'll end up losing money, resenting the client, and struggling to meet your own quality standards.

TIP

Tip 2 for Negotiating Your Fee: Dale Rose recommends negotiating on the scope of the work to be done instead of the fees you charge. In other words, deliverables should be sold at fixed prices, and the price should be determined based on the value of the product to the client and the amount of time and effort involved on your end. Rose has found that clients prefer not to have hourly billing, and only resorts to this when his company is already engaged with the client (e.g., you may request additional services for the hourly rate of x).

Ninety percent of those surveyed and interviewed stated that they used some sort of sliding scale when charging their clients. Most often, this means taking into account the resources of the client. But sometimes the scale is dependent upon the type of organization with whom consultants contract. For example, some consultants charge less for schools than they do for businesses regardless of their resource availability. It is helpful to be clear and consistent with your pricing methods. Since many of your jobs will come from word-of-mouth referrals, your clients may share information about what they paid you in the past. In order to maintain a fair and ethical practice (as well as image), you will want to be able to simply and quickly justify why you may give a particular nonprofit one rate and another nonprofit a lower rate for a similar service.

Some consultants have upper and lower limits of what they will charge. For example, as a graduate student and sole proprietor, Andrew White used a sliding scale, but kept his bottom limit above $25 an hour.

Elaine Biech (1999) argues that "pricing services too low is the biggest mistake that new consultants make" (pg. 43). Lower rates mean that you have to take on more projects to make ends meet (an overwhelming task for a newcomer). Taking on more projects also means you'll have less time to devote to any individual project or interacting with clients. She recommends charging a price that will allow you to do the job with "superior quality." Some consultants have also found that similar to other products and services, higher prices are equated with higher quality and lower prices are equated with lower quality. Very low prices may make you attractive to some clients, but may keep others away. For an example of a pricing worksheet and sample costs, see Appendix 7-1.

In addition, when negotiating fees you will want to avoid providing one price and then lowering that price to land the project. This implies that your first rate was padded and unnecessarily high. This will set a precedent for your negotiations with this client in the future (as well as potential clients referred by this client). Once you have established your credibility, either through great recommendations or based upon the initial meetings, then you are less likely to have potential clients try to talk you down in fees. Nonetheless, in the nonprofit arena, making exceptions based on available funds comes up much more than in the for-profit or government worlds.

TIP

Tip for When to Talk About Money: During exploratory meetings when a potential client is feeling you out, wait until it seems like you will work together, or the client asks you to tell them your fee. Many prospective clients will not like the idea of paying you an hourly rate before they know whether or not they want your services. But certainly do not wait until you are putting the proposal or statement of work together to discuss your prices. You do not want to waste your clients' or your own time if they cannot afford or are unwilling to invest in your services at the level you feel is appropriate or needed for your work.

TIMING OF PAYMENTS

In terms of the timing of the payments, often payment is spread out across the length of the project, but most informants explained that getting paid up front is both the most desirable and most difficult arrangement. With medium-sized contracts, Martha Henry requires one-third up front, one-third in the middle, and one-third at the completion of the project. With larger contracts, she requires monthly payments, or 75% up front. For small businesses, handling larger contracts can lead to a large tax burden if it comes at the end of the year, so it is best to negotiate a partial payment prior to year's end, and then spread out the rest of the payments after the first of the year.

Do not hesitate to renegotiate payment triggers in the contract when the project expands in time and/or deliverables. As clients can become friends, there is a tendency towards informality. However, if you expect payment upon completion of the project and the project expands, then you are further delayed in payment. Thus, project delays can quickly eat into your cash reserves.

PROPOSALS AND CONTRACTS

Proposals

A proposal is a common step in competing for a project and/or determining the scope of a project. The proposal should include what tasks and deliverables will be included in the project, roles and responsibilities to ensure tasks get done, a time line for completion of tasks and deliverables, and the costs or investment required to complete the project (monetary, manpower, time, materials, etc.). Often, consultants choose to include a background or purpose statement that provides an overview of the organization and their needs for the project.

TIP

> Tip for Keeping the Proposal and Contracting Process Moving Forward: Some consultants suggest including effective dates in proposals so you are not kept waiting for an inordinate amount of time to hear back from a client. For example, you could insert a short clause stating the terms of this proposal are effective through July 1, 2010.

Writing Contracts

There are many good resources for deciding what to include in a consulting contract. However, a good contract is specific to the topic area and the project to be completed. Ask colleagues for templates from which to build a contract that is comfortable for you. There are two general types of contracts in common use. The first type of contract is the informal, "Memorandum of Understanding" (MOU), or "Memorandum of Agreement" (MOA). MOUs/MOAs are often stripped down versions of project proposals, and are usually prepared by the consultant. Jolley, Wituk, Gregory, Thomas, and Meissen describe using MOUs with local organizations (and include a sample MOU) in Chapter 12, "Capacity Building with Faith-Based and Community Organizations: Lessons Learned from the Compassion Kansas Initiative." Peter Block (2001) provides a good description for the essential parts of this type of consulting contract. Block's template includes nine sections:

1. The boundaries of the analysis
2. Objectives of the project
3. The type of information you seek
4. Your role in the project
5. The product(s) you will deliver
6. What support and involvement you need from the client
7. Time schedule and costs
8. Confidentiality
9. Provision for post-project feedback

The other type of contract is a formal, legalese-type document. The formal contracts are most often prepared for consultants or clients by a contract lawyer. Often, clients will have standard contracts for all consultants or vendors that they will want you to sign. While most of these contracts are built to create clear guidelines for your working agreement, they are also designed to meet the needs of the client first and foremost. Contracts that are created by lawyers are often long and difficult for non-lawyers to understand. You'll want to check to see if there are any clauses that protect the client without protecting you. For instance, there may be language that caps the amount of money paid in case of project overrun, regardless of the increased amount of time or costs to you. Data ownership is another issue to examine carefully in client contracts. Susan Staggs (2004) recommends trying to have clients sign your contract, and if they won't, read theirs carefully before signing it. If you do not understand their contract, ask questions, and if you still feel uneasy, consult with a lawyer.

Additional Parts of Proposals and Contracts

Roles and responsibilities of consultant and consultee (client) need to be clearly established. Effective consultation requires that the clients and consultants define their respective roles and responsibilities prior to beginning the project. The client should clearly articulate information priorities, facilitate the consultant's access to information and personnel if needed, and be invested in the use of the consultant's findings. In addition, issues such as ownership of data and/or intellectual property should be articulated in the contract. Andrea Solarz explained that for her projects, "They buy it, they own it." If she wanted to publish from the data, she would write it into the contract.

WORKING THROUGH INSTITUTIONAL REVIEW BOARDS

When consultants put on their researcher hats for their clients and collect data, they need to consider proper ethical conduct with human subjects. When working on a federal research grant with a university or with an organization that has a review board, consultants will need to determine the process and guidelines for submitting their protocols to their Institutional Review Board (IRB) for approval. Under the federal guidelines, *research* is defined as a systematic investigation, including research development, testing, and evaluation, designed to develop or contribute to generalizable knowledge. Research that is used only for the purpose of improving an organization may not require review, unless it is designed to contribute to generalizable knowledge. Indicators of generalizable knowledge include, but are not limited to, the intent to extend conclusions beyond the program of interest or the intent to present or publish the information. Further, research that is organizational in nature, and does not involve data collection or information about individuals, may not require IRB review. You need to become familiar with IRB policies. Federal guidelines related to human subjects research can be found at the U.S. Department of Health and Human Services Office for Human Research Protections (http://www .hhs.gov/ohrp/).

Some social service agencies, such as departments of health and human services or child protective services, may have their own internal IRBs. Schools also sometimes have formal research review boards with particular guidelines related to consent processes and content, as well as research approval. If you are not affiliated with a university and the organization you are working with does not have a review board, formal institutional review is not required. However, if you wish to publish the work, some journals require studies to have undergone IRB approval. Independent IRBs do exist and reviews can be obtained through paying a fee. In any case, if IRB approval is required, you should be well aware of the processes, procedures, time lines, and fees (if any), as these factors will influence your consulting project.

All key informants stated they utilize an informed consent process (i.e., assent or consent forms) for every project that involves collecting data from human participants. Consultants ensure their consent process is consistent with the ethical guidelines of the professional associations to which they belong, such as the American Evaluation Association or the American Psychological Association. Examples of consent forms can be found on university IRB Web sites. Participants need to be informed about the purpose of the study, risks and benefits, and how the data will be used. When possible, individual records are held in confidence, and reports only provide information in the aggregate. In addition, confidential records are archived in a safe and secure manner (i.e., locked file cabinets, password protected files), de-identified when possible, kept for 3 years, and then destroyed (e.g., shredded). However, if the data does not contain any identifying information, it can be kept indefinitely. Other regulations that may need to be considered include the privacy and record-keeping guidelines outlined in the Health Insurance Portability and Accountability Act of 1996 (HIPAA), a federal law that protects the privacy of patients' health care records, and the Family Educational Rights and Privacy Act (FERPA) (20 U.S.C. § 1232g; 34 CFR Part 99), a federal law that protects the privacy of student education records.

Some universities also offer their IRB services to private companies, but costs and time lags are often prohibitive. Furthermore, businesses typically take a stance that is different from government or educational institutions. Their perspective leads them to focus more on gaining useful information rather than protecting the rights of individuals. See these IRB Web sites for more information on the topic: Western Institutional Review Board (WIRB) http://www.wirb.com/; Shulman Associates IRB http://www.sairb.com/; a guidebook from the U.S. Department of Health and Human Services is also available online at http://www.hhs.gov/ohrp/irb/irb_guidebook.htm.

Most informants explained that they often do not utilize review boards unless required. Reasons for this included excessive time added to the project and the high cost of non-university review board companies. Several informants stated they tried using state IRBs, but found that it took too long. A few even mentioned using private companies, but found this to be very costly. If the end goal of the consulting project is to serve the client's needs, rather than to create generalizable knowledge, use of an IRB is not needed, but of course, you must still treat participants ethically.

GETTING PAID

Make every attempt to track all of your time on each task. This helps keep you focused, ensures that all non-paid time is documented, and will help you plan more accurately for future projects. Set up a system to keep track of invoices before you get busy with multiple projects. This system will also come in handy when it is time to report earnings for taxes. Developing a good and trusting working relationship is important in every phase of the consulting process. The billing process is no exception. While it is natural to assume that you won't have a problem getting paid each time you sign a contract, delays in payment are common. While it is rare that clients refuse to pay for services rendered, funding problems and related delays are common in the nonprofit, educational, and government sectors. As an employee of a company, you can complain to your union or your state labor department if you do not get paid on time, and businesses are wary of heavy fines and bad morale among employees. However, as a self-employed consultant, there is no governmental agency that will help you get paid. Therefore, you need to be proactive and act as though your livelihood depends on getting paid for your work, because it does.

Make sure to send your bill immediately. Just as it is frustrating not to get paid in a timely manner, it can be troublesome for clients not to receive invoices when they are expected. Clients may procure (set aside) money ahead of time to make sure the money is there when they need it. However, procurements often have time frames, and can cause difficulties for your client if they are not closed out on time. For example, some budgeted accounts are frozen at the end of each fiscal year for accounting purposes, or for the purpose of determining how much money needs to be budgeted for the following year. In addition, the value of your work may be very clear a few weeks after the project is completed, but this apparent value may not be as clear several months later when there are other more pressing issues being dealt with. Thus, it is good practice to send invoices out as soon as you complete the task, provide the deliverable, or reach the agreed-upon point in the project when the next payment is due. Furthermore, many larger agencies, including the federal government, wait 30 days between the date they receive the invoice and the date they cut the check. So, if you wait a few weeks before sending the bill, it could be 45 or 60 days between when you complete the work and when you receive the check.

Remember that it is a lot harder to withhold payment from a person that you know as opposed to a company that sends letters. Therefore, calling clients usually works better than sending additional invoices. If you have contracted with a large institution or company, you may have to first contact someone in the accounts payable or purchasing department. But do not hesitate to let the person you contracted with know of the problem. If this doesn't work, www.nolo.com recommends speaking to management, or even the president of the institution or company. If you are not successful with phone calls, make an appointment to personally visit whoever is in charge of paying you.

TIP

Tip for Tracking Time Spent on a Task: Use timesheets for yourself and any employees you have. Your client(s) may want to know how much time you spent on various tasks. This information is also valuable to you so you can do a better job of estimating how much it costs to accomplish tasks for your next project.

TIP

Tip for Appreciating the Importance of Context: A common pitfall of the novice consultant is the tendency to stick with what has worked in the past. Try not to overuse pet solutions. Even if strategies have worked in the recent past, treat each project as something novel, and derive plans based on their unique situation, not on the skills you are confident in.

STAYING IN BUSINESS

Once you've got your business up and running, and you are busy, keep two things in mind. First and foremost, make sure you do an excellent job and provide top-notch service for your clients. This will likely make them satisfied with your work, seek your services in the future, and recommend you to colleagues. You will have pride in your work and feel comfortable taking on new and exciting projects. Second, don't forget to continue to build your network and market your skills. Staying in business requires that you have a continuous flow of clients.

CONCLUSION

In this chapter, we have identified several decisions and skills that are required as you contemplate which projects to engage in, set a pricing strategy, develop proposals, and navigate getting paid. Many of these initial decisions and planning skills will evolve as you gain more experience, yet each project will require you to think through the entire process up front in order to make the most appropriate plans for the project. It is important to keep track of your time on various types of tasks throughout the project so you can improve your efficiency, have accurate expectations of the work required to do a high quality job, and achieve your financial goals.

APPENDIX 7-1 Sample Billable Cost Estimates for a Consulting Project

Budget Assumptions:

1. Consultant time will be estimated at $150/hr. Billable time includes meeting preparation, meetings, planning sessions, workshop time, presentations, data analysis, report writing, and travel time. Billable time does not include background reading on content or methodology to prepare for the project, or any time associated with completing the project proposal, scope of work, or contract.
2. Administrative support time will be billed at $40/hr for data entry. All other support time (e.g., brief phone calls, email correspondence, mailings, billing, etc.) will not be billable.
3. In-town travel and any office equipment or supplies, or business-related expenses (e.g., insurance, taxes, professional development) are not billable.

Task	Hours	Fee	Billable Expenses	Total Billable Fee
1. Meetings with primary contact and organization leadership to determine scope of project and create agreement.	4			
2. Project planning/strategy sessions (two)	4	$600		$600
3. Literature review and information gathering specific to the project (post contract)	6	$900		$900
4. Design or find data collection tools (two meetings and research time)	10	$1,500		$1,500
5. Collect data (e.g., observations, focus groups, interviews, archival research, etc.)	15	$2,250	$300	$2,550
6. Data entry (support staff)	10	$400		$400
7. Preliminary data analysis and summary, and draft report	20	$3,000		$3,000
8. Review results with client, conduct additional analyses, and revise report as necessary	10	$1,500		$1,500
9. Produce 10 copies of report (support staff)	2	$80	$100	$180
10. Present report to executive administrators or board of directors	4	$600		$600
Totals	**85**	**$10,830**	**$400**	**$11,230**

A Client-Centered Approach to Winning and Losing New Business: What to Do If You Get the Project (And What to Do If You Don't)

Dale S. Rose and Elna Moore Hall

INTRODUCTION

For any consultant, winning a new project is a reason to celebrate; it is often the culmination of a great deal of hard work, time investment, and creative thought. It is an opportunity to do the work you have trained and prepared to do, and ideally, to be well compensated for doing so. Clearly, getting new business is a goal of your networking and marketing efforts, and the start to building a profitable business. For the new consultant, however, your reaction to winning project work can be a mixture of elation, uncertainty, and utter panic. What had seemed like a far off goal is now achieved, and you are faced with a critical decision: What do I do next?

For new consultants, a natural first reaction is to dive headfirst into the work, but this is not necessarily the best course of action at this stage of the project. Building a successful consulting practice involves more than the delivery of good technical work. It simultaneously requires cultivating solid partnerships with clients, and building their trust in you. This phase of the project cycle—the time period between winning the deal and starting the work—is the ideal phase to invest heavily in solidifying the client-consultant relationship, and this should begin before the actual work gets started. A strong relationship is likely to produce a steady book of business from that client organization over the long term.

This chapter will focus on common challenges faced at this stage of the project cycle, with a priority placed on strengthening the client relationship, and making decisions that balance short-term needs with the long-term vision for the consultant's practice. We will explain that how you present yourself as a client-focused consultant at this early phase sets the tone for this and future projects going forward. If you have won the opportunity to work with a client organization, this phase sets key expectations for how you will do the work, the type of partnership you will create, and whether each of you can ultimately view the completed project as a success.

We assert that there is a critical step—contracting—that must occur before project work begins in order to ensure its success. This step will be outlined in detail. We will also provide action plans for those difficult situations where winning a new project may not turn out to be a clear-cut victory for the consultant. In fact, not all wins are desirable for the long-term strategy of your business, and not all losses are detrimental. Alignment of your project work with your vision for your consulting practice should be a foremost consideration.

Finally, we will propose a strategy for turning a lost deal into an opportunity to maintain and cultivate that client relationship for possible future work. The new consultant who is turned down for a project may struggle with not knowing how to proceed after the loss. Not only is it disappointing to be turned down, but the pressures of cash flow and daily operations management can amplify that feeling of concern. Your initial reaction may be to withdraw from that client relationship in awkwardness or embarrassment, and to critique your proposal and sales efforts for possible shortcomings. It is important to consider winning or losing project work in the context of a much broader relationship with that prospective client organization, however, and to handle that win or loss accordingly. In fact, the consultant's response to winning or losing a project is a pivotal point in the life cycle of the client relationship that has the power to define it for the future.

The principles in this chapter hold true regardless of the size of the project or client organization. Realistically, all consultants will face both wins and losses in the pursuit of client work, so it is important to navigate each interaction artfully. The themes presented here borrow from an important business management process known as "Customer Relationship

Management," or CRM. CRM is a process that allows an individual or firm to remain highly connected to the interests, concerns, and purchase habits of their current or prospective customers. The information captured through the CRM process can be easily analyzed to create solutions to directly target those customers' needs. Many authors (cf. Dyche, 2001; Freeland, 2002) have described the CRM process in exhaustive detail, and it may be useful for the new consultant to review more literature specific to this topic. Our approach builds on CRM's basic concepts, but is tailored specifically to professional consulting services. While typical CRM methods tend to be software-dependent sales tools, our method simply builds on its generalized people-oriented approach to achieving authentic win-win relationships between clients and consultants.

CLIENT-CENTERED CONSULTING

Building a successful consulting business requires, among other skills discussed in this book, seeing every interaction with your client organization as an opportunity to enhance or deteriorate the quality of your relationship with them. While many people begin consulting because they are technically proficient in their specialty, technical skills alone are not enough to sustain a successful consulting business over time.

If you plan to grow a business, rather than simply operating as a hired gun, then projects are not a series of unrelated events, but rather milestones on a continuum of a long-term partnership. Successful consulting businesses operate from the premise that winning or losing a particular project is just a temporary state in the ongoing consultant-client relationship. Hence, the best consultants work on building and maintaining relationships, regardless of whether they get a particular deal. Often, clients will go months or years between projects, but if you maintain the relationship and continue to be a resource for your clients, when they do have work in your specialty you will be the obvious choice.

As Figure 8-1 illustrates, managing client relationships is something that should be considered at all phases of a consulting engagement. It is tempting to focus on relationship maintenance only during the phases before or after the project work is done. Many consultants are very active "networkers" and spend considerable time relationship building during the first few stages of the time line in Figure 8-1.

When a project is completed, consultants may re-engage in attending to the client relationship by conducting debriefing meetings, sending thank you cards, and other similarly focused activities. While this is important, the client-centered consultant understands that attending to the relationship

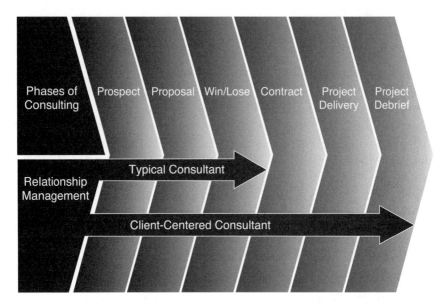

Figure 8-1 Managing consultant-client relationships at each phase of the consulting engagement.

is just as critical during the actual project delivery. Your clients will not remember how friendly you were at the cocktail party where they first got your business card nearly as much as they will remember how well you supported them and helped them to stay on task during the project. Focus on how to succeed by bringing a client-centered approach to the "win/lose" phase of this continuum. An engaging client relationship will almost certainly lead to future project work.

THE CLIENT-CENTERED RESPONSE TO WINNING THE PROJECT

If your hard work and dedication have resulted in getting hired for project work, it is a cause for celebration. Winning projects is a major milestone for a new business, and on a personal level, it validates that you can instill confidence and potentially add value to a client organization. Celebrating your win is important. Building a business, consulting or otherwise, requires endurance, and you need to celebrate these moments of success to energize and motivate you during periods of difficulty. If you work with a team of support professionals, include them in your celebration—their motivation and enthusiasm is just as necessary as yours. Even a symbolic action like framing the email from the client organization, or a simple champagne toast is something your whole team can look back upon with pride. We actually have a bell in our office that we ring when we receive a signed contract so the whole company knows every time we win a new deal.

When celebrating is done, it is time to plan the project, not to start the work. Seasoned consultants learn that even with the best-researched and best-written proposal, at this point you do not know everything you need to know about the problem situation or the client organization. In the selling phase, the client had to keep you at a certain distance and maintain formality. Now you are "on the team," and your client's disclosure to you can and should be different. Invariably, once you gain this entry, you will learn much more about the presenting situation, and it will no doubt influence how you will approach the work. There are many reasons why "jumping right in" to project work at the beginning of the relationship is ill-advised. Four of these reasons are outlined below:

- The consultant cannot presume that all of the project objectives are clear and have been discussed. For instance, what may appear to be a simple employee survey project may be intended to set in place broader changes in the organization that have not been previously discussed with the consultant. You need to be keenly aware of these broader objectives.
- The consultant and client roles during the project may not yet be clearly defined. It is important to keep in mind that you are a full partner with the client, not a subordinate, and you must negotiate with your client how that partnership will work.
- Time and dialogue are required to create the climate of openness and full disclosure that will help the consultant throughout the project. The client organization has shown confidence in you by hiring you for the work, but you are still a newcomer, and you must demonstrate that you are a trustworthy confidante.
- The consultant needs to be aware of concerns or fears the client has about the project. Depending on the nature of the work to be done, your client contact may have concerns about how the results of the study will affect their own job or their reputation, or whether your involvement in their organization reflects poorly on them (i.e., by completing a project they could not). If these concerns are not addressed before starting the work, you will face resistance from your client that you will not fully understand.

Consultants often project their own enthusiasm onto their clients and assume that the client shares their motivation to do the work. In fact, this is often not the case. Keep in mind that although you are being given an opportunity to demonstrate your expertise, your client is there because his or her organization has a problem it cannot solve independently—because they lack some specific skill or expertise. That deficit may or may not be a source of sensitivity for the client. Your client may share your interest in getting the project done, but the reasons behind it are likely quite different from yours. A consultant needs to clearly understand the client's motivation.

Start by engaging in an honest self-assessment of your own expectations and desires about the project. Ask yourself some critical questions about how you intend to work with your client, including the following:

1. Besides delivering strong technical work, do you have other goals you would like to accomplish during this project (i.e., broadening your expertise in a new area, building exposure within a client organization's industry, getting exposure to a specific leader in the organization, securing a solid client reference, etc.)?

2. Will you work on this project exclusively, or will you be engaged in other clients' projects concurrently?

3. Will you limit your involvement to the work listed on the proposal, or are you open to expanding the project scope if the client requests it?

4. Do you expect access to certain organizational leaders or experts, or invitations to key meetings and events in order to accomplish your work?

5. Do you plan to work on site at the client organization, or bring the work back to your office?

6. How will you define success for this project, and what is its end point (i.e., how do you know when you're done)?

Once you have clarified your own goals and assumptions, you must align them with the goals and assumptions of your client. This process of setting expectations, clarifying roles and responsibilities, and addressing any outstanding concerns before the start of project work is called contracting, and it is a pivotal trust-building exercise between consultant and client that cannot be overlooked in a successful partnership. Contracting is often thought of in legal terms, but in this context, the process goes beyond simple legal implications. Peter Block (1981) has described this phase of the client relationship extensively. In his view, contracting does not imply an obligation in the formal and legal sense, but refers to the act of: 1) creating shared expectations, and 2) documenting those shared expectations as an agreement. This document should be as detailed as is necessary to provide clarity to both the consultant and the client organization about how the work will be done, and it should serve as a self-contained roadmap for the remainder of the project. If done well, this agreement will also cement your client's role as your sponsor within the organization, which is likewise critical to your project's success.

As a client-centered consultant, you will attend to two objectives during the contracting stage: 1) gaining mutual agreement from the client about how the work will be done, and 2) continuing to build your client's reliance on you as a trusted advisor. Ed Schein, originator of the Process Consultation model of consulting (Schein, 1988), explains that these first few meetings with the client organization are in fact the beginning of the intervention, as you are already gathering diagnostic information about their organization's culture. You are also shaping how the client perceives you and your ability to address these challenges.

Your contracting meeting should include your project's sponsor, and this person may not necessarily be the same as your day-to-day client contact within the organization; if not, both people should attend. Ideally, other key individuals can attend the contracting meeting, particularly those who have the power to influence the outcome of your project and/or those whose active participation will be critical to its success. The meeting will serve as a valuable opportunity to learn more about how your client organization works. During this meeting, you will be able to judge the client organization's "degree of openness, spirit of inquiry, and authenticity of communication" (Schein, 1988).

After the contracting meeting(s), prepare an agreement that documents all decisions and commitments discussed. Generally, your agreement with the client should clarify:

- The client contact (the person who monitors your daily operations)
- The sponsor (the person who controls your funding)
- All project objectives to be accomplished
- The time line for all project phases, and estimated timing for delivery of final results
- The consultant's resource needs (i.e., access to data, people, meetings and activities, etc.)
- Communication between the client and consultant (how and when)
- A communication plan for the rest of the organization about the project (if appropriate)
- The billing model for the consultant's work (though it is assumed that the overall project cost has already been agreed upon)
- A method for handling out-of-scope requests
- Contents of the final work product/deliverables

There is no "standard" length to a contracting agreement. Their length and format vary, based on the type of client organization and scale of the project being conducted. We have seen effective agreements ranging from a clearly written 1-page email to a 65-page document. A good rule of thumb is to be concise but also comprehensive, and from that framework the consultant can determine the necessary length. Over time, however, if you find that you are conducting many projects of similar type and scale, you may choose to develop a contracting template that can be moderately customized for each client organization.

The contracting process will also allow you an opportunity to surface and address any inaccurate perceptions the client may have developed during the proposal process. Make sure that you have not been miscast as being an expert in an area where you are not. Lack of experience does not preclude you from taking on the work, but the client should have an accurate perception of your ability. Your client should also have a realistic perception of what your consulting approach will offer or solve. A well-designed job-training program, for example, can result in better informed employees, but it may not guarantee that all employees will become better, more motivated performers on the job. As an external consultant, you can generate tremendous results for your client organization, but it is unlikely that you will single-handedly rescue it from its various woes. Setting fair expectations for your involvement is key.

The contracting process also provides a window for the consultant to surface other non-project-related expectations that the client may bring to the partnership, so they do not derail the work later on. For example, many clients hope to have the consultant available as an external confidante, and intend to use the project as an opportunity to request informal feedback on their own effectiveness and professional reputation. The client may also ask the consultant for ad hoc opinions of their subordinates, or to mediate conflicts within the organization. These may or may not be appropriate expansions of the client relationship, and as a consultant you must measure whether these will lead to individual and organizational client relationships that are of benefit to you.

Some of these client expectations can be particularly challenging, and may test your comfort zone as a professional. For example, you will want to determine whether the client organization is hoping for legitimate, rigorous analysis, or simply a rubber stamp on decisions the organization has already made. You also want to know what will be done with the work product you provide to the client, and whether the data will be used for more than one purpose. We were once asked by a large client organization to create a performance review system that required managers to rank employees' performance into one of three categories: low, acceptable, and superior. At the end of the project, we found out that this ranking system would be used to justify layoffs of hundreds of employees, many of whom had not previously received negative performance reviews. Despite our objections, however, it was too late to stop that process from moving forward. It is always valuable to ask ahead of time how your work will eventually be used. If the response makes you uncomfortable, you have every right to respectfully decline to participate. All project work that you accept should make a positive contribution to the reputation of your business.

Your attention and sensitivity to these issues, as well as your candor in discussing them with your client, will do a great deal toward increasing your client's confidence in you. It demonstrates your integrity, that you are organized and strategic in your planning, and allows the client to have the comfort of knowing exactly what to expect over the course of the project work. Likewise, the dialogue will leave you with a much better understanding of the client organization you are preparing to support.

The amount of time needed to reach a solid contracting agreement will also vary widely from project to project, given not only the discussion time needed with the client, but the added delays of scheduling availability, review of draft agreements, and internal consensus building that may be necessary. Consultants should build allowances for these delays into their project planning. Reaching agreement in a large governmental agency may require a much different contracting process than doing so with a small, community-based nonprofit, and as a result the timing would look much different. While we encourage you to aim for a period of days or weeks instead of weeks or months to reach an agreement, it is worth investing as much time as necessary to ensure that your project begins with clear expectations for all involved. A thorough contract, supported by a detailed discussion, will prevent countless obstacles during your project work, and will keep you well-aligned with your client.

SPECIAL CIRCUMSTANCES IN WINNING PROJECTS

In consulting, few bits of wisdom are truer than the words, "even the best laid plans will go awry." This section addresses four special situations consultants may face after winning a proposed project. As with other situations described in this chapter, the consultant's response benefits from a long-term perspective on the client-consultant relationship.

Situation: You are offered a project that doesn't fit what you want to do, or the kind of work you are best suited to do.

One of the hardest decisions in the business of consulting is deciding which projects to accept and which ones to pass on to someone else. Even the biggest consulting firms make this choice, and it comes down to two basic considerations: 1) How well does the work fit with your core skills? 2) Can you afford financially to pass on the project? Both of these considerations are on a continuum, and Figure 8-2 can provide a framework for thinking about these issues when examining the viability of a project.

While most consultants early in the life of their business will tend to feel the pressure of cash flow issues first, a mutually critical point to consider is the extent to which the work fits with your skills and interests. What do you do best, and what type of work do you want to continue to do?

If you cannot imagine turning down business, you might consider making all of the boxes in this diagram "Yes," but doing so is ill-advised. Many inexperienced consultants take this approach by accepting every project they can; often, this choice is grounded in real concerns about cash flow because, at the start of their consulting careers, they may find themselves cash-strapped. Ironically, saying "no" to projects that do not fit your mission will likely generate more cash flow in the long run, because it will give you time to say "yes" to other work that will build a reputation certain to generate referrals.

If you still can't believe that it could be a good idea to turn down business, two examples may be helpful. Early in our career, when cash flow was a concern, we accepted a project evaluating a program for a small nonprofit that specialized in arts-based education. The project was sponsored by the organization's development director, whose primary concern was fundraising. She had secured a sizable sum from the client organization's biggest funder to "prove" the effectiveness of their program. Though we tried to involve the executive director to introduce the idea that the evaluation would also be a useful self-study for ongoing program improvement, she did not make herself available to discuss it. The study came to us in August with school starting in September, so we felt tremendous pressure to work quickly. Our study found no significant improvements in those students, and as a result, our client was furious—we had actually provided strong, scientifically credible evidence that their program wasn't any more effective than a typical curriculum! As it turned out, the development director was more interested in getting marketing material to secure more funding than trying to objectively understand and improve their program (which could have naturally led to more funding). The director of development and the executive director were so upset at the results, they actually hired another

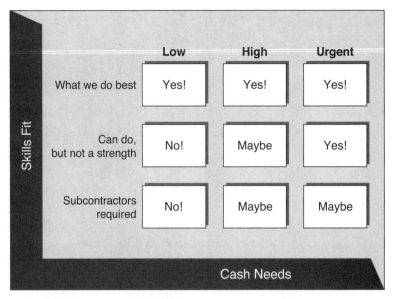

Figure 8-2 Balancing cash needs with skills fit when considering which consulting projects to accept.

consultant to write a brief stating that the results of our study (a randomized controlled experiment with over 600 students!) could be interpreted many different ways. Though we never worked with that client organization again, it served as an important early lesson about verifying shared expectations. Fortunately, we received consistent feedback that those who heard about the incident understood the high quality of the study, and felt that it illustrated our integrity more than anything. We would have had a much better chance of success with the client relationship if we had invested the time up front with both the sponsor and the executive director to clarify their expectations about the possible outcomes.

In another example, a consultant just starting his business (with cash flow concerns) was offered and eagerly accepted a project running statistical analyses for the human resources department at a large retail industry corporation. He was good with statistics and could do the work at a very high quality, so this became a fine—and safe—way to stay profitable. Sure enough, this led to many referrals and he soon found himself doing almost nothing but statistics for client organizations. After a while, short-term cash was less "urgent," and he began to realize that he had built a company with a reputation for number crunching, but he was not known for what he cared about most (leadership and organization development). It took almost 6 years of diligent effort for him to "undo" that reputation and start doing more of the work that he truly loves.

The best way to decide whether or not to accept a project is to ask the question, "Do I want more projects like this one?" The most common way consultants generate new work is by referral, so the projects you take today will beget you similar projects tomorrow.

Situation: You get a project that is too large for you to do on your own.

First-time consultants often start as a one-person firm, which can pose some challenges when it comes to winning larger projects. Often, one-person firms pursuing larger projects will cobble together a group of like-minded professionals, and rely on an existing client relationship to secure a larger than usual project. Perhaps the project is out of scope for you personally because of the volume of work in relation to the time frame for doing it, the range of locations where the work will be done, or because it requires multiple skill sets, only some of which you possess. In all of these circumstances, you must keep in mind that as far as your client is concerned, each subcontractor represents your firm, and their actions have a direct impact on your relationship with the client organization. If a subcontractor slips up, you have slipped up, and it is your client relationship that suffers.

When choosing how to involve subcontractors, make sure the main points of contact for the client relationship are always clearly in your hands. If you find that the core objective of the project is in a skill area outside of your expertise, you should consider passing on the project to the subcontractor whose skill is most in need. For example, if the project involves building an interactive Web site where you need to provide one section of the content but you will hire a programmer to create the Web site, you may not be the best point person for the project. Perhaps your client would be better served by allowing the programmer to run the project, and subcontract out to you for content. Your client will be grateful to you for recommending a high quality programmer, and your relationship will strengthen because they will see that you are interested in the client's well-being, not just in securing a large project. Good faith efforts, such as referring projects beyond your area of expertise, help your client see that you are genuinely interested in their well-being.

Using colleagues as subcontractors is tempting, but can be a risky way to deliver larger projects. Clients want a consultant they can trust who is focused on adding value through their services. When a consultant patches together a group of other professionals for large-scale work, it can make the client nervous to think that a loose collection of individuals, each with their own agenda, will be working on the project. The client trusts *you*, but they do not want to be in a situation where a long series of subcontractors is pointing at each other saying, "it was their responsibility to do that." Not unlike home construction, you may be able to act as a "general contractor" of sorts and pull together the efforts of others, but keep in mind that the buck stops with you. You need to have control of the project, and take absolute responsibility for every action taken. If, due to the nature of the project, you cannot guarantee to your client that you will take full responsibility, you risk jeopardizing the long-term relationship by pursuing the project. Effective contracting with the client becomes even more critical in these situations.

In our experience, the most effective way to use subcontractors is to build a small network of trusted and reliable colleagues that you work with regularly so you can assure clients (and yourself) that these professionals will do work you can stand behind personally. By working with the same individuals, you can also list each other on your Web sites as "affiliates," which adds to your credibility. No matter how often you have worked with a colleague, you still need to be the primary contact point for the client so that your management role is clear. Many friendships among colleagues and client-consultant relationships have been lost due to poor role clarity in these situations.

Situation: Immediately after you get a project, your sponsor leaves.

It is surprisingly common to have your primary client contact and/or project sponsor leave the organization or take on new roles within it during the course of your project. The project-oriented consultant sees this moment as a complete disaster. Often, the new person assigned to monitor your project will revise or reinterpret its parameters. In the worst case, you may find the new sponsor was against your project while you were proposing it. The client-centered consultant, however, sees these circumstances as pregnant with opportunity.

The client-centered consultant has built a solid relationship with the organization, not just with one individual. In nonprofit organizations, this often means making sure that the executive director is, at the very least, aware of your work, if not actively involved in contracting. Having established a clear and effective working relationship with the executive director, you can use the departure of your sponsor to influence the decision about who the new sponsor will be to assure a smooth transition. Also, because you have built solid relationships within this organization, you will undoubtedly make sure that you have exchanged contact information with the outgoing sponsor. It may be years before a new project comes up in the new organization, but hopefully this person will continue to use you as a resource and as a source of advice in their new position.

As for the immediate project at hand, the possibility of losing your sponsor highlights the importance of clear contracting, as discussed earlier in this chapter. When a project contract is clear and assumptions about the work are written rather than "unspoken," the new sponsor is likely to formulate realistic expectations. The contract will provide a clear guide along with a time line and expected deliverables. Approach this transition period by empathizing with the new sponsor, who is likely overwhelmed with new and unexpected responsibilities. Set aside the time to meet with the new sponsor, and listen openly to his or her concerns, thoughts, and expectations. While the temptation may be to tell the new sponsor what the project "should be," the client-centered consultant approaches these meetings as an important opportunity to understand the new sponsor's concerns, and to build a new relationship within the organization. As much as you may want to start the project right away and not miss any milestones on your time line, you need to allow the new sponsor to feel complete ownership for the project, and you need to be open to the possibility that he or she may want to change some things. If your focus is on the long-term relationship, then you will see that it is critical for the new sponsor to value the project. You should feel a strong sense of urgency to explore the impact of this transition on your relationship (and, as a by-product, your project). Changing project sponsorship is a critical incident in any client-consultant relationship, and this situation requires a timely response, preferably in person. For those procrastinators among us, meeting with this client is far more important than organizing your messy desk or cleaning up project files for recently completed work!

Situation: You are offered a good project but for substantially discounted (or pro bono) rates.

Eventually, every consultant will face the situation where they are offered a project they eagerly want to do, but the client organization wants to pay little to nothing for the work. This presents a very difficult decision, particularly for new consultants trying to establish themselves and build a reputation. Often the consultant's internal debate and indecision is further complicated by the cause that the organization supports. How can you turn down an organization that is helping eradicate hunger, for example? You may be tempted to ask yourself, "How many people could they feed with the fees I would usually charge?"

The airlines have this conundrum figured out when they remind us to "please put on your own mask before helping others." You need to take care of your own needs so you can maximize the benefits of your expertise for your clients. It may be easy to justify giving some time away if you think about a given project as a one-time event, but when you focus on building long-term client relationships, you quickly realize that doing free work is not a good long-term strategy for building your business. You must also realize that the client who is asking for a deep discount now will never be comfortable paying you market rates for your work in the future. Consider that by doing work for free, you have defined the relationship around your discounted price. You have established a pro bono mode of operating as acceptable, and have built a client relationship with this as one of the critical assumptions. Don't expect a client who gets something for free to be just as happy with the same work product when they have to pay for it.

Often, consultants who give their work away do not understand the value of the services they provide. Consider the value of a rigorously designed and implemented program evaluation study that demonstrates conclusively that a particular AIDS prevention program works far better than three popular and more costly alternatives. The organization implementing this program will be able to use your study to secure significant funding, expand its services, and garner broad public support. How much is that worth? Keep in mind that your work product in this case has a useful shelf life of perhaps 5 years. The client organization can continue to reference your study year after year during its fundraising and outreach efforts. If, for example, you charged $50,000 for the project and it led to $1 million in funding, the client will likely realize that your services were pivotal to securing that extra funding. At this point, you have established a healthy relationship where both you and the client organization understand the value of your work, and the client willingly pays you for your efforts. If you do this well enough, your client organization will begin to write your services into their annual budget as a de rigueur investment in their future. They will no longer view your services as a cost.

When a client asks for a discount, you should fearlessly articulate the value of your work. Ultimately, the client organization is most concerned with the benefits that your work will provide, and if those benefits are clear to them, cost will be a secondary and manageable concern. If they can get $1 million in funding out of a $50,000 investment in research, their decision will be easy. The important point is that you should not expect your client to know the value of your work unless you do. If you cannot articulate the specific and concrete benefits the client organization will receive from working with you, go back to the drawing board until you can. Good consultants are happy to explain the value of what they are providing; less successful consultants avoid this conversation.

Why do clients ask for pro bono work? Any consultant working with nonprofits must realize that the most popular metric for assessing the legitimacy of a nonprofit service agency is the percentage of funds that go to services, instead of "administrative overhead." Typically, agencies strive for less than 10% of their budget to be overhead. In almost all cases, consultants fall into the undesirable part of this equation. Hence, nonprofit agencies may actually have plenty of financial resources, yet they are heavily motivated by donors to pay you (as a member of the dreaded "overhead" class) as little as possible. If you are effective at articulating the value of your services, however, your client will have a very hard time NOT paying you what your services are worth because you are giving them something of value. If you cannot articulate the value that your services provide, find new services to offer.

THE CLIENT-CENTERED RESPONSE TO LOSING PROJECTS

Candor and active dialogue with the client are just as necessary when the consultant's proposal is not accepted as they are when you win the project. We have established that your agenda as a consultant and businessperson is to build mutually beneficial long-term relationships. Those relationships are much more significant than any individual project, and a "no" from a client organization at one point in time may lead to a "yes" at a later point. You can still present yourself as being a valuable advisor in the context of losing the deal—the key is to be authentic in your efforts. Being authentic, at any stage of a client relationship, is much more important than being smart or clever, and authenticity strengthens your credibility with the client (see Block, 1981, for an extended discussion of authenticity).

If you are interested in a long-term relationship with the client and have genuine concern for their needs, you will want to know why your proposal was turned down. Contact the client immediately after hearing their decision, and request a conversation (ideally in person) to find out the reason(s) behind it. Assuming this is a project you really wanted, and gave significant preparation and attention to winning, a formal, technical approach to this client conversation (such as the one below) is not authentic:

> We appreciate your notification of the decision you've made about consultant support for the scenario planning project. I realize you had many choices in whom to work with, and I am sure that ABC Firm will serve your needs effectively. We certainly hope we can work with your organization in the future, and we wish you success with the project.

Why is this approach insufficient?

- It ends the conversation. There is little motivation for the client to call you again.
- It doesn't show the client that you are genuinely concerned about their issues.
- You have created no opportunity to learn about their decision and why you were declined.

From a conversation like this, it will be hard to reinvigorate this client relationship going forward. By contrast, an authentic response allows you to put the relationship first and the project second:

> We are disappointed that we won't be working with you on this project. We have been enthusiastic about partnering with you, and felt that we had a great understanding of your needs and had proposed a powerful solution. Though I realize the decision is made, I would like to understand what was missing and what you preferred about the consultant you chose so that we can better match your needs the next time an opportunity arises. I'm quite eager for your feedback—can we meet over lunch to discuss it?

Why is this approach effective?

- It demonstrates a sincere interest in the client.
- It assumes there will be a long-term relationship and possible future work together.
- It opens the door for future meetings.

At the debriefing meeting with the client, your role stays the same: to listen well and to be responsive, and to show genuine concern for their needs. Demonstrate through your words and behavior that you are open to your client's feedback about your work, even if it is difficult to hear—you are modeling the trust that you eventually hope this client will place in you. New consultants often assume that when they don't win work, it must be due to a deficit in their technical skills. Often, this is not the case, and the decision may have very little to do with technical ability. Purchase decisions can be driven by multiple factors, including firm location, pre-existing internal relationships, or decisions handed down by leaders with very little involvement in the actual proposal review, among others. It is important not to personalize the feedback, but to use it as a helpful way to gain experience and information. In fact, it is valuable to ask, "What should we have asked you about, but didn't?" (Beich, 2001). You may be surprised by the client's willingness to share information with you. As the client shares feedback, read between the lines and listen for clues about what this organization values, and for possible other project opportunities that may exist. End the meeting by showing your appreciation for their feedback, and affirming your interest in partnering with them in the future.

After the meeting, continue to keep the client's interests and concerns active in your mind. Stay on top of trends in their industry. Clip a magazine article or send a book that has relevant information for them. Alert the client to conferences and workshops on this topic area, and ideally, offer to attend the event with them. Check in periodically to see if their issues are getting adequately resolved. Clearly, you do not want to become a nuisance to the client, but you want to maintain sufficient rapport that they view you as a valued resource and confidante. The key is to demonstrate that your interest in them goes far beyond the scope of the project that you proposed. Loss of a single deal does not equal the end of the relationship.

We recently lost a project with a utility company where we had built a strong relationship based on delivering a very high-quality training evaluation. During the initial engagement, we spent considerable time teaching the client's staff about evaluation and answering questions about how to use the information within the organization. When they requested an evaluation of a public outreach program about gas lines in residential areas, we happily wrote a detailed proposal, which was accepted. We were waiting for the initial payment before beginning the work when the director of training (the sponsor) called in a panic, having realized there were many legal and regulatory implications for the project. We immediately visited the client to discuss the project. In the first 5 minutes, the director shared with us that he had found several firms who specialized in this particular type of program (including legal support services). Realizing we were not the best firm for the job, we quickly shifted to helping the client think about how to select among the handful of specialists they had discovered. When we left the meeting, the client repeatedly thanked us for our help and asserted that they would be looking for the next opportunity to work together. While our initial intent with our visit was to "save" the deal, the fact is that when we walked into the meeting, we had lost the deal already. No amount of persuasiveness would have changed the client's mind, and rightfully so. The client had already found a better solution, and our best option was to reinforce the relationship and find a way to add value in the meeting. We lost the project, but we kept the relationship and are far more likely to get the next one!

CONCLUSION

When you are new to consulting, all marketing activity, whether it results in wins or losses, yields teaching moments and opportunities to gain experience that will make you more effective the next time you sell a project. These activities allow you access to past, present, and future clients, and the chance to enhance your relationship with them. We have reviewed some of the different paths a project can take after the consultant wins it, as well as a productive path to take when your proposal is declined. What all of our examples have in common is the emphasis on keeping the client relationship at the center of the agenda, and creating a 50/50 partnership with the client based on trust, authenticity, and mutual agreement on what will happen next.

In the case of a project win, contracting is the necessary next step before beginning the work. Though the consultant should engage in careful self-reflection, contracting discussions should happen promptly, while client focus and attention is high. And while the contracting discussion may seem to entail a daunting number of contingencies to consider, years of successful consulting experience suggest that these considerations are mission critical. Consulting work is dynamic; issues rarely stay the same over the course of a project. Therefore, establishing safeguards and clear boundaries around the project work allows the consultant and client to stay on task and work efficiently. Ideally, it will let you exceed client expectations, which will almost certainly lay the path for future project work.

Whether you win or lose a project, however, let your response to the situation reveal how you will support the client as their partner and trusted advisor in the future. Remember that much of your marketing will not originate from you. It will come from word-of-mouth communication about you within the client organizations and industries you pursue. If you have managed client relationships favorably and keep communication active, this favorable word-of-mouth recognition will yield many dividends over the life of your business.

Chapter 9

From Start to Finish: A Typical Evaluation Project

Kathleen Dowell

INTRODUCTION

This chapter provides an overview of how a typical evaluation project might proceed, from getting the contract to reporting and communicating final evaluation results. While the project described in this chapter is a good example of a typical project, it is important to note that not all evaluation projects proceed in this manner. This chapter presents just one of many possible project scenarios.

THE PROJECT

Overview and Description of the Program

The *Healthy Schools for Healthy Students* (*HSHS*) Pilot Project was a 3-year youth development project for an independent, not-for-profit public foundation in Maryland that focuses on enhancing health and wellness. The project was aimed at improving the social and emotional well-being of school-age children, and was fueled by the foundation's view that health is "much broader than merely the absence of disease or infirmity, but rather a state of optimal physical, mental, and social well-being." This philosophy influenced the foundation to consider the many aspects of young people's lives that contribute to their health and well-being, including family, peers, schools, and community.

The foundation initiated the *HSHS* Pilot Project by partnering with a local school system. The first phase of the project was an adolescent and youth wellness project. During the initial years of this phase, local leaders, parents, educators, and students were brought together to discuss the difficulties in maintaining relationships at the family, school, and community levels. Many of the participants in that process expressed concern about the many threats (risks) facing today's young people. These discussions led the foundation to implement an integrated approach to coordinate schools, families, and communities to assist children in becoming effective, caring, and productive adults. These efforts focused primarily on staff wellness, character education, and parent/community involvement in children's education.

The vision of the partnership between the foundation and the school system was that students, staff, parents, and extended families would achieve their maximum health and wellness potential. *Healthy Schools for Healthy Students* grew out of this partnership and was the name of the second phase of the original adolescent and youth wellness project. This phase incorporated a more systematic approach to the concept of whole school wellness by focusing on school culture, and it was during this phase that the foundation decided to incorporate an evaluation into the project.

To complement the foundation's broad definition of health that includes "a state of optimal physical, mental, and social well-being," the developmental asset model designed by the Search Institute in Minneapolis, MN, was chosen as the core strategy for the project. This framework is a positive, strength-based approach that supports the entire community's engagement in the healthy development of youth. It is grounded in research and has the capacity to mobilize parents, business, faith-based organizations, and schools in working together to build assets or "building blocks" to empower and sustain growth over time. There are 40 developmental assets grouped into 7 categories (support, empowerment, boundaries and expectations, constructive use of time, commitment to learning, positive values, social competencies, and positive identity). Research suggests that youth who possess more of these assets are less likely to engage in risky behaviors and more likely to engage in positive behaviors than youth who possess fewer of these assets. Research also suggests that developmental assets help students achieve both personally and academically (Scales, 2002; Epstein, 1994; North Central Regional Educational Laboratory, 1996; Catalano, Berglund, Ryan, Lonczak, & Hawkins, 1999). The foundation anticipated that the application of the Developmental Assets model would result in improved school climate, and ultimately, to improved student achievement.

The *HSHS* program was piloted in three schools—one elementary school, one middle school, and one high school. The schools were chosen to participate by the foundation because of their willingness to incorporate the developmental assets approach in their schools. Within each school, a school culture committee (made up of teachers, staff, students, and parents) was responsible for coordinating and overseeing the implementation of asset-building activities. In addition, the foundation had a grant facilitator who assisted the schools in developing and implementing these activities.

Each school was given leeway to select the types and intensities of activities and services that supported the developmental assets way of thinking into the everyday culture of the schools. Activities chosen by the schools included: assets education targeted toward students, staff, and parents; ongoing recognition of asset behaviors; promotion of adult-child relationships; leadership development; professional development; wellness-promoting activities; tools for communicating with parents; and outreach to parents. These activities were expected to be effective ways of "infusing" the schools with the asset development mindset and were thought to also foster the development of youth assets and improve school culture.

The Evaluation Context

The foundation had two primary goals for the evaluation. The first was to determine if the developmental assets approach to youth development would lead to: 1) positive youth outcomes, including improved academic achievement, decreased negative behaviors, and increased positive behaviors; 2) improved outcomes for teachers, including increased job satisfaction and retention; and 3) increased involvement of parents in schools. Ultimately, the evaluation was to focus on whether these outcomes would lead to improved school climate.

The second major goal of the evaluation was to determine if it was feasible to expand the project to other schools within the same school system. The foundation hoped that the evaluation would demonstrate positive outcomes associated with the project, which would, in turn, make other schools eager to adopt the same youth development strategy. Ultimately, the hope was that all schools in the school system would adopt the program and that school climate would improve across the board.

GETTING THE CONTRACT

Our company, Partners in Evaluation & Planning, LLC, is an independent evaluation and program planning consulting company. We had been in business for approximately 5 years when this project came along. We have two partners who own the company and who work full time in the business, and, at the time this project started, we also had a part-time research assistant who worked 20 hours per week. The bulk of our business is focused on evaluating programs that address family and children's issues (e.g., teen pregnancy prevention, education, early childhood development), and this project appeared to fit well with our areas of interest and expertise.

The foundation released the request for proposal (RFP) for this project to the Baltimore Area Evaluators, one of the local affiliates of the American Evaluation Association. The affiliate passed the RFP on to all members, including our company. The foundation was unknown to us, but because the project focused on youth development, we were particularly interested in responding to the RFP.

For our company, only about 10–20% of our work is the result of an RFP process. As with many consultants, most of our work comes to us through networking and from word-of-mouth from one client to another. Furthermore, we only choose to respond to a limited number of RFPs because of the time and effort required to prepare and submit proposals. Our success rate with RFPs varies, but generally we win approximately 40% of the proposals we submit.

Choosing to respond to RFPs takes careful consideration since the time for proposal writing is non-billable. We chose to respond to this RFP because the *HSHS* project fit nicely with our experience and interests, and we felt that we had a very good chance of getting the job. In the end, we decided that it was worth the risk (cost) to go for it.

Besides the risk/cost issues associated with RFPs, there are some other things to keep in mind if you choose to respond to an RFP that may increase your chances of success:

- First, be realistic about your experience and qualifications, and make sure that you are qualified to do the work; don't waste time responding to an RFP for work that you can't realistically perform.
- Highlight your unique qualifications to perform the work in order to set yourself apart from all of the other evaluators who may also be submitting proposals.
- Be sure to provide all of the information asked for in the RFP, even if it sounds unimportant or irrelevant.
- Neatness and organization count because how you prepare the proposal is a reflection of how you will do the actual work if you were to get the job.

Ultimately, you need to think strategically about responding to RFPs, and focus on those for which you have a reasonable chance of success.

For the *HSHS* project, the foundation wanted an evaluator to perform three major tasks:

- Assess how the *HSHS* project functioned in the school setting.
- Monitor how, and to what degree, the project activities were implemented.
- Determine the short- and long-term results of the project for students, staff, and families.

The RFP also specified a theoretical framework for the evaluation design (developmental assets), as well as specific data collection tools that needed to be used. In particular, the foundation requested that the major outcome of the evaluation—school climate—be measured by the *Profile of School Social and Learning Climate Survey*, a school climate survey that had been developed by the Search Institute. Use of this instrument was required by the foundation.

Unlike many other RFPs, this one included a specific budget amount ($60,000) for the 3-year project. Having an explicit dollar value made preparing the proposal much easier because we could determine exactly what tasks we could perform with the given budget. When we know the budget of a project at the proposal stage, we typically estimate how many hours each specific task will take and, thus, how much each task will cost. We then adjust our proposed approach based on whether or not the budget can adequately cover the cost of the proposed tasks. For this project, we wanted to include contextual, process, and outcome evaluation components, and we also wanted to use both quantitative and qualitative data collection methods. The challenge was figuring out specific methods that we could employ for each component of the evaluation while staying within the available budget. We did this by weighing the pros and cons of various approaches, dismissing those in which the cost outweighed the benefits that would be achieved, and including those that would yield the data we needed while keeping us within the budget limitations. It is not unusual to have to make concessions regarding methodology so that you can stay within the budget amount.

In preparing our response, we proposed the following:

- The formation of an Evaluation Advisory Team, which consisted of three foundation staff members, project staff, the principals from each of the three participating schools, the grant facilitator, and an administrator from the school system. The team was to meet quarterly to discuss progress and provide input into the evaluation.
- The creation of a project logic model that specified the expected short-term, intermediate, and long-term outcomes for the project

- A three-pronged evaluation approach that included: 1) a *contextual* evaluation to assess the environment/context in which the project was being implemented; 2) an *implementation* evaluation to assess how well and to what extent the project was implemented as planned; and 3) an *outcome* evaluation to assess project outcomes
- Both quantitative methods (surveys of students, school staff such as teachers, principals, and school culture committee members, and parents) and qualitative methods (on-site observations, student focus groups and interviews with school principals, school culture committee members, school system administrators, foundation staff, and project staff) to collect data
- Interim and final reports

We proposed using a participatory approach to the evaluation. That is, we emphasized participation of project staff and other stakeholders in all phases of the evaluation, from developing the logic model, to designing the data collection tools, to helping to interpret the findings. The specific ways in which project stakeholders were involved are described throughout the chapter.

As with all proposals we submit, we included a cover letter that essentially introduced our company, highlighted our qualifications to perform the work, and expressed our appreciation for their consideration of our proposal. The only attachments we included with the proposal were resumes for key evaluation staff. We did not attach any examples of our past work because this RFP did not ask for that type of information. In our experience, though, this is quite unusual, as most RFPs typically ask respondents to include samples of previous work.

The final proposal was 10 pages long and took about 2 weeks to prepare and submit. The proposal itself was detailed enough to give the foundation an idea of how we would perform the work, but general enough so that it was clear that the proposed advisory team would play a major role in the evaluation design process. For example, we did not propose any specific measures to be used for data collection because we typically develop or decide upon data collection tools in collaboration with the client. Also, we typically can't propose data collection tools prior to the development of the project logic model, which specifies the expected project outcomes (see Appendix 9-1 for a copy of the proposal). We were contacted by the foundation approximately 2 weeks after submitting the proposal and were invited for an interview with staff from the foundation. To prepare for the interview, we read through the proposal several times so that we could present our approach without having to read directly from the proposal. The interview lasted about an hour and was fairly typical in that we gave a presentation of our proposed approach to evaluating the *HSHS* project, and the interviewers asked questions to further clarify how we would approach the project. During the interview, the foundation staff described to us their expectations for the evaluation. Most importantly, because of the desire to replicate the project in other schools, the evaluation needed to be technically sound, providing the foundation with reliable data, based on scientifically sound data collection methodologies.

The proposed qualitative data collection approaches proved to be a sticking point—one of the foundation staff members was very skeptical of the use of qualitative data collection methods, believing that qualitative data was nothing more than "anecdotal" information that was not "scientific." Concerns were expressed that qualitative data would not be "scientific" enough to help determine if project outcomes were achieved. At the time, it became apparent that he held this view because he was not knowledgeable about the different qualitative methods that can be used to collect reliable data. He often referred to qualitative data as "anecdotal" data, and he did not want the evaluation to use anecdotal information to demonstrate changes in project outcomes. So, much of the interview was spent educating the staff on the various qualitative data collection techniques, the value of collecting qualitative data, and the reliability of such data. In the end, this issue did not seem as though it would cause problems, as the person who questioned the qualitative approach was open to hearing about how we could use that type of data to help inform the evaluation.

At the conclusion of the interview, the foundation told us that they would contact us in a few days with their final decision. We were very happy with how the interview went—we got the impression that they were leaning toward hiring us for the project, and we were very interested in continuing to work with them based on what we learned in the interview. As promised, the foundation called us within a couple of days and offered us the job.

For most projects, we have a standard contract that we ask clients to use (although in some cases client organizations have their own contracts that they want to use or must use, and we will defer to that). For this project, we drew up the contract after being offered the job, and sent it to the foundation for review and final approval. There are times when a client will make changes to our standard contract and we are usually willing to make such changes. In this case, the foundation did not request any changes to the contract. The contract was finalized and signed before we began work on the project.

PLANNING THE EVALUATION

As with most projects that we work on, the *HSHS* evaluation began with a kick-off meeting of the Evaluation Advisory Team. The length of a kick-off meeting varies from project to project and depends largely on what we want to accomplish during the meeting. For this project, we wanted to incorporate the development of the logic model into the meeting, mainly because the members of the team were extremely busy and getting them all together for an additional logic model meeting would have been extremely difficult. Because the development of the logic model was on the agenda, the kick-off meeting was an all-day meeting.

At the kick-off meeting, the team:

- Finalized the project work plan and established time lines for completion of various tasks
- Established a communication protocol between the project staff and the evaluators
- Created the program logic model

The Project Logic Model

Creating the program logic model was the first step in designing the *HSHS* evaluation. The bulk of the project kick-off meeting was devoted to developing the logic model, with evaluation team members working collaboratively to identify and agree upon the expected short-term, intermediate, and long-term outcomes for the project. While the ultimate outcome (improved school climate) had already been identified as such, the group worked on identifying the other outcomes that would lead up to achievement of improved school climate. As with most projects, development of the logic model was a long and arduous process; however, the value of having the model outweighed the effort involved in putting the model together. In addition, the team members all believed in the usefulness of having the model so they were enthusiastic about creating the model. Team members' passion helped the process go more smoothly.

When we work with clients to create a program logic model, we typically begin by showing a short PowerPoint presentation about logic models—what they are, how we use them in evaluation, what components are included in the model, how we define short-term, intermediate, and long-term outcomes, and how we distinguish outcomes from outputs. Taking the time to make this presentation is critical, as most clients are not familiar with a logic model or the terminology we use in creating a model.

Educating clients about logic models helps them better understand the process of creating a model.

When creating the actual logic model, we use a consensus process in which we encourage all stakeholders to ultimately agree not only on the activities and outcomes for the project, but the linkages between the activities and outcomes. As with any process involving a fairly large group of people, disagreements occur and need to be discussed. This project was no exception. Part of the advantage of having a diverse group of people making up the evaluation team is that they all bring different perspectives to the project. This, however, can also be one of the drawbacks. For the *HSHS* project, principals had different perspectives than the project staff, who had different perspectives than the school system administrators, who had different perspectives than the foundation staff. The key to developing the logic model is getting all participants to see and understand others' perspectives, and to have an open mind about including those perspectives in the logic model.

We used a systematic approach with this group. Starting with program activities, we asked everyone to identify the activities that made up the *HSHS* project. Everyone was asked to share their ideas without regard to what others may have been thinking. Once that list was developed, we then went through each activity one by one and asked for agreement on whether the activity was a component of the project or not. Participants were encouraged to disagree or reword the activities and to discuss their opinions with the group. Ultimately, we would reach consensus about what activities to keep in the model and which ones to exclude. This process proceeded in the same manner for each remaining component of the logic model—short-term outcomes, intermediate outcomes, and long-term outcomes. Once these components were all agreed upon, participants worked together through long discussions to determine the exact pathway of outcomes.

The logic model created a visual display of how the project was expected to work and provided an easy way for team members, as well as other stakeholders who were not as closely associated with the project, to understand the theory behind the program. The final logic model was completed about 2 weeks following the kick-off meeting. During those 2 weeks, we prepared an initial draft of the model, distributed the draft to the Evaluation Advisory Team members for comments and suggestions, and then made changes to the model based on their suggestions. We believe it is critical to allow participants to comment on the model because it helps them to understand the model better, and it also increases their "buy-in" to the model since they had a hand in its development. The *HSHS* logic model is displayed in Figure 9-1.

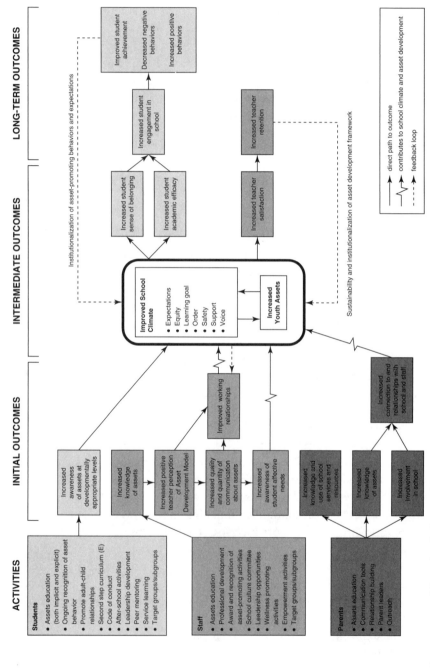

Figure 9-1 Healthy Schools for Healthy Students: Program Logic Model

The Evaluation Plan

The next step in planning the evaluation was the development of the evaluation plan. The plan was based on the logic model drafted at the project kick-off meeting. The evaluation plan specified the final evaluation questions for the contextual, implementation, and outcome evaluations; data collection methods and data sources for collecting data to address the research questions; and a time line for implementation of the plan. The plan also specified the data collection methods, data collection time points, and data sources for each of the outcomes specified in the program logic model. The evaluation plan served as the guide for implementing the *HSHS* evaluation. The plan was very useful for the stakeholders who were involved in the evaluation, as it served as a "road map" for the evaluation team, and let them know what they could expect as the evaluation unfolded. Table 9-1 contains selected excerpts from the *HSHS* evaluation plan and shows the types of data collection strategies planned.

As with all evaluations that we conduct, the evaluation plan served as a guide for the Evaluation Advisory Team. The plan was reviewed at each quarterly meeting of the advisory team to determine if we were on track with the evaluation. Because evaluations never run as smoothly as planned, the goal was not to strictly adhere to the plan. Instead, the goal was to make sure all evaluation tasks outlined in the plan were completed in a reasonable time frame.

Data Collection Tools

Once the evaluation plan was finalized, the next step was the creation of data collection tools. The process of developing data collection tools varies from project to project—sometimes, tools exist that measure the outcomes in which we are interested, and, other times, we have to develop our own tools because appropriate ones do not exist. For this project, it was a mixture of both.

The major outcome of interest for this project was school climate. This outcome was measured both quantitatively and qualitatively. For the quantitative measure, an existing tool was available (the Profile of School Social and Learning Climate, developed by the Search Institute). The existing tool was developed for high school and middle school students; since the *HSHS* project also included an elementary school, we adapted the tool for the elementary school.

In addition to the questions already on the school climate survey, we added questions that would provide us with data to measure the other

Table 9-1 *HSHS* Evaluation Plan and Data Collection Strategies

Evaluation Questions	Data Collection Method(s)	Data Source(s)	Data Collection Schedule
Contextual evaluation			
How receptive were staff members to using the developmental assets framework as a vehicle to change school culture?	Interviews	Foundation and school stakeholders, key teacher/asst. principal, school culture committee chair	February–April Yr 1
How satisfied were staff members with the support/training?	Interviews Staff survey	Key teacher/asst. principal Other staff	February–April Yr 1, Yr 2, Yr 3 May Yr 1, Yr 2, Yr 3
What differences existed among the elementary, middle, and high schools in incorporating the program into the schools?	Interviews	Foundation and school stakeholders, key teacher/asst. principal, school culture committee chair	February–April Yr 1, Yr 2, Yr 3
Implementation evaluation			
To what degree were the strategies/ approaches learned in the training implemented throughout the school community?	Interviews Observation	Grant facilitator, key teacher/asst. principal, school culture committee chair School site	February–May Yr 1, Yr 2, Yr 3
To what degree were the activities in each school's action plan implemented?	Interviews Observation	Grant facilitator, key teacher/asst. principal, school culture committee chair School site	February–May Yr 1, Yr 2, Yr 3

/ continues

Table 9-1 *HSHS* Evaluation Plan and Data Collection Strategies (continued)

Evaluation Questions	Data Collection Method(s)	Data Source(s)	Data Collection Schedule
What are the strengths and challenges to the actual operation of the program?	Interviews	Grant facilitator, key teacher/asst. principal, school culture committee chair	February–May Yr 1, Yr 2, Yr 3
	Observation Focus group	School site Parents	
Outcome evaluation			
What effect did *HSHS* have on school climate?	Profile of School Social and Learning Climate	Students	Baseline (staggered for each school: Sept, Dec, Jan) and May Yr 1, Yr 2, and Yr 3 (all schools)
How effective was *HSHS* in improving students' achievement in school?	Standardized tests scores, report cards, school records	School system	Baseline (school year) and May Yr 1, Yr 2, and Yr 3
How effective was *HSHS* in promoting positive behaviors among students?	Student survey or focus group Staff survey	Students Staff	May Yr 1, Yr 2, and Yr 3 May Yr 1, Yr 2, and Yr 3

outcomes of the project. To come up with these questions, we spent several days researching existing tools from which we could draw questions. Most of our search for existing tools was conducted via the Internet, although we also had to make several library visits to get copies of some tools. The elementary school survey is included in Appendix 9-2.

Finally, we created staff and parent surveys that included questions about school climate, as well as other project outcomes. Staff surveys were administered to teachers, teachers' assistants, administrators, and other support staff at the three participating schools. Copies of these surveys are included in Appendix 9-3.

For the qualitative data, we developed: 1) focus group protocols for students and school staff; and 2) interview protocols for the principals, school culture committee chairs, the project's grant facilitator, and the foundation staff.

The student focus group interview questions explored their feelings about school, how school helped them, how being in school made them feel, and the extent to which their parents were involved in school (see Appendix 9-5). Staff focus groups explored their impressions of the developmental assets framework, activities they implemented at their schools, the types of support they received from school administrators to implement the project, and perceptions of staff satisfaction (see Appendix 9-6). Interview protocols included questions regarding the receptiveness of school staff to implementing the *HSHS* project, staff satisfaction with training that was provided on the developmental assets, barriers to implementing the project, the capacity of the schools to implement and sustain the program, and what other schools should know about implementing the project.

In keeping with our participatory approach to this evaluation, the Evaluation Advisory Team was very involved in helping to develop both the surveys and the qualitative protocols. Drafts of surveys and qualitative protocols were reviewed by team members several times before they were finalized and ready for use in the field. Involving the team at this stage helped to ensure that the right questions were asked, and that they were asked in the right manner. This improved our chances of obtaining the data we needed. The school staff was integral to the data collection process, as well.

Some team members were concerned that parents would not take the time to complete a lengthy survey and that students would not have enough time during class to complete the surveys. However, the issue was discussed among the team members and they decided that getting the data we needed to adequately measure the project outcomes was important enough to keep the surveys as they were. In the end, it took about a month and a half to get all of the surveys and qualitative protocols finalized.

COLLECTING THE DATA

Student Data

Student data were collected in two ways. First, the Search Institute administered the *Profile of School Social and Learning Climate Survey* to the middle and high schools because the foundation already had a contract with the Search Institute to do so. Once the surveys were administered to these two schools, data were entered by the Search Institute, and the raw data files were sent to us for analysis.

The process that the Search Institute used for student surveys presented a problem for us—they did not use ID numbers or other types of codes to identify student surveys, so we were in a position of not being able to track individual students over time. Instead, we would only have school-level data. This, unfortunately, was not the approach we wanted to take, but we were unaware of this until we began the data collection process. After much discussion about ways we might track surveys over time, the evaluation team decided that we would have to abandon that idea and simply aggregate the data at each time point, and compare overall findings from one time point to another.

Since we had additional questions for the middle and high school students beyond what was asked on the *Profile of School Social and Learning Climate Survey*, we were responsible for administering another survey to those students to ask the additional questions. The processes we used to administer these surveys, as well as the surveys for the elementary school, are described below.

School personnel, in particular the teachers and principals, were an integral part of helping to collect the student data. For the survey data, we enlisted the help of the principals and teachers to administer the surveys during the regular school day. This gave us the advantage of getting a high response rate, since the students were a "captive audience," and the teachers were able to get the vast majority of students to complete surveys. Surveys were administered at the beginning of the project and then every spring for the remainder of the project. Thus, we ended up with a baseline and several follow up surveys for each student.

We also enlisted the help of the principals to complete the student focus groups. At each data collection time point, we conducted one focus group at each school. Principals selected the students who would participate, and helped with the logistics, such as reserving a room and scheduling the time. The groups typically included 8–10 students, and were held during the students' normal lunch time. Often, the groups ran slightly longer than the half hour allotted for lunch, but the teachers were very cooperative in letting students out of class for the additional time (usually about 15 extra minutes). We provided pizza and drinks. This worked out well, as it didn't take students away from class time, and the kids were happy to talk and be fed at the same time.

Staff Data

The staff surveys were left in each teacher's mailbox and a collection box was left in each school's main office. Staff members were asked to complete their surveys and then simply drop their completed surveys into the collection box. While many staff members were responsive to the initial request, the principals, once again, were very helpful in nudging along and persuading those who had not yet completed the survey to participate on time. Because the principals were so highly invested in the project and the evaluation, they assumed this role for us, and were just as anxious as we were to have their teachers respond in a timely fashion. Teacher response rates at all three schools exceeded 90%.

Parent Data

We mulled over several options for administering the parent surveys. For example, we discussed doing phone interviews, but this option was too expensive given the budget available. We also considered using a Web-based survey, but there was a substantial portion of parents who did not have access to the Internet at home. After much discussion, we finally decided to send the survey home with students. This also had its drawbacks, including the possibility, especially among the middle and high schools, that the students would not deliver the surveys to their parents/caregivers. Despite this challenge, the team felt that this approach was the best option available.

In each parent survey packet we included a letter explaining the purpose of the survey, the survey itself, and an envelope for returning the survey to the school. Parents completed the surveys anonymously. Collection boxes for the parent surveys were also left in the main offices of the schools, and students were instructed to give the surveys to their teachers, who were asked to put the completed parent surveys in the collection boxes. Response rates for parents were low to moderate, ranging from 11% for the high school, to 67% for the elementary school.

REPORTING THE RESULTS

We established a schedule for submitting preliminary evaluation reports, as well as a final evaluation report. Towards the middle of the first year of the project, foundation staff members were very eager to begin learning about the findings from the evaluation. This was a change from our original plan, but we have found that a request like this is not unusual. Clients are often eager to hear about evaluation findings as soon as data have been collected. Usually, we try to accommodate these requests if it is reasonable to do so. In this case, we had enough data to provide the foundation with some very preliminary results, and so we granted their request.

At the time of their request, we didn't have enough outcome data collected to determine what impact the program was having. So, we decided to provide the foundation with a preliminary report that focused solely on the contextual and implementation evaluations. This allowed the foundation to get some feedback about the project while giving us more time to collect enough outcome data to be able to report on project outcomes. Although the foundation would have liked to receive more information at that point in time, we explained to them why we couldn't provide them with anything more, and they reluctantly accepted that decision.

The first preliminary report was submitted approximately 7 months after beginning the evaluation. Most of the first preliminary report focused on implementation issues, such as the extent to which: 1) the schools had adopted the principles of the asset development model, 2) teachers and other school staff were helping to implement the program, and 3) school leadership was supporting teachers' efforts to implement the program. In addition, we described the effectiveness of training that school staff had received about asset development, barriers and challenges encountered, and school staff perceptions of changes in students' behaviors.

Once adequate outcome data had been collected, we began to provide the foundation with yearly reports. These reports provided updated data on the contextual and implementation evaluations, as well as preliminary outcome findings. The final report was submitted approximately 2 1/2 years after the start of the project. The final report included recommendations for program improvement (see Appendix 9-8 to view the executive summary). Staff at the foundation, as well as other members of the Evaluation Advisory Team, spent several weeks after the submission of each report reviewing the findings and the report drafts. They were very helpful in interpreting findings, and many of their suggestions were incorporated into the final drafts. Foundation staff also helped to further craft the recommendations.

While evaluation findings were presented in report format, results were also presented in person at debriefing sessions with the Evaluation Advisory Team. Presenting the findings in person was helpful for two reasons. First, it gave us the opportunity to present the major findings of the evaluation to the team, some of whom did not have time to read the full reports.

Many times, the people who make decisions about the fate of a project do not have time to fully read and digest a full evaluation report, but they would benefit from knowing the highlights of the evaluation. Debriefing sessions make up for this by providing project staff with the important information they need to make informed decisions about their programs. Second, it provided the opportunity to dialogue about the implications of the findings as plans for program expansion went forward. We have found that these types of in-person debriefings are invaluable in getting clients to understand and ultimately use the results of an evaluation and are a very useful supplement to written reports.

The evaluation ended prematurely and quite unexpectedly. At the end of the second year of the project, the foundation started to move forward with plans to initiate a community-wide asset building campaign that would encompass the entire geographic area served by the school system that participated in the *HSHS* Pilot Project. The desire to take the asset building model to a community level shifted the foundation's focus from completing the pilot to establishing the broader program. Thus, the foundation decided to end the pilot evaluation early, and spend its resources on planning and implementing the community project.

LESSONS LEARNED

Every evaluation project is an opportunity for learning and growth. Challenges, problems, setbacks, etc., are all part of the normal evaluation process. The *HSHS* project was no exception, as we faced a number of challenges and learned a number of lessons over the course of the project.

Evaluators Need to Be Educators

As described earlier, one of the foundation staff members was very skeptical about the use of qualitative data collection methods. The skepticism was so great that throughout the entire evaluation process (from the initial interview to the final report), our role became that of educator—educating project staff on qualitative data collection and its usefulness in evaluation. Many times, even though our job title is "evaluator," we are often educators as well, informing project staff about the evaluation process so they gain an understanding of what evaluation is all about. Educating project staff about evaluation is crucial, as they are more likely to understand and support the evaluation if they understand how the process works, and how the process will benefit them in the end (i.e., by demonstrating the impact of their program).

You Have to Sell Your Services

The evaluation business is getting more competitive every day, with more and more consultants going into business and competing for work. To get a contract, you have to really sell yourself as an evaluation "expert" by emphasizing your strengths, experience, and credentials. For this project, we took this approach in both the proposal and in the initial interview with the foundation staff. It was important for us to distinguish ourselves as better than other applicants by emphasizing what we could do better than our competition. At both points in time we emphasized our experience working with youth of all ages (which was important for this project), and in evaluating outcomes over the long term (also an important component of this evaluation).

Participatory Approaches Make a Difference

Engaging the *HSHS* project staff and other stakeholders in the evaluation proved to have huge benefits. It was clear from the beginning that the evaluation would not run smoothly without the full support and involvement of the principals from the three *HSHS* schools. Having to work through school systems to get evaluation data can be a tough job, but having the principals support the evaluation process made data gathering much easier. In the end, the principals were eager to make the evaluation successful because they had helped with the planning and design from the very beginning. It gave them a sense of ownership.

While the participatory approach often has huge benefits, there are also drawbacks to this approach, including:

- Additional time spent sorting out differing stakeholder opinions and perspectives
- Potentially less scientific rigor if the theoretical model and tools are too "homegrown" and not based on valid theories and reliable evaluation tools
- Less objectivity on behalf of the evaluator if the "partnership" is taken too far

However, if care is taken to minimize these challenges, the benefits of the participatory approach outweigh the challenges. Benefits include:

- Stronger logic (theoretical) model development that is based on opinions and perceptions of a variety of stakeholders, including administrators, funders, participants, and, most of all, those who work with the program on a daily basis

- Better buy in from all stakeholders in the evaluation process because they have been consistently involved in the process of design, implementation, and debrief of results
- Cleaner data, especially if data collection is based on program level staff administration of tools. Since staff have been included in the entire process of developing the plan, they are more likely to put the necessary effort into getting good data.
- There is a higher likelihood that data will be used to benefit the program at both the program director level and the administrative level. When stakeholders understand (and have been part of) the process of the evaluation, they are more likely to feel closer to the results, and to find the results useful to them.

For this project, the participatory approach was well accepted, and the Evaluation Advisory Team's members thoroughly enjoyed being a part in the process.

Nothing Is Written in Stone

When the *HSHS* evaluation began, the project was expected to last for 3 years. Due to unforeseen circumstances and the changing priorities of the foundation, the project was terminated after 2 years. There will be times when projects don't follow the expected course. For this project, the early termination was due to the foundation being extremely anxious to move onto the next phase of the project, which was a community-wide adolescent health and wellness promotion initiative. Not wanting to wait until the planned conclusion of the evaluation to move forward, they made the decision to move forward as soon as some positive results were found. This was a political decision rather than a decision based on problems with the evaluation. At the time the evaluation ended, the foundation expressed interest in having us work with them to evaluate the larger initiative, but that never came to fruition. To our knowledge, the community initiative has not been evaluated.

CONCLUSION

Overall, the *HSHS* evaluation was a positive experience for us. We got the opportunity to work with a diverse group of people who were enthusiastic about the evaluation component of their project, and who were invested in making sure the evaluation was conducted as rigorously as possible and ran as smoothly as possible. We were also able to expand on our experience working with youth, and we gained valuable experience in designing surveys for a wide age range of students. Finally, we learned effective ways of collecting and analyzing long-term data from different populations.

The *HSHS* evaluation was by no means perfect. We faced a number of challenges over the course of the project, including:

- Documenting the "program" was difficult because the activities that could be included as an *HSHS* activity varied from school-to-school, and were not always clearly defined.
- Because of the constraints of data collection and the existing relationship of the foundation with the Search Institute, all survey data collected by the Search Institute was school-level versus individual-level, and that restricted the types of analyses we could conduct.
- The selection of the participating schools was suspect since there was no definitive selection criteria.
- Premature use of evaluation data for political purposes resulted in the early termination of the evaluation so that the client could move forward with their new initiative.
- Client expectations were (too?) high, and this is not unusual, but it did make pleasing the client difficult at times.

If the budget for this project had been larger, we would have made several changes to the evaluation design, including:

- More qualitative data collection, particularly more on-site visits to the schools to observe and document program activities
- The inclusion of control or comparison schools so that we could better associate changes in program outcomes to the actual program
- Additional efforts to collect data from parents, including telephone interviews

These changes would have made the evaluation stronger, and would have provided the foundation with a more rigorous methodology.

APPENDIX 9-1: Proposal for Evaluation of the *Healthy Schools for Healthy Students* Pilot Project

Partners in Evaluation & Planning, LLC (Partners), proposes to work with the Horizon Foundation and Howard County Public Schools to evaluate the *Healthy Schools for Healthy Students* (*HSHS*) Pilot Project. In this capacity, Partners will provide leadership in the development and implementation of an evaluation protocol that examines the context, implementation, and outcomes of the program. Specifically, Partners will:

- Assess how the project functions in the school setting.
- Monitor how, and to what degree, project activities are implemented.
- Determine the short- and long-term results of the project for students, staff, and families.

Partners is dedicated to ensuring that the evaluations we design and conduct are scientifically strong, user friendly, and realistic. It is our goal to build programs and organizations that integrate data into ongoing program operations and decision-making processes. Therefore, it is vitally important to us that staff and stakeholders are involved in many phases of evaluation, and that they understand the results of evaluation. In the end, we believe this creates better services. To support this participatory approach, we will include the *Healthy Schools for Healthy Students* Evaluation Advisory Team in planning and implementation of the evaluation, as appropriate. The team's knowledge and expertise will be essential in the development and implementation of the evaluation, and the utilization of the evaluation findings.

> This proposal describes the tasks to be completed during the 3-year pilot project. Ultimately, the project will provide the Horizon Foundation and Howard County Public Schools with evaluation results that may be used in decision-making about the program, so that services are provided at an optimal level, and the program is achieving desired results for students, staff, and families.

1. EVALUATION DESIGN

The evaluation study will include the following tasks:

- Design a plan for evaluating the 3-year project.
- Develop key evaluation questions with input from the Evaluation Advisory Team.
- Identify data techniques and data sources.

- Create a work plan with a time line that indicates key data collection and reporting activities.
- Collect and analyze qualitative and quantitative data.
- Prepare and present annual interim reports and a final report.

Partners' approach for accomplishing each of these tasks is described next. An estimated time line for completing each of these tasks is displayed in Exhibit 1.

1.1 Design Plan for Evaluating the 3-Year Project

Designing a sound evaluation plan for this project will be the key to its success. The evaluation plan will form the foundation of all activities to be performed during the 3-year project period. Partners proposes to work collaboratively with the Evaluation Advisory Team in the development of such an evaluation plan. Initially, Partners will meet with members of the Evaluation Advisory Team to discuss the goals and objectives of the project and identify the key components of the 3-year project. Based on this preliminary meeting, and in conjunction with review of relevant *Healthy Schools for Healthy Students* materials and documents, Partners will prepare a draft evaluation plan. The draft plan will include final evaluation questions for the contextual, implementation, and outcome evaluations; data collection methods and data sources for collecting data to address the research questions; and a time line for implementation of the plan. The draft plan will be submitted to the Evaluation Advisory Team for review and comment. The plan will be revised as appropriate, and a final evaluation plan will be submitted to the team for approval.

To ensure that the evaluation plan continues to meet the needs of the Horizon Foundation and Howard County Public Schools, Partners proposes to hold quarterly meetings with the Evaluation Advisory Team. These meetings will provide Partners and the team with opportunities to discuss progress on the evaluation, identify barriers and potential solutions to those barriers, share findings, and determine if the evaluation plan needs to be revised.

1.2 Develop Key Evaluation Questions

There will be three levels of evaluation included in each of the three school settings: context, implementation, and outcome. Therefore, three sets of key evaluation questions will be developed relating to each of the three types of evaluation. The evaluation questions already developed by the

Horizon Foundation will serve as the starting point for generating a final and comprehensive list of questions. The preliminary sets of questions are identified below.

The contextual evaluation will be guided by the following preliminary evaluation questions:

- What are the demographics (and characteristics) of the pilot schools?
- How receptive were staff members to using the developmental assets framework as a vehicle to change school culture?
- What types of support/training activities were provided for school staff?
- How satisfied were staff members with the support/training?
- What action plans were developed for implementing specific initiatives?
- What barriers were evident that restricted efficient and effective planning?
- How were these barriers addressed and overcome?
- What types of orientation programs were provided for parents?

The implementation evaluation will be guided by the following preliminary evaluation questions:

- To what degree were the strategies/approaches learned in the training implemented throughout the school community?
- How receptive was the school community to the programs/activities/events that were conducted?
- To what degree were the activities in each school's action plan implemented?

The outcome evaluation will be guided by the following preliminary evaluation questions:

- What changes occurred for students in: support and empowerment; commitment to learning; positive values; social competencies; positive identity; and boundaries, expectations, and constructive use of time?
- What changes occurred for staff in: working relationships, working environment, and collaboration with families and the community?
- What changes occurred for families in: connection to school and staff; involvement in school activities; and knowledge and use of school and community resources and services?

These sets of preliminary questions will be discussed during Partners' initial meeting with the Evaluation Advisory Team (described in Section 1.1). At that meeting, team members will be asked to participate in a discussion about additional evaluation questions that should be included. These additional questions will be incorporated into the draft evaluation plan. In assisting the Evaluation Advisory Team in developing a final set of evaluation questions, Partners will focus on the needs and interests of the team members, and will attempt to ensure that all key evaluation questions are:

- Appropriate to the pilot project's goals and objectives
- Focused on addressing issues that other stakeholders may be interested in
- Measurable

Evaluation Advisory Team members will have the opportunity to review and comment on the final set of evaluation questions when they review the draft evaluation plan. Changes to the evaluation questions will be made based on their comments, and the final, revised list of key evaluation questions will be included in the final evaluation plan.

1.3 Identify Data Collection Techniques and Data Sources

Based on preliminary information, we anticipate that a variety of both quantitative and qualitative data collection techniques will be used for this evaluation. The specific data collection techniques to be used will depend heavily on the type of evaluation (contextual, implementation, or outcome), and the key evaluation questions for each type of evaluation. Preliminary approaches to collecting data for each of the evaluations are described next.

Contextual Evaluation

Based on the preliminary set of questions for the context evaluation, Partners will use two primary methods of data collection: 1) interviews with key stakeholders from the Horizon Foundation and from Howard County Public Schools; and 2) focus groups at each of the three participating schools with staff involved in the *HSHS* project. During Year 1, interview and focus group protocols will be developed to gather in-depth information as to how sites received training and support regarding the developmental assets framework, whether action plans were developed, how action plans were implemented, and barriers and strengths of the process. The purpose of the investigation will be to provide a picture of the larger context in which the HSHS program is operating. We will explore differences across schools to determine if the three schools are having different experiences.

Additional data collection methods will be used as necessary to address any new evaluation questions identified by the Evaluation Advisory Team.

During Years 2 and 3, follow-up interviews and focus groups will be held with key stakeholders and staff included in Year 1. Questions will be developed based on Year 1 data and will likely be targeted at ascertaining changes in program operation and contextual factors during Years 2 and 3.

All interviews and/or focus groups will be tape-recorded, and the tapes will be transcribed. Hard copies of the transcripts will be analyzed for themes and content related to the evaluation questions. Presentation of the findings from Years 1 and 2 will be included in the interim annual reports. The final project report will include a summary and analysis of the contextual evaluation data across all 3 years of the evaluation. Staff and stakeholders will be debriefed on the results of the context evaluation prior to submission of the interim reports or final report for strategic improvement purposes, as necessary.

Implementation Evaluation

To address the preliminary implementation evaluation questions, Partners proposes to implement a case study approach to learn how the HSHS project is being implemented at each of the three schools. The case study approach is very useful for the in-depth study and comparison of events across different groups. As such, a case study approach will allow us to gather detailed information about the implementation of the HSHS project in the elementary, middle, and high school settings, and identify similarities and differences in implementation, and the factors that affect implementation for each of the schools.

The case study will involve several methods of data collection. First, observations of each school will be used to document the implementation of the program. As possible, during Year 1, a researcher will spend 2–3 days at each school participating in activities, and interviewing staff, students, and parents. This will allow us to gather firsthand documentation about the implementation and operation of the program at each school. During Years 2 and 3, follow-up observations will take place to document changes in operation over the course of the project.

Second, interviews will be conducted with stakeholders from the Horizon Foundation and the Howard County Public Schools, and with school staff. The interview and focus group protocols developed for the contextual process evaluation (described previously) will include questions pertaining to the implementation evaluation. During Year 1, questions will focus on the integrity of project implementation throughout the school community, and how activities were integrated at the local site. During Years 2 and 3, questions will be targeted at ascertaining any improvement in program operations during Years 2 and 3. As appropriate, additional interviews will be held with key community collaborators to gather information from their perspective. Other data collection techniques will be used as necessary to address any additional evaluation questions identified by the Evaluation Advisory Team.

All interviews and/or focus groups will be tape-recorded, and the tapes will be transcribed. The transcripts will be analyzed for themes and content related to the evaluation questions. Presentation of the findings from Years 1 and 2 will be included in the interim annual reports. The final evaluation report will provide a summary and analysis of the data across all 3 years and across the three school settings. Staff and stakeholders will be debriefed on the results of the context evaluation prior to submission of the interim reports or final report for strategic improvement purposes, as necessary.

Outcome Evaluation

Prior to determining the data collection methods and sources for the outcome evaluation, the Evaluation Advisory Team and other stakeholders will be asked to participate in a process to develop a logic model (or program theory). The purpose of developing this model is to clarify the outcomes and contributing factors of the *HSHS* program. Logic models are useful tools for both program administrators and evaluators for establishing the linkages between what a program does, and the outcomes it expects to achieve. Using the logic model design established by United Way of America (see Figure 1), Partners will facilitate the group of stakeholders in identifying the resources that go into the program, the types and amounts

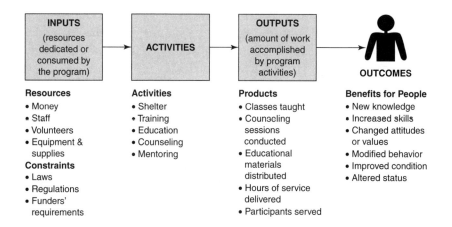

Figure 1. Sample United Way Program Logic Model

of services that are provided, and the initial, intermediate, and long-term outcomes expected of the program.

Once the logic model is created, Partners will develop a measurement plan that will identify indicators for measuring each outcome (measurement statements), and instruments proposed to collect data to track each outcome. A data collection schedule will be established in the measurement plan for staff and site leaders and will include an explanation of procedures for implementing consent procedures, establishing client confidentiality, and submitting data. The logic model and associated measurement plan and data collection schedule will be incorporated into the evaluation plan.

The *Profile of School Social and Learning Climate Survey*, created by the Search Institute, will be used to establish a profile of the middle and high school's social and learning climate, and to measure changes that occur throughout the pilot. Partners will work closely with the Evaluation Advisory Team to identify appropriate means of measuring changes in social and learning climate at the elementary school. One option is to modify the *Profile of School Social and Learning Climate Survey* to be applicable to the elementary school setting. Other options will also be explored.

Once the measurement plan has been finalized, Partners will conduct a 1-day training for all appropriate staff on the implementation of the plan. The training will include a review of data collection instruments, procedures for collecting data, procedures for informed consent, and processes and schedule for submitting data to Partners for analysis.

1.4 Create Work Plan and Time Line

Once Partners has completed tasks 1–3, we will develop a final work plan and associated time line that depicts, in detail, key data collection and reporting activities. This work plan will be submitted to the Evaluation Advisory Team and to the Horizon Foundation no later than 2 weeks following approval of the final evaluation plan.

1.5 Collect and Analyze Qualitative and Quantitative Data

The work plan and time line described in Section 1.4 will form the basis for all data collection activities. Partners will follow the established time line for the collection and reporting of all data. Partners anticipates that data collection will begin in February and will continue for the duration of the 3-year evaluation.

1.6 Prepare and Submit Interim and Final Reports

At the end of Year 1, Partners will submit an interim report that summarizes findings from the contextual, implementation, and outcomes evaluation from Year 1. The report will include summaries of all data analyses and will highlight overall evaluation findings, key findings for each of the three schools, and comparisons across schools in terms of implementation and preliminary outcomes. A similar report focusing on Year 2 findings will be submitted at the end of Year 2. The Year 2 interim report will also include a comparison of Year 1 and Year 2 findings. Both reports will highlight the implications of the findings for various groups of stakeholders.

Within 30 days of the end of the contract, Partners will submit a final evaluation report. This report will provide a synthesis of findings from all 3 years of the evaluation and will include cross-school comparisons, as well as comparisons across years. The report will include a discussion of the implications of the findings for project improvement, understanding what works and what does not work, and possible expansion to other schools.

2. BUDGET

2.1 Budget Summary

BUDGET SUMMARY

	Year 1	Year 2	Year 3
Personnel			
Dr. Christy Lynch	$12,240	$8,640	$8,640
Dr. Kathleen Dowell	$10,800	$7,920	$7,920
Administrative Assistant	$800	$400	$400
Contractual Services			
Data Entry Assistant	$1,060	$490	$490
Other			
Copying	$100	$50	$50
TOTAL	**$25,000**	**$17,500**	**$17,500**

2.2 Year 1 Budget Narrative

Dr. Lynch will provide 136 hours of consulting time @ $90/hour. She will be responsible for overseeing the implementation and development of all products of the contextual and process evaluations. She will also serve as the main contact for the project.

Dr. Dowell will provide 112 hours of consulting time @ $90/hour. She will be responsible for consultation on outcome evaluation, instrument development, and will conduct outcome analyses and provide end-year reports.

Administrative Assistant will provide 32 hours of time @ $25/hour. She will be responsible for all administrative functions, such as document preparation, mailings, copying, etc.

A subcontractor/research assistant will be hired by Partners to complete data entry.

2.2 Years 2 and 3 Budget Narrative

Each year, Dr. Lynch will provide 96 hours of consulting time @ $90/hour. She will be responsible for overseeing the implementation of and development of products of the contextual and process evaluations. She will also serve as the main contact for the project.

Each year, Dr. Dowell will provide 88 hours of consulting time @ $90/Hour. She will be responsible for consultation on outcome evaluation, instrument development, and will conduct outcome analyses and provide end-year reports.

Each year, an Administrative Assistant will provide 16 hours of time @ $25/hour. She will be responsible for all administrative functions such as document preparation, mailings, copying, etc.

Each year, a subcontractor/research assistant will perform data entry.

3. PROJECT TIME LINE

Exhibit 1 displays a Year 1 proposed time line for completion of tasks 1–6, as described in Section 1 of this proposal.

Exhibit 1. Sample Time Line of Proposed Evaluation Tasks—Year 1

MONTH

TASK	Month 1	Month 2	Month 3	Month 4	Month 5	Month 6	Month 7	Month 8	Month 9	Month 10	Month 11	Month 12
Quarterly Evaluation Advisory Team Meetings				✓			✓			✓		
Task 1. Design Plan for Evaluating the 3-Year Project												
Initial meeting with Evaluation Advisory Team	✓											
Submit draft evaluation plan		✓										
Comments from team		✓										
Submit final evaluation plan			✓									
Task 2. Develop Key Evaluation Questions												
Initial meeting with Evaluation Advisory Team	✓											
Submit draft evaluation questions with draft evaluation plan		✓										
Comments from team		✓										
Submit final evaluation questions with final evaluation plan			✓									

/ continues

Exhibit 1. Sample Time Line of Proposed Evaluation Tasks—Year 1 (continued)

MONTH

TASK	Month 1	Month 2	Month 3	Month 4	Month 5	Month 6	Month 7	Month 8	Month 9	Month 10	Month 11	Month 12
Task 3. Identify Data Collection Techniques and Data Sources												
Initial meeting with Evaluation Advisory Team	✓											
Submit draft data collection techniques and sources with draft evaluation plan		✓										
Comments from team		✓										
Submit final data collection techniques and sources with final evaluation plan			✓									
Task 4. Create Work Plan and Time Line												
Submit draft work plan and time line to team				✓								
Comments from team				✓								
Submit final work plan and time line to team					✓							

/ continues

Exhibit 1. Sample Time Line of Proposed Evaluation Tasks—Year 1 (continued)

TASK	MONTH											
	Month 1	Month 2	Month 3	Month 4	Month 5	Month 6	Month 7	Month 8	Month 9	Month 10	Month 11	Month 12
Task 5. Collect and Analyze Qualitative and Quantitative Data												
Identify and obtain/develop data collection instruments			✓	✓								
Data collection for contextual evaluation						✓	✓	✓				
Data collection for implementation evaluation						✓	✓	✓	✓	✓		
Train staff on outcome data collection procedures					✓							
Data collection for outcome evaluation						✓	✓	✓	✓	✓	✓	✓
Data analysis							✓	✓	✓	✓	✓	
Task 6. Prepare and Submit Interim Report												
Prepare and submit Year 1 interim report											✓	✓

During Years 2 and 3, data collection will continue for the contextual, implementation, and outcome evaluations. A Year 2 interim report will be submitted in August of year 2. The final evaluation report will be submitted no later than September 30 of year three.

4. KEY TEAM MEMBERS

Staff of Partners in Evaluation & Planning have extensive experience and proven capabilities in evaluation design, research methods, data collection, data analysis, report preparation, and dissemination of evaluation results. Partners is a consulting company, founded in 1995, that provides high quality program planning and evaluation services to nonprofit, government, and private social service and health organizations. Partners' services include, but are not limited to, program evaluation design and implementation, needs assessments, data collection, tool development, data analysis and reporting, strategic planning, and grant writing. Partners also provides training and technical assistance to programs and organizations that desire assistance in carrying out program evaluation and strategic planning activities. A select list of Partners' past clients include Delaware HIV Consortium, Delaware Division of Public Health, Youth Crime Watch of America, The Family Tree (Maryland Child Abuse Prevention Agency), Maryland Department of Human Resources (Social Services), Maryland Department of Transportation/Highway Safety Office, Family and Children Services of Central Maryland, Baltimore City Head Start, and the Baltimore City Police Athletic League. Partners' staff has over 20 years of combined experience in program evaluation, program planning, and grant writing.

The project will be under the direction of *Christina Olenik Lynch, MSW, PhD,* the Founding Partner of Partners in Evaluation & Planning. She will be responsible for coordinating and overseeing the project, preparing data collection tools, facilitating the collection of data, analyzing data, and preparing reports. Dr. Lynch has been working with human service and health organizations for more than 15 years. Starting out in direct service and moving to program management and evaluation, she has worked in a variety of service areas, such as juvenile justice, child abuse prevention, homelessness, youth development, teen pregnancy, and job training and placement. Since 1995, Dr. Lynch has provided consulting services to government, nonprofit, and private agencies in the areas of program evaluation, strategic planning, and grant writing. Dr. Lynch's expertise includes process and outcome evaluation, focus groups, developing measurement tools, and writing research reports. Dr. Lynch has a Masters of Social Work degree, and a PhD in Social Work.

Kathleen Dowell, PhD, a Partner with Partners in Evaluation & Planning, will be involved with development of data collection tools, data collection, data analysis, and report preparation. Dr. Dowell has more than 12 years of experience in all phases of evaluation, including research design, data collection, data analysis, and report writing. Dr. Dowell's areas of expertise focus on issues related to children and families, and include adolescent pregnancy prevention, HIV prevention, sexuality education, substance abuse treatment, and child abuse and neglect prevention. Dr. Dowell has conducted numerous evaluation projects, involving the collection and analysis of both quantitative and qualitative data. From 1993 through 1997, Dr. Dowell was responsible for research and evaluation activities in the Maryland Governor's Office for Children, Youth and Families. From 1997 through 2002, Dr. Dowell worked as a consultant for Caliber Associates, where she managed a large multisite evaluation of substance abuse treatment programs for women and their infants and children. Dr. Dowell has a Masters of Arts degree in Clinical Psychology, and a PhD in Policy Sciences.

APPENDIX 9-2: Survey of School Social and Learning Climate Elementary School Student Survey

We are asking you to take this survey to find out what your school is like. This survey is voluntary. You do not have to take this survey, but we hope you will. We need your help!

DO NOT write your name on this survey. No one but you will know how you answered these questions.

Please mark only one answer for each question. Fill in the bubbles neatly with a #2 pencil. Do not make any other marks on the survey.

Please read each question carefully. Select only one answer for each question. Please be as honest as you can. Even though some of the questions may sound the same, it is very important for you to answer all the questions carefully.

HOW TO MARK YOUR ANSWERS

- Use black lead pencil only (#2).
- Do not use pens or markers.
- Make marks that fill the whole circle.
- Erase any answers you want to change.
- Do not make any extra marks on the survey.
-

EXAMPLES	
RIGHT	WRONG
○○●○	○○✕○

Thank you for taking this survey!

PART ONE. Please answer the following questions about yourself.

1. How old are you?
   - O 7 years old, or younger than 7
   - O 8 years old
   - O 9 years old
   - O 10 years old
   - O 11 years old
   - O 12 years old, or older than 12

2. Are you a boy or a girl?
   - O Boy
   - O Girl

3. What grade are you in?
   - O 3rd grade
   - O 4th grade
   - O 5th grade

4. How long have you been at this school?
   - O Less than 1 year
   - O 1–2 years
   - O 3 or more years

5. How would you describe yourself? (Check all that apply)
   - O White
   - O Black/African-American
   - O Asian or Pacific Islander
   - O Hispanic or Latino/Latina
   - O American Indian/Native American/Alaskan Native
   - O Middle Eastern/Arab
   - O Other: _____

6. What language do you speak most of the time?
   - O English
   - O Spanish
   - O Other: _____

7. What language do you read most of the time?
   - O English
   - O Spanish
   - O Other: _____

PART TWO. Mark how much of the time you feel the following statements are true.

The teachers at my school . . .

		Never	Some of the Time	Most of the Time
1.	care about me.	O	O	O
2.	tell me when I do a good job.	O	O	O
3.	listen to me when I have a problem.	O	O	O
4.	expect me to do well in school.	O	O	O
5.	listen when I have something to say.	O	O	O
6.	treat students fairly.	O	O	O
7.	expect all students to follow the rules.	O	O	O
8.	only notice me when I do a good job.	O	O	O
9.	help students learn new things.	O	O	O

Keep on Trucking . . .

Students at my school . . .

		Never	Some of the Time	Most of the Time
10.	are expected to work hard to get good grades in school.	O	O	O
11.	treat other students from different backgrounds the same.	O	O	O
12.	do well if they try hard.	O	O	O
13.	treat each other with respect.	O	O	O
14.	do not let other students bully someone.	O	O	O
15.	think that school is important.	O	O	O
16.	don't work very hard.	O	O	O
17.	try to get good grades.	O	O	O
18.	listen to what I have to say.	O	O	O

You are doing "A" OK!

How true are these statements about your HOME?

In my home, there is a parent or some other adult . . .

		Never	Some of the Time	Most of the Time
19.	who thinks that school is important.	O	O	O
20.	who wants me to do my best.	O	O	O
21.	who cares about my schoolwork.	O	O	O
22.	who asks me about my homework.	O	O	O

How often are these statements about your FRIENDS true?

My friends at school . . .

		Never	Some of the Time	Most of the Time
23.	encourage me to work hard in school.	O	O	O
24.	work hard so they will do well.	O	O	O

How often are these statements about your SCHOOL true?

		Never	Some of the Time	Most of the Time
25.	My school is a safe place to be.	○	○	○
26.	Most students follow the rules.	○	○	○
27.	Other students bother me when I am doing my schoolwork.	○	○	○
28.	Teachers here respect me.	○	○	○
29.	Teachers let students bully other students.	○	○	○
30.	My teachers help me when I need it.	○	○	○
31.	My teacher cares about me even when I don't do well on my schoolwork.	○	○	○
32.	I can count on other students to help me.	○	○	○
33.	Some students don't have to follow the rules.	○	○	○

You're doing great!

How often are these statements about YOU true?

		Never	Some of the Time	Most of the Time
34.	I feel like school is a waste of time.	O	O	O
35.	I get to help make decisions in my classroom.	O	O	O
36.	I can be successful even if I don't do well in school.	O	O	O
37.	I like to learn new things at school.	O	O	O
38.	I would like to go to a different school.	O	O	O
39.	I work hard at school.	O	O	O
40.	I can do well in school even if the work is hard.	O	O	O
41.	I am afraid I will be hurt at school.	O	O	O
42.	I can figure out things if I really try.	O	O	O
43.	I can really be myself at this school.	O	O	O

Please turn the page . . . almost done!!

How often are these statements about YOU true?

		Never	Some of the Time	Most of the Time
44.	I think most of my schoolwork is too easy.	○	○	○
45.	I get to help make class rules or choose activities to do at school.	○	○	○
46.	I believe that doing well in school will help me be successful.	○	○	○
47.	I am confident that I can do all of my schoolwork this year.	○	○	○
48.	I feel like I am an important part of this school.	○	○	○
49.	I can share my ideas and ask questions at school.	○	○	○
50.	I just give up when my schoolwork gets hard.	○	○	○
51.	I get to choose the reward for being good at school.	○	○	○
52.	I feel like I make a difference at my school.	○	○	○

Yeah!!! You reached the finish line!!!

Thank you.
Please give your survey to your teacher.

APPENDIX 9-3: *Healthy Schools for Healthy Students* Staff Survey

> Deep Run Elementary School is participating in a pilot project called Healthy Schools for Healthy Students. We are conducting this survey to obtain feedback from teachers and staff of Deep Run Elementary School. Completing the survey will only take a few minutes of your time. ***The survey is anonymous, so please <u>do not put your name on it.</u>*** Your responses will be combined with those of other staff, and your name will not be used in any reports that are written about this survey. We will use the results of this survey to make this school the best it can be in helping children succeed.

PART ONE. Please rate your opinion of the following statements by circling the number that best represents how you feel about each statement. In the "**BEFORE**" column, think back and indicate how you felt at the very **beginning of the school year** (last September). In the "**NOW**" column, indicate how you feel now.

1 indicates you **strongly disagree** with the statement
2 indicates you **disagree** with the statement
3 indicates you **agree** with the statement
4 indicates you **strongly agree** with the statement

If you don't know if you agree or disagree, please circle the "**don't know**" option.

<u>Remember:</u> Circle one number in the "BEFORE" column **AND** one number in the "NOW" column.

	STATEMENT	How you felt BEFORE (in September)	How you feel NOW
1.	I am knowledgeable about developmental assets.	1 2 3 4 Don't know	1 2 3 4 Don't know
2.	I understand the relationship between developmental assets and children's attitudes and behavior.	1 2 3 4 Don't know	1 2 3 4 Don't know
3.	I understand my role in developing/nurturing assets in students.	1 2 3 4 Don't know	1 2 3 4 Don't know
4.	I am knowledgeable about students' emotional needs.	1 2 3 4 Don't know	1 2 3 4 Don't know
5.	I respond appropriately to students' emotional needs.	1 2 3 4 Don't know	1 2 3 4 Don't know

STATEMENT	How you felt BEFORE (in September)					How you feel NOW				
6. Most students care about doing well in school.	1	2	3	4	Don't know	1	2	3	4	Don't know
7. Most students complete homework assignments.	1	2	3	4	Don't know	1	2	3	4	Don't know
8. Most students feel positive about their friendships.	1	2	3	4	Don't know	1	2	3	4	Don't know
9. Most students are sensitive and empathetic to others.	1	2	3	4	Don't know	1	2	3	4	Don't know
10. Most students are aware of the impact of their actions on others.	1	2	3	4	Don't know	1	2	3	4	Don't know
11. Most students try to solve conflicts in a peaceful way.	1	2	3	4	Don't know	1	2	3	4	Don't know
12. Most students get along with people from different cultures or ethnic backgrounds.	1	2	3	4	Don't know	1	2	3	4	Don't know
13. Most students avoid situations that might place them in danger.	1	2	3	4	Don't know	1	2	3	4	Don't know
14. Most students feel good about themselves.	1	2	3	4	Don't know	1	2	3	4	Don't know
15. Most students feel positive about their future.	1	2	3	4	Don't know	1	2	3	4	Don't know
16. Most students treat one another with respect.	1	2	3	4	Don't know	1	2	3	4	Don't know
17. Most students treat teachers with respect.	1	2	3	4	Don't know	1	2	3	4	Don't know
18. I spend too much time dealing with student discipline issues.	1	2	3	4	Don't know	1	2	3	4	Don't know
19. I have a good relationship with most students.	1	2	3	4	Don't know	1	2	3	4	Don't know
20. I feel optimistic about our students.	1	2	3	4	Don't know	1	2	3	4	Don't know
21. Our school has a good relationship with parents.	1	2	3	4	Don't know	1	2	3	4	Don't know
22. Our school treats parents with respect.	1	2	3	4	Don't know	1	2	3	4	Don't know
23. Our school involves parents in a meaningful way.	1	2	3	4	Don't know	1	2	3	4	Don't know

STATEMENT	How you felt BEFORE (in September)	How you feel NOW
24. In our school, parents and staff are able to work collaboratively.	1 2 3 4 Don't know	1 2 3 4 Don't know
25. Our school is respected by the community.	1 2 3 4 Don't know	1 2 3 4 Don't know
26. Our school involves community members in a meaningful way.	1 2 3 4 Don't know	1 2 3 4 Don't know
27. I have a good working relationship with most of my colleagues at Deep Run Elementary School.	1 2 3 4 Don't know	1 2 3 4 Don't know
28. I feel supported by my colleagues.	1 2 3 4 Don't know	1 2 3 4 Don't know
29. I am treated with respect by my colleagues.	1 2 3 4 Don't know	1 2 3 4 Don't know
30. My role within the school is meaningful.	1 2 3 4 Don't know	1 2 3 4 Don't know
31. In this school, my opinions are taken seriously.	1 2 3 4 Don't know	1 2 3 4 Don't know
32. In this school, I have the opportunity to provide input on a regular basis.	1 2 3 4 Don't know	1 2 3 4 Don't know
33. I am excited about coming to work each day.	1 2 3 4 Don't know	1 2 3 4 Don't know
34. I am satisfied with my job.	1 2 3 4 Don't know	1 2 3 4 Don't know

35. Compared to the first 3 months of this school year, do you think students at this school now are exhibiting more, fewer, or about the same amount of **positive** behaviors **toward other students**?

   a. Exhibiting more positive behaviors toward other students

   b. Exhibiting fewer positive behaviors toward other students

   c. Exhibiting about the same amount of positive behaviors toward other students

36. Compared to the first 3 months of this school year, do you think students at this school now are exhibiting more, fewer, or about the same amount of **positive** behaviors **toward staff**?

   a. Exhibiting more positive behaviors toward staff

   b. Exhibiting fewer positive behaviors toward staff

   c. Exhibiting about the same amount of positive behaviors toward staff

37. Compared to the first 3 months of this school year, do you think students at this school now are exhibiting more, fewer, or about the same amount of **negative** behaviors **toward other students**?

   a. Exhibiting more negative behaviors toward other students

   b. Exhibiting fewer negative behaviors toward other students

   c. Exhibiting about the same amount of negative behaviors toward other students

38. Compared to the first 3 months of this school year, do you think students at this school now are exhibiting more, fewer, or about the same amount of **negative** behaviors **toward staff**?

   a. Exhibiting more negative behaviors toward staff

   b. Exhibiting fewer negative behaviors toward staff

   c. Exhibiting about the same amount of negative behaviors toward staff

PART TWO. Using the same scale as in PART ONE, please rate your current opinion of the following statements. Again, if you don't know if you agree or disagree, please circle the "**don't know**" option.

STATEMENT	HOW YOU FEEL NOW				
	Strongly Disagree	Disagree	Agree	Strongly Agree	Don't Know
39. Focusing on asset development among students is a good idea.	1	2	3	4	Don't know
40. The *Healthy Schools for Healthy Students* project has improved our school culture.	1	2	3	4	Don't know
41. There has been an appropriate amount of communication about developmental assets among school staff members.	1	2	3	4	Don't know

STATEMENT	HOW YOU FEEL NOW				
	Strongly Disagree	Disagree	Agree	Strongly Agree	Don't Know
42. The communication about assets that has taken place among staff has been productive.	1	2	3	4	Don't know
43. I have been able to apply asset-building strategies in my classroom.	1	2	3	4	Don't know
44. I have been able to build assets in students through my relationship with them.	1	2	3	4	Don't know

PART THREE. **Please help us improve our efforts by sharing your thoughts and suggestions with us.**

45. Thinking about the *Healthy Schools for Healthy Students* Pilot Project, what do you feel has worked well so far?

_____

_____

_____

_____

46. What do you think could be done differently?

_____

_____

_____

_____

47. Do you have any additional comments or suggestions?

_____

_____

_____

_____

PART FOUR. **Please tell us a little about yourself.**

48. What is your current position?

    ☐ Teacher → What grade(s) do you teach?_____

    ☐ Teacher's assistant

    ☐ Other support staff

    ☐ Administrator

    ☐ Other, please describe _____

49. How long have you been employed by Deep Run Elementary School (including this year)?

    ☐ Less than 1 year

    ☐ 1–2 years

    ☐ 3–4 years

    ☐ 5–9 years

    ☐ 10–14 years

    ☐ 15–19 years

    ☐ 20 years or more

50. How long have you worked in the field of education, in general (including this year)?

    ☐ Less than 1 year

    ☐ 1–2 years

    ☐ 3–4 years

    ☐ 5–9 years

    ☐ 10–14 years

    ☐ 15–19 years

    ☐ 20 years or more

51. What is your gender?

    ☐ Male

    ☐ Female

52. How old are you?

    ☐ Under 20

    ☐ 21–30 years old

    ☐ 31–40 years old

    ☐ 41–50 years old

    ☐ 51 years old or older

53. How would you describe yourself? *(Please check all that apply)*

☐ White

☐ Black/African-American

☐ American Indian/Alaskan Native

☐ Hispanic/Latino/Latina

☐ Asian

☐ Middle Eastern/Arab

☐ Pacific Islander

THANK YOU FOR YOUR TIME!

APPENDIX 9-4: *Healthy Schools for Healthy Students* Parent/Caregiver Survey

Deep Run Elementary School is participating in a pilot project called *Healthy Schools for Healthy Students*. We are conducting this survey to obtain feedback from parents/caregivers of children enrolled at this school. Completing the survey will only take a few minutes of your time. ***The survey is anonymous, so please <u>do not put your name on it.</u>*** Your responses will be combined with those of other families, and your name will not be used in any reports that are written about this survey. We will use the results of this survey to make this school the best it can be in helping your child succeed. **<u>When you have completed your survey, please place it in the return envelope, seal the envelope, and return the survey to school with your child.</u>**

***In this survey, the term "child" refers to any child residing in your home who attends Deep Run Elementary School, whether you are the child's parent, stepparent, foster parent, guardian, relative, or other caregiver.

PART ONE. **Please tell us a little about your child or children.**

1. Did your **oldest** or **only** child who attends Deep Run Elementary School attend Deep Run for 6 months or more during the school year?

    ☐ Yes → Please **continue**

    ☐ No → Please **skip to** PART FOUR **(question #34) of the survey.**

PART TWO. **Thinking of your <u>oldest or only child</u> attending Deep Run Elementary School, please answer the following questions.**

1. CHILD'S AGE (Circle one)	2. CHILD'S GENDER (Circle one)	3. CHILD'S GRADE (Circle one)	4. # OF YEARS AT DEEP RUN ELEMENTARY (Circle one)
5 6 7 8 9 10 11	Male Female	K 1 2 3 4 5	1 2 3 4 5 6 7

5. What is your relationship to this child? (*Check one*)

    ☐ Parent

    ☐ Stepparent

    ☐ Grandparent

    ☐ Other relative

    ☐ Foster parent

    ☐ Other, please describe _____

Again, thinking only of this child **(your <u>oldest</u> or <u>only</u> child attending Deep Run),** please complete items **6–19.** These questions ask you to think of this child and respond to several statements about the child. Please circle the number that best matches how you feel about each statement. In the "**BEFORE**" column, think back and tell how true the statement was at the very **beginning of the school year** (last September). In the "**NOW**" column, please tell how true the statement is **right now.**

    1 indicates the statement is **never** true

    2 indicates the statement is **rarely** true

    3 indicates the statement is **sometimes** true

    4 indicates the statement is **almost always** true

If you are unsure about a statement, please circle the "**don't know**" option.

<u>Remember</u>: Circle one number in the "BEFORE" column **AND** one number in the "NOW" column.

MY CHILD . . .	How true was this statement BEFORE (in September)?	How true is this statement NOW?
6. Cares about doing well in school.	1 2 3 4 Don't know	1 2 3 4 Don't know
7. Completes his/her homework assignments.	1 2 3 4 Don't know	1 2 3 4 Don't know
8. Likes reading books or magazines for pleasure.	1 2 3 4 Don't know	1 2 3 4 Don't know
9. Feels good about his/her friendships.	1 2 3 4 Don't know	1 2 3 4 Don't know
10. Tries to make others feel better.	1 2 3 4 Don't know	1 2 3 4 Don't know
11. Tells others how s/he is feeling.	1 2 3 4 Don't know	1 2 3 4 Don't know
12. Gets along with people from different cultures or ethnic backgrounds.	1 2 3 4 Don't know	1 2 3 4 Don't know
13. Avoids situations that might place him/her in danger.	1 2 3 4 Don't know	1 2 3 4 Don't know
14. Tries to solve conflicts in a peaceful way.	1 2 3 4 Don't know	1 2 3 4 Don't know
15. Feels good about him/herself.	1 2 3 4 Don't know	1 2 3 4 Don't know
16. Feels positive about his/her future.	1 2 3 4 Don't know	1 2 3 4 Don't know
17. Feels that school staff cares about him/her.	1 2 3 4 Don't know	1 2 3 4 Don't know

18. Compared to the first 3 months of this school year, do you think your child now is exhibiting more **positive** behaviors, fewer **positive** behaviors, or about the same amount of **positive** behaviors?

    a. Exhibiting more positive behaviors

    b. Exhibiting fewer positive behaviors

    c. Exhibiting about the same amount of positive behaviors

19. Compared to the first 3 months of this school year, do you think your child now is exhibiting more **negative** behaviors, fewer **negative** behaviors, or about the same amount of **negative** behaviors?

    a. Exhibiting more negative behaviors

    b. Exhibiting fewer negative behaviors

    c. Exhibiting about the same amount of negative behaviors

PART THREE. The following questions ask about <u>your own</u> experiences with and opinions of Deep Run Elementary School during this school year. Please answer each question by circling the number that best corresponds to your feelings or experiences. Again, in the "**BEFORE**" column, think back to the very **beginning of the school year** (last September). In the "**NOW**" column, please answer thinking about **right now**.

1 None   **2** A little bit   **3** Some   **4** A lot

Remember: Circle one number in the "BEFORE" column **AND** one number in the "NOW" column.

HOW MUCH DO YOU KNOW ABOUT . . .	BEFORE? (in September)	NOW?
20. the *Healthy Schools for Healthy Students* project at Deep Run Elementary School.	1 2 3 4	1 2 3 4
21. developmental assets for children and youth.	1 2 3 4	1 2 3 4
22. the relationship between developmental assets and children's attitudes and behaviors.	1 2 3 4	1 2 3 4
23. services available through Deep Run Elementary School.	1 2 3 4	1 2 3 4
TO WHAT EXTENT . . .		
24. Do you use services available through Deep Run Elementary School?	1 2 3 4	1 2 3 4
25. Are you involved in Deep Run school activities?	1 2 3 4	1 2 3 4

For questions 26–33 in the table below, please use the following answer choices. Please circle the number that best represents how you feel about each statement.

1 indicates you **strongly disagree** with the statement

2 indicates you **disagree** with the statement

3 indicates you **agree** with the statement

4 indicates that you **strongly agree** with the statement

If you are unsure about a statement, please circle the "**don't know**" option.

Again, in the "**BEFORE**" column, think back and indicate how you felt at the very **beginning of the school year** (last September). In the "**NOW**" column, indicate how you feel right now.

STATEMENT	How you felt BEFORE? (in September)	How you feel NOW?
26. I feel as if I am a part of Deep Run Elementary School.	1 2 3 4 Don't know	1 2 3 4 Don't know
27. I respect the staff of Deep Run Elementary School.	1 2 3 4 Don't know	1 2 3 4 Don't know
28. I feel respected by the staff of Deep Run Elementary School.	1 2 3 4 Don't know	1 2 3 4 Don't know
29. I have a good relationship with the staff of Deep Run Elementary School.	1 2 3 4 Don't know	1 2 3 4 Don't know
30. The staff of Deep Run Elementary School values my opinion.	1 2 3 4 Don't know	1 2 3 4 Don't know
31. The staff of Deep Run Elementary School encourages me to be involved in school activities.	1 2 3 4 Don't know	1 2 3 4 Don't know
32. The staff of Deep Run Elementary School encourages me to be involved in my child's education.	1 2 3 4 Don't know	1 2 3 4 Don't know
33. I am glad my child attends Deep Run Elementary School.	1 2 3 4 Don't know	1 2 3 4 Don't know

PART FOUR. **Please tell us a little about yourself (OPTIONAL).**

34. What is your gender?

☐ Male

☐ Female

35. How old are you?

☐ Under 20

- ☐ 21–30 years
- ☐ 31–40 years
- ☐ 41 or older

36. How would you describe yourself? (*Check all that apply*)

- ☐ White
- ☐ Black/African-American
- ☐ Hispanic/Latino/Latina
- ☐ American Indian/Alaskan Native
- ☐ Asian
- ☐ Middle Eastern/Arab
- ☐ Pacific Islander

37. What is your marital status?

- ☐ Married
- ☐ Divorced/separated
- ☐ Single, never married
- ☐ Widowed
- ☐ Living with a partner

38. What is your level of education?

- ☐ Some high school
- ☐ High school graduate/GED
- ☐ Some college or technical school
- ☐ College graduate or beyond
- ☐ Other, please describe: _____

39. How long have you lived in your current neighborhood?

- ☐ Less than one year
- ☐ One to three years
- ☐ Four to six years
- ☐ Seven to nine years
- ☐ Ten years or more

40. What is your total household annual income?

- ☐ Less than $2,500
- ☐ $2,500 to $4,999
- ☐ $5,000 to $9,999
- ☐ $10,000 to $19,999

    ☐ $20,000 to $39,999

    ☐ $40,000 to $99,999

    ☐ $100,000 to $199,999

    ☐ $200,000 to $499,999

    ☐ $500,000 or more

41.   Do you have any other thoughts or comments that you would like to share?

_____

_____

_____

_____

THANK YOU!

APPENDIX 9-5: *Healthy Schools for Healthy Students* Contextual Evaluation Interview Protocol

1. What is your role in the *Healthy Schools for Healthy Students* initiative? How did you first become involved in the project, and how do you see your role evolving over time?

2. How did the idea first come to the Horizon Foundation and the school system to integrate the Search Institute's framework? What is your observation of the relationship between the *Healthy Schools* project and the Search Institute? What has been exchanged in the relationship?

3. How receptive were staff members to using the developmental assets framework as a vehicle to change school culture? Was it positive/negative? What examples can you share of their reactions?

4. What types of support/training activities were provided for school staff? When were they provided? And were school staff able to make suggestions on the training they were interested in?

5. How satisfied have staff members been with the support/training? What has been the best part of the support/training? What could use improvement?

6. Were action plans developed for implementing specific initiatives at the schools? What process was used to develop the plans? What stakeholders were involved? How will plans be updated?

7. What barriers were evident that restricted program planning across the three schools and within each school, specifically? Have these barriers been addressed? If so, how?

8. What are the strengths and challenges to incorporating the ideology into the school systems? How has it taken shape as a program in each school?

9. What differences have there been to incorporating the program in an elementary, middle, and high school? What are some of the characteristic differences of the schools?

10. What has the capacity been for the schools to build the program? What resources were in place, and what new ones were needed to implement the program? How does leadership and vision impact on its incorporation?

11. Describe the relationship between the school system and the Horizon Foundation. Has it been positive or difficult? What examples can you share that help describe what you have seen?

12. In your opinion, how sustainable is the program? What are the contributing factors to making it a long-term program?

13. Overall, how satisfied have you been with the development and implementation of the *Healthy Schools* project?

APPENDIX 9-6: *Healthy Schools for Healthy Students* Student Focus Groups

1. What do you like best about school? What are some of your favorite things to do at school?
2. What don't you like about school?
3. What are your favorite things to learn in school?
4. What do you think about the teachers at this school? How do they help you learn?
5. What activities are you in at school (i.e., sports, dance, theater, student government, etc.)
6. How do you feel when you come to school? Happy? Sad? Scared?
7. Do any of your parents help out at school? What kinds of things do they do?
8. What do your parents do at home to make sure you finish your school work?
9. How could school be better? What would make you feel happier about being at school?
10. How does school make you smarter?
11. How does school make you a good person?

APPENDIX 9-7: *Healthy Schools for Healthy Students* School Culture Committee Focus Group

1. How were you first introduced to the *Healthy Schools for Healthy Students* project, and how did you feel when you first heard about it?
2. What is your impression of the developmental assets framework? How have you been able to integrate it into school activities?
3. What type of training have you received on the developmental assets framework, and how helpful was the training?
4. How has the developmental assets framework helped you understand students' emotional/social needs? Do you feel there is an impact on their academic achievement after these needs are understood?
5. How were the strategic plans developed for the *Healthy Schools for Healthy Students* initiative? What did you think of the process? Has the plan been implemented as expected?
6. What are some of the activities you have actually implemented and how well did they work out? How has the communication about youth assets increased in this school?
7. How do you feel about the support you have received from the school system and Horizon staff in implementing the activities? What improvements would you like to see in this regard?
8. Overall, how well do you think staff get along at this school? How would you characterize the relationships among staff?
9. How satisfied are you with working at this school? What key elements keep you working here?
10. What are some of the overall strengths and weaknesses of the *Healthy Schools for Healthy Students* project?
11. What impacts have you seen on children, staff, and parents as a result of the program? What assets have you observed in students? Has there been an increase in parent involvement? How have staff relationships changed?
12. Do you have any other thoughts or suggestions about the program?

APPENDIX 9-8: *Healthy Schools for Healthy Students* Principal Interview Protocol

1. What is your role in the *Healthy Schools for Healthy Students* initiative? How did you first become involved in the project, and how do you see your role evolving over time?
2. What is your observation of the relationship between the *Healthy Schools* project and the Search Institute? What has been exchanged in the relationship?
3. How receptive were staff members to using the developmental assets framework as a vehicle to change school culture? Was it positive/negative? What examples can you share about their reactions?
4. What types of support/training activities were provided for school staff? When were they provided? And were school staff able to make suggestions on the training they were interested in?
5. How satisfied have staff members been with the support/training? What has been the best part of the support/training? What could use improvement?
6. Were action plans developed for implementing specific initiatives at the schools? What process was used to develop the plans? What stakeholders were involved? How will plans be updated?
7. What barriers were evident that restricted program planning within this school? Have these barriers been addressed? If so, how?
8. What are the strengths and challenges to incorporating the ideology into the school systems? How has it taken shape as a program in each school?
9. What has been unique in incorporating the program in an elementary, middle, and high school? What are some of the characteristic differences of the schools?
10. What has the capacity been for the schools to build the program? What resources were in place, and what new ones were needed to implement the program? How does leadership and vision impact on its incorporation?
11. Describe the relationship between the school system and the Horizon Foundation. Has it been positive? Has it been difficult? What examples can you share that help describe what you have seen?
12. In your opinion, how sustainable is the program? What are the contributing factors to making it a successful, long-term program?
13. Overall, how satisfied have you been with the development and implementation of the *Healthy Schools* project?

APPENDIX 9-9: Year 1 Report Executive Summary

1. Introduction

Fueled by the desire to improve the health and well-being of Howard County's young people, the Foundation initiated the *Healthy Schools for Healthy Students* (*HSHS*) Pilot Project by partnering with the Howard County Public School System. The vision of this partnership is that students, staff, parents, and extended families will achieve their maximum health and wellness potential. Planning for the project was a collaborative effort to ensure that the project goals align with both the Horizon Foundation's mission and emerging priorities of the school system. This phase incorporates a more systematic approach to the concept of whole school wellness by focusing on whole school culture.

To complement the Foundation's broad definition of health that includes "a state of optimal physical, mental, and social well-being," the developmental asset model designed by the Search Institute in Minneapolis was chosen as the core strategy for the project. This framework is a positive, strength-based approach that supports the entire community's engagement in the healthy development of youth. Supported by research on the role of assets in helping students achieve both personally and academically, the Horizon Foundation anticipates that the application of the developmental assets model will result in improved school climate and, ultimately, to improved student achievement.

The *HSHS* project was implemented at three schools during the school year: Deep Run Elementary School, Burleigh Manor Middle School, and Reservoir High School. Schools were given leeway in the types and intensity of activities and services that support the developmental assets way of thinking into the everyday culture of the schools. Activities chosen by the schools included:

- Assets education targeted toward students, staff, and parents
- Ongoing recognition of asset behaviors
- Promotion of adult-child relationships
- Leadership development
- Professional development
- Wellness-promoting activities
- Tools for communicating with parents
- Outreach to parents

These activities were thought to be effective ways of "infusing" the schools with the asset development mindset, and simultaneously fostering the development of youth assets and improving school culture.

2. Methods

Under contract with The Horizon Foundation, Partners in Evaluation & Planning, LLC is conducting a 3-year evaluation of the *Healthy Schools for Healthy Students* Pilot Project. To capture the process of supporting schools in the implementation of *HSHS*, the actual implementation of *HSHS* within the school setting, and the outcomes achieved by the project, the evaluation was designed to focus on three primary activities:

- *Context evaluation* to describe the school settings in which the initiative was implemented and the larger systems context of the project;
- *Implementation evaluation* to monitor, assess, and document how, and to what degree, project activities were implemented; and
- *Outcome evaluation* to identify and document the initial, intermediate, and long-term outcomes for students, staff, and parents.

The contextual and implementation evaluation together constituted the process evaluation. Data for the process evaluation were collected via focus groups with students, school staff, and parents; interviews with project stakeholders, including Horizon Foundation staff, school administrators; review of historical documents; and observation of activities and classrooms at each of the three participating schools.

The outcome evaluation was based on a project logic model that was developed by project stakeholders. The logic model identified expected outcomes for students, staff, and parents/caregivers. Data collection tools were then developed to measure outcomes for each of these three groups. Tools administered during the school year included:

- School climate survey (students)
- Student asset survey
- Staff survey
- Parent/caregiver survey

3. Process Evaluation Results

3.1 Contextual Evaluation

The *Healthy Schools for Healthy Students* initiative is staffed by several people at the Horizon Foundation and Howard County School System. The project is overseen by the President and CEO of the Horizon Foundation, Richard Krieg, and the Superintendent of Howard County Schools, John O'Rourke. The Horizon Foundation also has a Project Coordinator for the *Healthy Schools* initiative, Peggy Alexander, and a Director of Evaluation,

Dr. Phyllis Utterback. Much of the direct support for *Healthy Schools* comes from the Grant Coordinator, Razia Kosi, who is an employee of the school system and acts as a liaison between the schools and the foundation. Each school's program is overseen by its principal and directed by a school culture committee.

In general, the school system was very receptive and open to the developmental assets framework. To them, it tied in well with their character education efforts that encourage students to become "ethical, responsible adults." While the school system sees the assets development framework as one of many options within the context of their character development efforts, the Horizon Foundation sees it as something broader, and prefers not to include it within character development.

The selection of schools for the pilot project also played an important role in the potential integration of developmental assets in the school system. Each school was selected primarily because of the motivation and interest of the principal. The selection of pilot schools was a convenience sample more than anything, and primarily predicated on the support and motivation of the school principals. There are some unique characteristics that define each school. There was some concern that not all schools had an opportunity to be selected for the project.

Two levels of training were provided to school staff; one was the Search Institute Conference and the other was training provided by the grants coordinator and project director at Horizon. Both training efforts were beneficial.

All schools ran into some barriers in implementing the project. At Deep Run, the teaching staff became overwhelmed early in the school year with additional paperwork and academic requirements from the school system leaving little time for focusing on other activities. At Burleigh Manor, there was a settled stability and a highly integrated school culture committee (including students and parents) that allowed the program to grow. At Reservoir High, much of the focus during the year was on all the aspects of starting a new school from scratch, binding up some time that might have been spent on the program. Ensuring implementation of developmentally appropriate activities for students of varying ages also became an issue, especially for older students.

Positive aspects of the project were identified. One positive aspect was the heightened awareness about using the asset framework as a philosophy within the school system. Most respondents felt the program is not only sustainable, but will grow in the Howard County School System. Many suggested that the cost for the program is low, and once the philosophy is integrated, will really entail little cost for individual schools.

3.2 Implementation Evaluation

In planning for the project, planning committees at each school identified activities intended to target specific assets. Activities for students included academic support, advising, and special awards and recognition for positive behavior. Staff activities included wellness clinics, collaborative meetings, and special celebrations. Parent activities included workshops, PR materials, and special activity nights. Lack of planning time during the last school year was an issue for all schools.

Students varied in their receptivity to the activities. Younger students were more accepting, especially when the activity included some sort of reward. Older students, however, felt that some of the activities were too childish.

Challenges in implementing the project included lack of parental involvement, staff already feeling overwhelmed with other responsibilities, and lack of communication about the project among staff. Overall, participants were positive about the project, and expressed excitement at being able to influence school culture and promote asset development among students.

4. Outcome Evaluation Findings

4.1 Students

Deep Run Elementary School

In terms of school climate, Deep Run Elementary students reported high levels of all school climate domains in both March and June, with the exception of voice, which was quite low for both administrations. There was a significant increase between March and June in only one domain—academic expectations. Males reported lower levels of both academic expectations and learning goal orientation, suggesting that males may not perceive that the school emphasizes learning and academic excellence to the extent that females do. In terms of grade, results indicated that younger students (3rd graders) perceived lower levels of voice and support than older students. Black students reported significantly lower levels of support than both White and Asian students. Staff, parents/caregivers, and students reported high levels of assets among the students.

There were no changes in sense of belonging, academic self-efficacy, or school engagement between March and June. However, females scored higher than males on these domains, 3rd graders scored lower than 4th and 5th graders on school engagement, and Asians scored higher than all other races on school engagement.

Both staff and parents reported changes in student behaviors, reporting decreases in negative behaviors and increases in positive behaviors. Student reports of behavior corroborated these findings.

Student achievement was quite high. Trends in achievement data will be explored more fully in subsequent years of the evaluation.

Burleigh Manor Middle School

In terms of school climate, females were higher than males on academic expectations, equity, safety, and student academic culture; and 8th graders scored lower on all domains of school climate than either 6th or 7th graders. Burleigh experienced significant decreases in equity, learning goal orientation, and support between October and June; however, these changes were very small, likely do not indicate any real change in these domains, and probably have little, if any, programmatic significance. Instead, these changes were probably statistically significant due to the large sample size.

Staff and parents reported high levels of assets among students. Students also reported high levels of assets, but 8th graders scored lowest on possession of assets. Eighth graders also scored lowest on sense of belonging, academic self-efficacy, and school engagement.

Student achievement was quite high at Burleigh. High percentages of students performed well on the Maryland School Assessment, and the majority of students are performing at or above grade level. In subsequent years, as more achievement data are collected, trends in achievement can be examined to determine if changes are occurring.

As with Deep Run Elementary, student reports of negative behaviors were low. Staff and parents supported these findings, reporting that they have seen a decrease in negative behaviors among Burleigh students and an increase in positive behaviors. Students at Burleigh were likely to see bullying, with older students more likely to see bullying than younger students. Older students were also less likely to report the bullying to an adult.

Reservoir High School

Reservoir High experienced statistically significant decreases in all school climate domains from December to June; however these changes were extremely small. Most likely, the changes do not reflect any real changes in school climate but, rather, are due to the large sample size of the survey. In June, females scored higher than males on safety, student academic culture, and achievement motivation, suggesting that efforts to nurture these domains of school climate may need to focus on male students. Minority students scored lower than other students on safety and equity (Black students were lowest) and student academic culture (Hispanic students were lowest).

Students at Reservoir scored moderately on possession of assets, as did staff. Parent reports of assets were quite high, indicating that parents felt that students possessed a high degree of all three assets. There were a few minor differences between males and females, according to parents. For example, parents reported a slight increase in commitment to learning among females and a slight decrease for males. They also reported an increase in positive identity for females and a slight decrease for males.

In terms of sense of belonging, there was a slight decrease in this domain from December to June for all students, although the change was probably not programmatically significant. Ninth graders reported a significantly lower sense of belonging than 10th graders. Results for academic self-efficacy were similar to those for sense of belonging. There was a slight decrease in this domain from December to June for all students, although the change was very small and probably not programmatically significant. Ninth graders reported significantly lower academic self-efficacy than 10th graders. Engagement in school was moderate for all students, with no differences between 9th and 10th graders on this domain.

Student achievement was quite high at Reservoir. Scores on the Maryland School Assessment were good. Changes in student achievement will be explored further in future years, when more data have been collected.

Student reports of negative behaviors were low at Reservoir. Staff and parents also reported positive trends in behavior, with more positive behaviors and fewer negative behaviors at the end of the school year. Students at Reservoir were likely to report seeing a student bullying another student, but were not likely to report the incident. As with Burleigh Manor Middle, older students seem very likely to be exposed to aggressive and violent behavior at school, but for reasons not yet explored, are not likely to report such behavior to school staff.

4.2 Staff

Deep Run Elementary School

Knowledge of the *HSHS* project and the assets development model increased significantly during the year, with staff reporting greater understanding of developmental assets, the relationship between assets and students' behaviors and attitudes, and ways that they can help nurture assets in their students. Most staff were also very positive about developing assets, suggesting that it is a good idea to nurture these characteristics in students. Most staff also reported having the opportunity to incorporate asset development strategies into their classrooms.

On the other hand, staff remarked that communication about assets and the *HSHS* project has not been as broad as it could have been, with some staff stating that they really don't know what the *HSHS* project is or what its purpose is. Staff who haven't received a lot of information about the project were likely to report not using asset strategies in the classroom.

In terms of student needs, Deep Run staff reported that they already had a high level of student needs at the beginning of the school year; therefore, there was no increase in knowledge over the course of the year. However, staff did report an increase in their responsiveness to student needs from September to May.

Satisfaction with working relationships and with their jobs in general was quite high. Staff reported feeling as though they worked well with their colleagues, feel supported by their colleagues, and feel respected by their colleagues. Most staff were extremely satisfied with their jobs, and staff reported an increase in their perception that the school takes their opinions seriously.

As for the project's impact on school climate, staff were unsure whether or not the project itself had improved the climate at Deep Run. Less than half the staff thought that school climate had improved because of the project.

Burleigh Manor Middle School

In terms of knowledge and attitudes toward the *HSHS* project and the asset development model, findings for Burleigh Manor were very similar to those for Deep Run. Staff at Burleigh experienced significant gains in knowledge of the asset development model, the relationship between assets and students' attitudes and behaviors, and their role in nurturing assets in their students. Most of the staff also agreed that focusing on assets is a good idea, and this was supported by the fact that most teachers reported using asset development strategies in their classrooms.

Communication about assets among the staff has been good at Burleigh Manor this year. Staff reported high levels of communication about the model and the project. Most staff also felt that the communication that has taken place has been productive. Staff also appear to be using what they are learning in the classroom.

Staff had quite high perceptions of their knowledge of student needs and their responsiveness to those needs. In both September and May, staff reported that they were knowledgeable about student needs, and they also reported that they are able to respond appropriately to those needs. There were no changes on these items from September to May.

Staff relations at Burleigh are quite positive. Most staff reported having good working relationships with their colleagues, feeling respected by their colleagues, feeling supported by their colleagues, and having their opinions taken seriously at school. These findings were reflected in the high levels of job satisfaction also reported by Burleigh staff. Staff at the school clearly enjoy their positions and are satisfied with their jobs.

In terms of the effect of the *HSHS* project on school culture, over half the staff felt that the project has contributed to an improvement in the culture at Burleigh. The improved school culture may also be contributing to their high levels of satisfaction with their jobs.

Reservoir High School

At Reservoir High, staff had positive attitudes toward the *HSHS* project. Most staff reported that the model was a good idea and that focusing on assets was important. Most staff also experienced significant gains in knowledge regarding assets, the relationship between assets and students' behaviors and attitudes, and how they play a role in nurturing assets in their students. Many of the staff reported applying their knowledge of assets in the classroom, by using strategies designed to promote assets in students. Communication about assets, however, was moderate; staff may desire more communication among staff members on this model and how it fits with their roles at school.

Staff at Reservoir experienced several important changes from September to May. For example, staff reported an increased knowledge of students needs, and also reported increased responsiveness to those needs. Staff also experienced better working relationships, more support from colleagues, and more respect by colleagues. In both September and May, job satisfaction was high, another positive indicator of working relationships at the school.

In terms of school climate, a sizable proportion of the staff were not sure of the project's impact on school climate. For this school, it may take a year or two for the impact to be known, as the new school is basically "building" a school climate as it evolves.

4.3 Parents/Caregivers

Deep Run Elementary School

Parents/caregivers at Deep Run reported increased knowledge and use of school resources and services. However, in May, still less than one-third of parents/caregivers reported actually using school services and resources. On a positive note, parental/caregiver involvement in school activities increased significantly from September to May. Parents/caregivers also reported increased knowledge of assets, but at the end of the year, less than half of the parents/caregivers knew about the *HSHS* project.

Finally, parent/caregiver-school relationships improved over the course of the school year. Parents/caregivers reported significant improvements in their relationship with the school. Parents reported: 1) increased feelings of being a part of Deep Run; 2) increased feelings of being respected by school staff; 3) increased perception that the school values their opinions; and 4) increased staff encouragement for them to be involved with their child's education. Parents/caregivers also reported that they respect the staff of the school and are glad their children attend the school. Staff concurred with parent/caregivers, reporting good relationships with parents, treating parents with respect, working collaboratively with parents, and involving parents in a meaningful way. Students also reported that their parents are involved in school, by being concerned about their schoolwork.

Burleigh Manor Middle School

Burleigh Manor parents/caregivers reported small increases in knowledge and use of school services. Still, at the end of the year, less than one-quarter of the parents/caregivers reported using school resources and services "a lot" or "some." Knowledge of the *HSHS* project among Burleigh parents/caregivers was quite low—less than one-third of the parents/caregivers knew about the project at the end of the year.

Parents/caregivers reported only slight increases in involvement in school activities from September to May. Student reports mirror these findings, with a small decrease in parental/caregiver support on the school climate survey, and with 8th graders reporting the lowest level of parent/caregiver support.

Both parents/caregivers and staff reported good relationships with each other. Parents/caregivers reported an increased sense of being a part of the school, increased feelings of being respected by staff, and an increased perception that staff value their opinions.

Reservoir High School

Parents/caregivers at Reservoir reported increased knowledge and use of school services and resources. Use of services was higher at Reservoir than at the other two schools, with over half of the parents reporting use of services. Reservoir parents/caregivers also reported greater knowledge of assets in May compared to September. However, while more parents knew about the project at the end of the year, less than one-third of parents were aware of the project

Parental/caregiver involvement and support were moderate, with half of parents/caregivers reporting being involved in school activities. School climate data from the students, however, suggest a small decrease in parental support.

Finally, school-parent/caregiver relationships appear to be quite good at Reservoir. Parents/caregivers reported an increased feeling of being a part of the school, probably a reflection of the school being new, and parents needing time to become part of the school's "community." Over half of the parents agreed with all other statement reflecting their relationships with the school, suggesting that parents/caregivers perceive these relationships to be quite positive. Staff concurred, reporting increases in treating parents with respect and involving parents in a meaningful way.

5. Recommendations

RECOMMENDATION #1: **Discuss more clearly the issues of character education versus developmental assets in the context of ensuring a "home" for the developmental assets model in the school system.** Finding an appropriate place to fit this project into the school system will be necessary to ensure its long-term sustainability and acceptance by other schools. Discussions with school administrators will help to further explore this issue.

RECOMMENDATION #2: **Explore the plans for expansion and sustainability of the program in more detail, ensuring that all stakeholders have a clear vision for this.** Without planning now for the future sustainability of the project, the project will not likely continue beyond the 3-year grant funding cycle. All project stakeholders should be involved to ensure a clear and common vision for all.

RECOMMENDATION #3: **Create training programs within each school that are decided upon by the school culture committee for long-term integration.** Again, planning for future sustainability will be predicated on staff acceptance of the project and their ability to implement the project appropriately. Staff would benefit from training sessions designed to increase knowledge of the project, as well as their ability to implement the project within the school.

RECOMMENDATION #4: **Define the Grants Coordinator role within each school individually, based on need and motivation of the school culture committee.** Defining the role of the Grant Coordinator will help all stakeholders be clearer about responsibilities and expectations.

RECOMMENDATION #5: **Explore more fully the issues of parental/caregiver involvement.** Staff would like to see parents become more involved in supporting the school's efforts to develop youth assets. Future planning for activities for parents/caregivers should take into consideration some suggestions from parents/caregiver themselves. One way to increase parent/caregiver involvement may be to focus on activities where students and parents/caregivers are in attendance together.

RECOMMENDATION #6: **Make sure there is an appropriate amount of time and attention paid to action planning.** This past year, staff felt that there was not enough time to adequately plan the project. Spending more time on planning will benefit all involved and support better implementation of project activities.

RECOMMENDATION #7: **Explore the development of new activities at each school that are unique to the project and that are more developmentally appropriate for older students.** In addition to building on what schools are already doing, project staff should explore the possibility of designing and implementing new activities at each school. Further, new activities need to be tailored to each grade level so they are developmentally appropriate and accepted by the students.

RECOMMENDATION #8: **Focus efforts on specific subpopulations within each school.** For example, at Deep Run, efforts to improve voice, sense of belonging, academic self-efficacy, and school engagement may need to focus more on male students. Third graders may need more opportunities to express their "voice." At Burleigh, 8th graders need to be targeted on all domains of school climate, and efforts to improve academic expectations, equity, safety, and student academic culture may need to target male students. At Reservoir, efforts on safety, student academic culture, and achievement motivation need to target male students, and efforts to improve safety and equity may need to focus on minority students.

Chapter 10

Developing and Maintaining Long-Term Consulting Relationships

Gary W. Harper, DePaul University, Maureen Blaha, National Runaway Switchboard, and Carlos Samaniego, Project VIDA

INTRODUCTION

The focus of this chapter is on developing and maintaining long-term consulting relationships, particularly those between consultants and community-based nonprofit organizations. Here we define "long term" as those consulting relationships that continue for a minimum of two years. It is important to note at the outset that having a long-term consulting relationship does not mean that the community-based organization (CBO) is dependent on the consultant, but instead that both entities are growing together. In the world of consulting, you will find that there is a range of different types of consulting jobs, as well as a range of clients. There will be some clients that you will enjoy working with and with whom you feel a connection, and then there will be other clients where you will complete your contract and then (gladly) part ways. This chapter is focused on the former.

Given the focus of this book on providing guidance and direction regarding effective consultation, we thought it would be helpful for the reader to learn about long-term consultation relationships from both the side of a consultant *and* an agency who hires consultants. Having both perspectives will give the reader unique insights into what their potential clients may be thinking and doing throughout the course of the relationship, which will assist the consultant in being more understanding and effective in his or her work.

In order to accurately portray the views of both consultants and clients, we include one consultant and two representatives from CBOs who have worked with a variety of consultants. Both consultant and CBO authors have experience working in long-term consulting relationships, some of which have lasted 10 years or more. In addition, the consultant author has been engaged in long-term consulting relationships with both CBO authors. The insights and ideas presented in each section were collaboratively developed by all of us, regardless of our affiliation or role, in order to give a more complex and comprehensive view of long-term consulting relationships.

The first section offers some insights into the benefits of developing and maintaining long-term consulting relationships, first from a community-based organization (CBO) perspective, and then from a consultant perspective. In addition to general benefits for each party, we offer some consultant and agency specific benefits. In the next two sections of the chapter, we provide information regarding the types of issues that CBOs may consider when forming and maintaining long-term consulting relationships, then we provide insights regarding issues that consultants may consider when forming and maintaining such relationships. The final section offers some conclusions regarding long-term consulting relationships.

BENEFITS OF LONG-TERM CONSULTING RELATIONSHIPS

There are several benefits to developing and maintaining a long-term consulting relationship between a community agency and a consultant, otherwise we wouldn't have written this chapter! We will first discuss the general benefits of long-term consulting relationships for both consultants and clients, followed by a few benefits specific to consultants and CBOs. The general benefits will be organized into three broad areas: a) familiarity and comfort, b) team work and synergy, and c) commitment and dedication.

General Benefits

With regard to familiarity and comfort, we have found that after working together for an extended period of time, each party learns about and becomes accustomed to the other's work ethics, working styles, and patterns of communication. This can create a sense of comfort since both parties know what to expect in their relationship, and do not have to spend time trying to figure out how to best work with the other. Having this understanding over time will decrease the preparatory time needed to start a new project, thus leading to more efficient development and execution of projects.

Familiarity also leads to an understanding of each other's strengths and weaknesses, resulting in more cohesive and collaborative teamwork. Such knowledge can assist the team in appropriately dividing tasks and creating both a better process and end product; thus increasing the likelihood of reaching the project goals. This synergistic type of relationship can result in a project that is more efficient and effective than any project that either party alone could create and execute since it's capitalizing on the best qualities of each group. It can also add depth and richness to the work that is conducted, which typically could not be achieved with less familiar partners.

Commitment to the collaborative team and dedication to the end product develop as consultants and CBOs work together. This is critical for both parties, since a consultant does not want to work with an agency that will not be committed to fulfilling their roles and responsibilities on a project, and the same goes for an agency not wanting an under-committed consultant. As trust and respect are developed between an agency and a consultant, a combined sense of accomplishment and pride often develops when working on a project. This can increase the likelihood that both parties will actively work to see the project through to fruition in a collaborative manner. Friendships may also develop between consultants and various staff members of community agencies. These friendships can be both professionally and personally fulfilling, and bring a special sense of companionship that "together, we've made a difference."

Combined commitment and dedication to the continued working relationship and to each other can also result in additional benefits. Both parties may be able to use each other's expertise and credibility in non-project-related activities as they arise. This may take the form of a CBO serving as a professional reference when the consultant is attempting to acquire new clients, or the consultant providing the CBO with background information or research for a new project they are considering.

Consultant and CBO-Specific Benefits

From the consultant's perspective, having a long-term client means that you will have the potential to participate in multiple agency projects, thus providing yourself with a relatively steady flow of income. This is an important reality factor if you are going to consult as your primary source of income, since it can give you a sense of comfort knowing that you will be receiving paychecks on a regular basis.

You will also have the ability to work with your long-term clients to contribute to the writing of grant proposals, which can assure that the project being proposed is feasible and able to be accomplished given the proposed budget and time frame. Many consultants have had experiences in which they have been asked to consult with a new agency on a project after funding has already been received, but the grant writer was not realistic or practical with the stated outcomes. Working collaboratively with an agency on grant writing can be beneficial for all involved, since the agency ends up having a more accurate and sophisticated grant proposal (especially when including areas where the consultant has expertise, like program evaluation), and the consultant has a job completing consultation tasks that he or she proposed instead of tasks generated by someone who may not have the same expertise.

Community agencies also experience some specific financial and programmatic benefits from long-term consulting relationships. At a practical financial level, a CBO can save money by continuing to hire the same consultant for various projects since they typically do not have to pay fringe benefits to consultants as they do with their traditional employees. In addition, they do not have to provide a work space and accompanying office equipment and supplies (e.g., desk, chair, computer, phone, etc.) for a consultant. For small CBOs that are on tight budgets, these can be very critical cost savings. We have found that for some agency projects, it also may be easier to find outside financial resources or grants to fund a consultant-based project rather than one that involves the hiring of staff members specifically because the overall price tag may be cheaper.

Having a long-term consultant also improves agency programs since the consultant typically has areas of expertise that are not found among agency staff members, thus expanding the agency's scope of knowledge. So, for a CBO, having a long-term consulting relationship can be like adding a part-time staff member who comes with unique areas of expertise, but does not require all of the financial and physical resources of a traditional employee. This can result in growth and expansion of the services offered by the CBO. One example of how a long-term consulting relationship has improved an agency program is the development and expansion of an HIV-prevention program for African-American and Latino young men who have sex with men. This program was initiated when the consulting relationship first began, and over an 11-year period, the exponential growth, refinement, and longevity of the program (especially in a time of severe budget cuts for HIV-prevention programs) have been strongly influenced by the long-term efforts of the consultant. The consultant has been able to bring national and local intellectual input and pro bono human resources to the program, which has served to enhance and expand the program. The consultant also has been able to work with the program staff members over time to create and continually modify their own evaluation systems, and to use these data to further improve the program.

In addition to the direct fiscal and programmatic benefits, we have found that a long-term consultant can also assist with the depth and breadth of an agency's dissemination efforts. One example from our collaborative work involves the dissemination of a national runaway prevention curriculum, which was co-developed by staff members from one author's CBO, and the consultant and his staff members. Based on the consultant's work on this curriculum, prior history of consultation activities, and the consultant's areas of expertise, the CBO author asked the consultant to participate in a local press conference announcing the release of the prevention curriculum. As a result, both authors were invited by a Federal Congressperson to Washington, DC, to introduce the curriculum at another press conference on Capitol Hill. The press conference was coupled with a legislative briefing, so the authors co-presented at the briefing on issues related to both the agency and the content area (i.e., runaway youth). The consultant's participation resulted in a more in-depth briefing that also included an extensive presentation of complementary information regarding homeless youth.

DEVELOPING A LONG-TERM CONSULTING RELATIONSHIP: CLIENTS' PERSPECTIVES

When CBOs desire to establish a long-term consulting relationship with a consultant, there are several factors they should consider. We will discuss these issues in two broad developmental stages: a) researching and selecting a consultant, and b) starting a relationship with a consultant. We hope to offer insights into what is happening "on the other side" when you are developing a relationship with your clients. Keep in mind that these factors are most likely influencing an agency's actions regardless of whether or not they are viewing you as a potential long-term consultant. Agencies want consultants who can perform for them, so once you have proven your worth as a consultant, the agency may then invite you to participate in another project and work toward building a long-term relationship. Thus, you should approach each organization as a potential long-term client, and realize that they will be assessing the situation to determine whether or not to use your services again in the future.

Researching and Selecting a Consultant

It is very important for CBOs to "do their homework" before hiring a consultant. This should involve both internal and external exploration, where the agency first learns more about what they truly want and need for their proposed project(s), and then critically examines what type of consultant can best meet those needs. In doing an internal assessment, members of the CBO need to think through what they will need with regard to their *consultation project*, as well as what they want and need with regard to their *consultant*. One approach that we have found to be useful in terms of thinking about the consultation project is to have the agency consider the end of the story first—so at the end of the project, what do we want to be able to *do* or *say*? In a perfect world, what will our end product *look like*, how will it *function*, how will it be *utilized*, and how will it be *maintained*?

Once the agency has an idea of their desired consultation project outcomes, they can then think about the type of consultant that will best help them reach their end goal. The following are some questions that have been helpful in our thinking about what type of consultant is desired:

1. *What type of expertise do we need to have a successful project?* For example, do we need someone who has expertise and experience in research, program evaluation, brand awareness, staff compensation, or national industry and geographic comparisons of job functions? Do we need someone who is familiar with the population served by the agency, or is expertise in the task-related area (e.g., organization development, process evaluation, concept mapping, etc.) more important?

2. *What type of consultation and leadership style best matches our agency culture and staff members?* For example, is our agency one that provides opportunities for all staff members to offer input, and thus would work well with a consultant who is nonhierarchical and collaborative? Do we have a more hierarchical agency that only incorporates input from the executive director and upper management, and thus may work well with a consultant who is viewed as a professional expert who offers specific guidance and advice?

3. *How accessible of a consultant do we need?* Do we need a consultant we can call directly with any immediate questions or requests, and he or she will consistently respond to our needs within 24 hours or less? Are we comfortable with sending e-mail questions or requests that are then addressed during the next regularly scheduled meeting with the consultant?

Once the agency has taken the time to explore their consultation project and consultant needs, then it's time to seek out the best person for the job. We have found that although it is tempting to jump into a consulting relationship with the first consultant that appears to fit the bill of what we need, especially when working under a tight deadline from funders, it is best to take the time to really learn about potential consultants first. In our experience, it has been helpful to cast a wide net, and to explore a range of different types of consultants who have the expertise that is needed for our project. This is one place where you as a consultant can make the job of CBOs much easier by providing easily accessible information, through a Web site or printed materials, to potential clients regarding the following:

- areas of expertise
- consultation experiences
- styles of consultation
- services available
- availability (this will be discussed in greater detail in the next section)

Some CBOs may also decide to create a Request for Proposal (RFP), and distribute it through multiple channels in order to have a larger pool of consultants from which to choose.

Once potential consultants have been identified, we have found that it is best to request references from prior clients first, and then interview all appropriate candidates. Although calling and checking references can be a time-consuming process, it typically pays off in the long run since agencies can learn a great deal about the consultant from talking with her or his previous clients. The interview process typically entails participation from a range of individuals working in the agency, especially if the agency is seeking to hire a consultant with whom they hope to work for an extended period of time. We find it helpful if consultants distribute printed materials during the interview that outline the services that can be provided (along with a Web site address), as well as some sample reports or products from previous consulting jobs. The interview team will typically include both those who will work directly with the consultant on the project(s), as well as key stakeholders in the agency whose buy-in and commitment are needed. Some agencies may also involve members of their board of directors, especially if the goal is to select a consultant with whom the agency hopes to work for a long time.

Once the interviews have been conducted and the references checked, then the CBO must make their final decision about who to invite to be their consultant. This decision should be one that involves multiple voices and perspectives, and considers all of the information gathered about each consultant. Although some agencies may be tempted by a lower price tag, we have found that sometimes cheaper consulting relationships end up being more expensive in the end. So as a consultant, it is not advisable to try and promote yourself as having the lowest price at the expense of experience, expertise, or substance.

Beginning a Relationship with a Consultant

Once the agency has gone through the process of researching and selecting a consultant, it is time to begin negotiations with that person in order to establish the parameters of the working relationship. The CBO and consultant should openly discuss each other's expectations, goals, and boundaries for the relationship, including clear delineations of responsibilities. Agency staff members will need to be as clear as possible about what they need the consultant to do, and what they themselves have the time, experience, and skills to do on the project. Time frames for the expected work should also be discussed. Scopes of work set by funders, as well as the required end products (both those mandated by the funder and those mandated by the agency's needs), will need to be discussed so that the consultant is clear about what he or she, as well as the agency, will need to produce. The final product from such negotiations will be a mutually agreed upon contract that clearly details the focus and scope of the contracted work, and delineates the expectations of both the client and the consultant.

When the expectations of the consultant and the consulting project are being negotiated with the consultant, a parallel process should occur within the agency whereby CBO staff members are aware of what will be expected of them and what they can expect from the consultant. Some staff members may think that the consultant will be taking over responsibilities for them, or that the consultant will now serve as a staff member, or supersede the role of their current supervisors. It is important that members of the agency do not see the consultant as a "magic bullet" who will solve all of the agency's problems.

As the contract is negotiated and the consultant begins to visit the agency more, staff members can play a critical role in helping the consultant learn about the history, mission, and vision of the agency. We have found that although our CBO staff members are typically quite busy with their workloads and multiple roles, it benefits the agency to have them set their typical duties aside when the consultant is present in order to help him or her become acclimated to the agency. This involves both formal and informal learning activities, such as describing elements of current programs and services, reviewing annual reports and promotional materials, discussing some of the challenges that have occurred when meeting scopes for funders, and sharing a meal and talking about the reasons for working at the agency. This personal time is very important in ensuring that the key personnel who will work with the consultant feel comfortable working with him or her, and see him or her as an ally, not as an outsider who will be criticizing his or her work.

DEVELOPING A LONG-TERM CONSULTING RELATIONSHIP: CONSULTANTS' PERSPECTIVES

When a consultant is seeking to establish a long-term consulting relationship with a CBO client, there are several factors they should consider, as well. We will discuss these issues in two similar broad developmental stages: a) seeking and securing a client, and b) beginning a relationship with a client.

Seeking and Securing a Client

In some situations, you may seek out a potential client with whom you would like to develop a long-term consulting relationship, and in other cases, they will find you. In the former, you may identify a CBO with whom you have had previous contact, or you may identify an agency whose mission, values, and services are in line with your own personal and professional interests. Before selecting a potential client, you should take the time to learn as much as you can about the agency by engaging in a wide range of activities, such as:

- carefully examining the agency Web site (if they have one)
- reading agency program materials/publications, reading any articles written about the agency
- reviewing past annual reports
- talking to clients/stakeholders of the agency/organization
- talking to past/current consultants
- making a visit to the agency

This can be a time-consuming process, but having such information will be very valuable, both in deciding which agency to approach and in developing the initial relationship.

If you do decide to approach an agency instead of them approaching you, you may need to offer some pro bono services to demonstrate your sincere interest and commitment to their agency or cause. If they have an existing need and funding for the project, this may not be necessary, but in many cases when you are making a "cold call" to an agency and seeking to establish a relationship, you often have to demonstrate both your skills and commitment before they are willing to hire you on an official basis for fee-for-service projects.

Some agencies also may seek you out as a consultant. In order for this to occur, you have to make yourself visible to potential clients. This includes having both printed materials and a Web site so that potential clients can quickly access information about your services, past consulting experiences or training, fee structures, and other pertinent information. If you have specific areas of expertise or concentrations, either with regard to your specific services (e.g., process evaluation, board of directors, development, etc.) or populations of interest (e.g., homeless youth, HIV prevention, etc.), it is beneficial to list these in your promotional materials and on your Web site. We have found that CBOs often prefer to work with consultants who have a shared interest in the population(s) they serve, so detailing this information may make you stand out from other potential consultants. Also, Web page authors can increase the ranking on a Google search of their Web page through techniques such as HTML commenting and adding multiple links, so it may be beneficial to work with someone who has such expertise when creating your Web site.

Regardless of whether *you* seek out the client or the client seeks out *you*, a successful consultant will need to do some background homework before establishing a long-term consulting relationship. If *you* approached the agency and followed our advice above, then you will have a solid base of background knowledge about the agency. If the agency approached *you*, then it would be beneficial to take the time to learn about the agency using some of the techniques we've already discussed (e.g., examining the agency's Web site, reading the agency's program materials/publications, etc.). When working with any client it is helpful to make sure that you (as the consultant) and the agency are a good fit for the project, and it is particularly important when establishing a potentially long-term relationship with a client.

In addition to learning about the agency, it is important to learn as much as possible about the specific project for which they would like to hire you. This may be accomplished through reading Requests for Proposals (RFP), attending bidders' conferences or informational sessions, examining program announcements on funders' Web sites, or just having multiple phone calls or e-mail dialogues to ensure you have a clear understanding of what they are hoping to gain. You need to make sure that you have the skills and expertise required to accomplish the stated objectives, the time to put into successfully completing the project, and that the project fits within your fee structure. It is better for the long-term relationship to pass on some projects that don't match your skill set, time frame, or financial needs, than to try and make them fit.

Once you are confident that you, the agency, and the specific project are all a good match, it is time to have a formal interview or meeting with the agency to solidify the formation of a consulting relationship. This meeting is extremely important, since all of the prior steps may have occurred over the phone or via e-mail. This may be the first time that the agency staff members meet you face to face. When developing a potentially long-term relationship, this meeting is even more critical, since it is an opportunity for each party to figure out whether or not they can work together over time.

As is often said, you only get one chance to make a good first impression, and this is certainly the case in the world of consulting. Just like other long-term relationships, the first meeting can set the tone and pace for subsequent encounters, so you want this to be a smooth and successful event. It is important to review your background materials about the agency and the project prior to this meeting, and to bring with you samples of your prior work and contact information for references. Adequate preparation will result in a more productive and enjoyable first meeting.

This meeting is a time for you to learn about the agency and for the agency to learn about you. It is important to be realistic and clear about what you *can* and *cannot* deliver, and make sure you don't make promises you can't keep. It will be useful to share your experiences with the agency, and to let them know about your consultation and work styles. You should also take this opportunity to have the agency answer any remaining questions you have about the agency or the specific project. It will be helpful to learn about the agency's past experiences in working with consultants—what worked and what didn't work. If discussions of these prior relationships do not naturally surface during the course of the first meeting, you may direct the conversation by making a statement such as the following: "I realize that different agencies have a range of both positive and negative experiences with consultants. In order to provide you with the best services possible, I would be very interested in learning more about your agency's prior working relationships with consultants—what you felt worked well for your specific agency and what you would have changed." This can be very valuable information in forging your relationship with the agency.

In our roles as both consultants and clients, we have found that during that first meeting we often get a sense of the potential for developing a sustainable working relationship—"This is a great fit . . . I can imagine working with this person for a long time," or "I really don't think this is going to work." However, the reality is that some consultants *and* CBOs are good salespeople, and the proof will be in the quality of the developing relationship and the project deliverables. Therefore, it is important to be patient and monitor the progress of your work with the agency to determine whether or not it will truly become a long-term consulting relationship.

Beginning a Relationship with a Client

Several of the general relationship development factors that we discussed earlier with regard to the CBO's role in beginning a relationship with a consultant apply here, as well. In addition, you should be clear about what *you* can provide to the agency, given the scope of the project and the budget, and what will be required from the agency and its staff members. Since you, as the consultant, will likely have more knowledge regarding what will be needed in order to complete the desired project, it will be important for you to take a key role in realistically outlining specific roles and responsibilities for all team members. This should take into account both the needs of the project and the time constraints, and the experience and skills of each individual who is assigned to work on the project.

In order to assess the potential role of each team member from the agency, it is important that you spend time with each person to learn about his or her background and experiences. This learning process can also serve the purpose of giving agency staff members the opportunity to learn more about you as a consultant and as a person. These early interactions are critical to the establishment of trust and buy-in from CBO staff members—factors that are extremely valuable when developing a long-term consulting relationship.

As the consultant, you will also need to work with the CBO in these early days to develop a feasible project plan that will meet the needs of the agency and their funder(s). The agency will rely on you to bring your experience in projecting the time, skills, and resources (human and financial) needed to successfully complete the project. This process will also require that you work with the CBO to create an accurate and feasible time line for the project. It is sometimes helpful to walk the agency through all of the specific steps that will be required to complete the project, and then collectively decide on the amount of time that will be needed for each step, taking into account potential barriers and setbacks. This step-by-step process can also be helpful in determining whether or not the initially projected budget will be adequate. Throughout this process, it is important that you are engaged in active dialogue with all members of the team, and that you do not make assumptions about the agency staff members and their skills or abilities. You may be surprised what some individuals are capable of doing when given a chance to truly contribute.

As previously discussed, the final culmination of these initial conversations is a contract. For agencies with which you hope to continue to work, the development of the initial contract is just as much about developing a mutually beneficial working relationship as it is about developing a written agreement for the work that will be completed. As a consultant, this is time for which you may not be paid, but it is a substantial investment in the future of your working relationship with the CBO.

MAINTAINING A LONG-TERM CONSULTING RELATIONSHIP

Once you have developed an initial relationship with a CBO with whom you wish to forge a long-term consulting relationship, there are several steps you need to take in order to maintain that relationship. Many of these steps are essential to any type of consulting relationship, but are especially critical when working with a potential long-term client. Instead of breaking this part of the chapter into two separate sections focused on the CBO and the consultant, we decided to discuss maintaining a long-term relationship as one integrated section, with some separate advice offered to meet the unique needs of either the CBO or the consultant. This decision was made to highlight the fact that at this point, the two entities—consultant and agency—are working together in a synergistic fashion to accomplish a goal or to create a product. Thus, both parties will need to combine forces to develop, nurture, and maintain the relationship.

We have found five essential elements that have been useful to consider and address when attempting to maintain a productive and mutually beneficial long-term consulting relationship. These are presented here as the 5 R's—Relationship building, Responsiveness, Resource allocation, Remain focused, and Reevaluate. The 5 R's offer guidance for maintaining long-term consulting relationships by reminding us about the diversity of factors that should be considered in order to continually grow and develop as a consulting team. The following sections offer more detail regarding the 5 R's.

1. Relationship Building

Both consultants and clients should keep in mind that when working together on a contracted project, they are indeed engaged in a relationship of sorts. For those wishing to keep this relationship intact over time, there are several factors that can help to build a strong, mutually beneficial relationship. One of the key elements of any successful relationship is clear communication from both parties. Both the consultant and the client need to keep the lines of communication open, and find multiple ways to ensure that each party is both *hearing* and *being heard*.

It is also important to assure that there is shared meaning when communicating, since the message that one party intends to send to another may not be heard or interpreted in the same way. This can occur when the consultant and/or client uses specific jargon or acronyms that are not fully understood by the other. For example, if a client is funded through a specific government-funding source, such as the Family Youth Services

Bureau, agency staff members may refer to that source as FYSB. In order to understand the multiple stakeholders that are involved in the allocation of such funds, it is helpful for the consultant to know that such funding actually comes from the federal government through the U.S. Department of Health and Human Services in the Administration for Children and Families. Shared meaning related to terms that are used to describe the populations of focus for agencies (e.g., high-risk families, homeless youth), as well as the methods used by consultants (e.g., focus groups, process evaluation), are other critical examples.

Part of maintaining productive communication involves understanding each other's preferred styles and modes of communication. Some CBOs may have a more relaxed and casual style of communication, whereas others may be more formal. The mode of communication can vary greatly, too. Some CBOs may prefer e-mail, phone calls, face-to-face meetings, faxes, or other forms of communication. Part of that style may also be the types and amount of information that is shared using different modes of communication. Some CBOs may prefer to pick up the phone and call you to discuss minor issues, while waiting for face-to-face meetings for more significant concerns. As the consultant, you should attend to these factors and work to establish mutually productive patterns of communication. This may mean changing the way you prefer to communicate, and adapting to the needs of the CBO. After all, they are hiring you to complete a task, and this often requires adapting to different communication patterns.

Another aspect of building your relationship with an agency has to do with accessibility. This is a factor for both the consultant and the CBO to consider. The client has to ensure that the staff members who are involved in the project are accessible to the consultant, and the consultant has to ensure that he or she is available when needed by the client. If the consultant cannot reach staff members who are involved in the project, or if the CBO cannot reach the consultant when needed, delays may occur, and frustration and resentment may begin to build. Accessibility is very important in the early stages of developing a long-term relationship, since this may serve as a signal for the client about your level of commitment and dedication as a consultant. If the CBO becomes frustrated with your lack of accessibility, they may choose to seek out the services of another consultant for their next project. Issues of accessibility should be viewed, though, through a lens of moderation. You should not be expected to be at the beck and call of your client, and you, too, should not expect members of the CBO to be available on your time schedule whenever you need them.

Respect is another key element in building a productive relationship with a client. Just as with communication and accessibility, respect is a two-way street. As a consultant, you need to be respectful of the skills and abilities that staff members in your CBO possess. Some individuals may incorrectly assume that staff members working in community agencies do not have the same level of training or expertise as the consultant, especially when the consultant has an advanced degree. This is not the case, and we have found that those working in CBOs often have an extensive array of both traditional and nontraditional educational and experiential backgrounds. Another aspect of respect for you as a consultant to consider is being aware of the multiple demands that many CBOs have on them, and respecting their time commitments related to these tasks. This may mean that during a time when CBO staff members are pressed for time (e.g., before a big fundraiser or health fair), you may need to either take on greater levels of responsibility or delay aspects of the project until the competing project is complete.

The CBO, on the other hand, should also respect your time commitments and your role on the project. You will be under contract to perform particular tasks with the agency, and should be careful about agreeing to do additional work. Early in the relationship, some consultants seeking to form a long-term relationship may work outside the scope of their contract to show their dedication and commitment to the agency and the project, but this can be a slippery slope. Be careful that your excitement about the project and the population of interest does not turn into a situation where you feel like you are being taken advantage of, or your time is not being respected.

The last aspect of relationship-building between a consultant and CBO that we would like to emphasize is to work toward building trust between both parties. There is no secret recipe for how to build trust, and this typically occurs over time as you continue to work with an agency. The prior aspects of relationship building that we've discussed all contribute to building trust—communication, accessibility, and respect—and thus, are very important as you work to develop a long-term consulting relationship. Trust is not something that is easily obtained, and you will find that you both have to work to develop a sense of trust in your relationship.

2. Responsiveness

In order to maintain a mutually beneficial relationship between a consultant and a CBO, both parties need to be responsive to each other and to the needs of the project. As a consultant, you should be responsive to the needs of your client, and you should do so in a timely manner. By this we mean that if your client makes a reasonable request for information or resources, you should do your best to provide it to them in the most expeditious manner possible. This also means that the CBO should be responsive to your needs, as well. You may require data or information from the agency related to the project, and an agency's lack of responsiveness can lead to feelings of frustration or resentment. It is important that you are being realistic in these requests, and that you are mindful of competing demands on the agency that may impact their responsiveness. This is a place where having open and established lines of communication will assist you in being able to make an assessment of whether or not your request is feasible.

Another aspect of responsiveness has to do with completing assigned tasks in a timely manner. Staff members in the agency and the consultant will have assigned tasks with accompanying deadlines in order to keep the project on task and on time. If either party does not strive to complete tasks in a timely manner, such neglect may be viewed in a negative manner. Especially early in a relationship, your inability as a consultant to meet your task-related deadlines may send a message to the CBO that either you are not truly committed to the project, or that you are not competent to complete all of the required tasks.

3. Resource Allocation

Consulting projects can vary greatly in terms of the amount of resources—financial, physical, and human—that are required to complete them. When developing a contract with a client, it is important that you as the consultant are realistic about what *you* will provide, and that you work with the agency to be realistic about what *they* can provide. When seeking external funding for a project, it may be helpful to build in a "cushion" with regard to resource requests, just in case there are unexpected barriers that arise during the course of the project.

Throughout the consulting relationship, it will be necessary for each party to continually monitor the resources that are needed to complete the project, and that they each fulfill their commitments with regard to those resources. If one party does not allocate the resources promised, this can have a detrimental effect on the success of the project, and also on the ensuing relationship. If an agency feels that you have not been honest with the types of resources you will be bringing to the table, and that you are not committing the needed resources to make the project a success, they will likely not desire a long-term relationship with you.

Similarly, if an agency does not uphold their end of the deal with regard to resources, you may find that they are not the best partner for a long-term relationship. It is important, however, to find out why an agency may not be fulfilling their financial obligation to you. If they are receiving funding from outside sources for the project, they may have to wait until they receive the funds from the funder before paying you. This is often the case with smaller CBOs, where they may not have a fiscal reserve from which to draw payment for you, as opposed to larger agencies that have such luxuries. If the resources they promised are in terms of physical or human resources, then you should also assess the reasons for such inability to fulfill their initial commitments. Staff turnover is high in some agencies, and the person who was originally dedicated to your project may no longer be employed at the agency. When attempting to maintain a long-term relationship, you may find that you are more comfortable with cutting the agency some slack and giving them more time to deliver on the resources.

4. Remain Focused

As consultants and agencies work together on a long-term project, it is imperative that both parties remain focused on the ultimate outcome of the consultation project. Especially when the project continues for a prolonged period of time, and the consultant and client become more comfortable with each other, it is easy to get distracted from the desired end point. This may result in expanding the project beyond the original scopes, or drifting in new directions. Although those immediately involved in the project may actually view this as a positive outgrowth of a burgeoning relationship, such divergence can result in the original project objectives not being met. This, in turn, may concern funders, agency upper administration, or an agency's board of directors. These parties may see the lack of focus on and completion of the original scope as a sign that the consultant is not competent, and thus, may seek out another consultant for future projects.

In order to maintain a productive long-term relationship, you as the consultant may have to be the one to keep the overall team focused. One way to remain focused on the project's end point is to continually review the project time line with your client to ensure that the team is staying focused and on schedule, and to make adjustments to the time line as a group when necessary. In doing this, it is also helpful to celebrate the small successes that are made along the way to keep agency staff invested in the project. A problem that we have seen in some CBOs is that different agency staff members may lose interest in the project over time, so as a consultant you will have to find innovative ways to keep them focused and engaged. This may involve changing the types of tasks individuals complete, creating awards for outstanding contributions, using charts or diagrams to track a project's progression, or hosting small celebrations for reaching project time line milestones.

5. Reevaluate

As relationships grow and progress, both internal and external factors may impact the various parties involved in consulting relationships. Over time, different aspects of the CBO may shift, including personnel, leadership, service priorities, funding streams, and location. You, as a consultant, also may change over time as you gain new skills and more experience, especially when working long term with one or more agencies. Given all of these potential changes, it is important to create an ongoing process of evaluation and reevaluation that is focused on the organizational structure and functioning of your partnership with the CBO, and how that relates to the project at hand.

This reevaluation process can take various forms and can have a variety of foci. With some agencies, you may choose to do this on a more informal basis, whereby you create an opportunity to share feedback among all members of the project team at regular intervals. This may take place in lieu of or as an adjunct to a regular team meeting, or you may wish to set a separate time aside for the feedback and evaluation meeting. If informal methods are used, you want to be sure that you have created ample opportunities for team members to openly express their honest opinions. More formal evaluation modalities may be used, as well, such as having team members complete anonymous paper-and-pencil evaluation forms on a regular basis, or having all team members participate in feedback focus groups facilitated by a neutral third party. These various approaches require different resources in terms of financial and time investments, so some partnerships may be limited by these parameters. In a multisite project that involved a range of partners, we used multiple formal methods to continuously reevaluate the organizational structure and functioning of the partnerships. These methods were useful in helping to identify potential "systems failures" or areas of concern. They also provided insights into potential solutions and assisted the partners in working collaboratively to improve their relationships.

The focal areas for the reevaluation may vary across projects, and also at different time points within the same project, depending on what types of information will be the most useful to the sustainability of the partnership. These evaluations should also include a mix of explorations of what *is* working and what *is not* working. Such information will assist you in determining what aspects of the consultation project, as well as the project team, are working well and should be sustained, and what aspects are in need of revision or elimination. Regardless of the modality or the focus of the reevaluation, it will be critical to create an action plan for how you and the other members of the project team can work together to resolve any potential conflict. For example, during one project, a new consultant joined an existing long-term partnership between a CBO and a small group of consultants, and a member of the CBO team had a negative reaction to the new consultant. This resulted in decreased productivity and subtle attempts to sabotage the work of the new consultant. During a reevaluation interview with this staff member, it was revealed that she was concerned that the new consultant was "taking over" her role on the project. This led to a collaborative examination and clarification of each person's role on the project, as well as a restructuring of the project's organizational chart.

As you are conducting these waves of reevaluation, it is also important for you as the consultant to continually evaluate the capacity of the agency to conduct some of the project tasks without your assistance. Keep in mind that having a long-term consulting relationship does not mean that the CBO is dependent on the consultant, but instead that both entities are growing together. By having CBO team members take over some aspects of the project, you not only are building sustainable capacity within the organization, but also are freeing yourself to engage in additional or higher level tasks. We have found that when the consultant teaches agency staff members new skills, this often strengthens the existing relationship for the future, and assists in building the trust that is needed in order to have a successful long-term consulting relationship.

CONCLUSIONS

In this chapter, we have attempted to offer insights from both consultants and CBOs regarding long-term consulting relationships. We reviewed the benefits of such partnerships, and then detailed issues to consider in both the development and maintenance of these relationships. Our goal was to offer the reader a view of "both sides of the coin," instead of the traditional approach of talking to a *consultant* about how a *consultant* experiences a particular consulting situation from a *consultant's* perspective. By including the voices of both consultants and clients in the writing of this chapter, the reader will hopefully have a more balanced and comprehensive picture of what all parties experience in long-term consulting relationships.

Although there are many benefits to long-term consulting relationships, there can be challenges if both parties do not actively work to maintain a balanced and mutually beneficial partnership. Be careful not to get too complacent in your long-term consulting relationships to the point where you either offend your collaborative partners by taking them for granted, or you get too comfortable with the status quo and fail to push each other to continually produce your best work. In addition, both partners need to continually respect the non-partnership commitments of the other, and make sure not to overstress the relationship by pushing limits with inappropriate demands or requests. Like any relationship, you will need to continually reevaluate what is working and what is not, and then make appropriate changes to ensure the success of your collaboration and your projects.

Another caution that we would like to offer is to monitor for any signs that CBO staff members are becoming dependent on the consultant. We have seen some CBO staff members who begin to rely too heavily on the consultant, and thus neglect to execute their work-related tasks. It is important that members of the CBO keep in mind that the consultant is not another agency staff member, but is indeed an outside *consultant*. Thus, although the consultant may offer input regarding the structure and content of various projects, it is typically not her or his role to produce physical items for the prevention programs such as flyers and brochures. If not adequately addressed, dependency on the consultant may lead program personnel to misuse the consultant relationship, which may result in mistrust and frustration on the part of the consultant.

As you can see, developing and maintaining long-term consulting relationships is not necessarily an easy task. It can take a great deal of extra time and effort, especially in the beginning phases, but we feel that the long-term benefits outweigh the short-term investments of additional time and resources. We have all experienced great benefits from our personal long-term consulting relationships, and we honestly like and respect each other after all these years—after all, we did decide to write this book chapter together!

Chapter 11

Consulting with Small Community-Based Nonprofit Organizations: Insights and Understandings

Douglas F. Cellar, Gary W. Harper, and Leah C. Neubauer,
DePaul University

OVERVIEW

The following chapter chronicles some insights and understandings based on our collective experience consulting with small, nonprofit, community-based organizations (CBOs). We begin the chapter with a description of the initiation and development of our consulting center within a large urban university, and then discuss insights and understandings we have gleaned working with a number of small, diverse CBOs. Specifically, we describe in more detail the following 10 insights and understandings: 1) finding our niche was key, 2) the effects of passion are paradoxical, 3) preparation builds the foundation for entering into a partnership, 4) nurturing a partnership is a balancing act, 5) funding sources influence the consulting relationship, 6) boards of directors are omnipresent, 7) volunteers are sovereign, 8) project scope is easy to underestimate, and it expands, 9) a comprehensive framework links consulting, advocacy, and research, and 10) reflection and planning streamline future work.

These sections were included in the chapter because they reflect significant issues that we have confronted since our consulting center became operational. We believe our experience represents some common themes that emerge when working with small CBOs. We are not claiming that what we have done is the best or the only way to consult with CBOs, but rather we share our experience in the spirit that it may be useful to those considering a career in consulting and/or working with small CBOs. While the consulting experiences depicted in this chapter occurred in a university center, we believe our experience can be useful to those working in centers and other contexts, as well. Our experience working with these organizations has been exciting, satisfying, and even fun. The experience, however, can be very different from working as a consultant with larger organizations, and is not always an easy road to travel.

FINDING OUR NICHE WAS KEY

The idea for the creation of a consulting center was generated by members of our psychology department charged with exploring alternative means to enhance graduate student funding in our department. Challenges with funding made it difficult to recruit our top doctoral candidates, and students who entered our program needed additional sources of funding to live in Chicago. Several faculty were already involved in contractual work related to community and industrial/organizational psychology, and these consulting projects frequently involved graduate students. In combination, we had experience working with a variety of organizations, including large corporations, public safety forces, governmental agencies, and large and small nonprofits. We felt that a center could provide a structure for faculty and student consulting that would create a more stable source of funding for graduate students, an applied learning experience for graduate students, and a valuable service to the community.

Initially, the authors and other interested faculty and students began envisioning the mission of the center and identifying a potential client base. We began this process by considering the consulting work we had done in the past and requests for consulting services that we had received. The authors' educational backgrounds were primarily in clinical-community and industrial/organizational psychology. Based on our initial conversations regarding the demand for consulting services in the nonprofit sector and some consulting work we had done for CBOs, it became clear to us that the combination of services offered by clinical-community and industrial/organizational psychologists were in high demand. We also concluded that few CBOs consider projects that combine expertise from these two fields, yet often community and organizational psychologists engage in similar types of consulting work. For example, through several program evaluation projects conducted by one of the authors, it became apparent that there were human resources and organizational issues that were important to address in order to improve the effectiveness of the services that the CBOs offered. In these situations, it became clear early on in the consulting relationship that in order to successfully implement and evaluate agency programs, the roles, responsibilities, and chain of command for various staff members needed to be clarified within the structure of the CBO. Given the frequent need to address both organizational and programmatic issues, working together, we were able to provide the client organizations with more comprehensive services.

Based on our experiences and discussions with faculty, students, and clients, we became convinced of the viability of a joint center that would bridge both industrial/organizational and clinical-community psychology. We developed an initial list of potential services we could offer, and began to consider the types of organizations that we would target as a client base. Selection of the initial proposed services was based on the type of work we had already been doing individually as consultants, and activities students typically performed in their internships. Our menu of services contained specific listings of various aspects of program evaluation, program development/capacity building, human resources management, staff training and development, and organizational change. We wanted to start with a wide range of services in order to maintain flexibility as we went through the process of defining our niche.

We decided that service-focused nonprofit organizations would be an excellent fit with our goals and the mission of the university, which emphasize social justice and community service. Furthermore, such organizations could provide a wide range of training opportunities for our students, and were a good fit with the services that we could offer. At this point, we were leaning toward smaller CBOs, but had not ruled out the possibility of working with larger nonprofit organizations.

We developed and submitted a proposal for creating our center, including our mission and a list of potential services, to the university for approval. We believed there were a number of advantages to creating a center within the university, given our goals of training students and providing services to CBOs. Agencies often value partnering with an academic institution because it enhances their credibility with funding sources and boards of directors. Working with a university center provides a simple descriptive label that is easily communicated to individuals outside the organization. There is also value to the university in that its partnership with community agencies contributes to a positive image of the university, and in our case, fit with the service-oriented mission of our university.

An advantage for students is that they can be paid through the university for their project work and, as agents of the university; they are covered by university insurance. In addition, faculty can choose to reduce their teaching load to work on contracts and receive credit for the consulting work that they do when their performance is evaluated. Finally, though not specifically requested in our proposal, the university generously provided start-up funding and space for the center.

We also knew there were some disadvantages to consulting through a university center. Universities tend to have policies and internal processes regarding external funds that were designed to accommodate research grants, not consulting contracts. The bureaucratic structure has, at times, been cumbersome for negotiating contracts and managing funding streams for projects, as consulting projects are often more fluid and more uncertain than research grants. Also, there are policies restricting the amount of money a faculty member can be paid beyond his or her academic salary in many academic institutions. From our perspective, an academic center makes sense as a vehicle for consulting if the primary goal of those involved is to provide professional training and funding for students. If one is more inclined toward consulting as a business, other outlets may be a better choice. For example, many academics form their own private consulting groups or work with an existing consulting firm on a part-time basis.

After obtaining university approval for the center, we created an ad hoc advisory committee of 11 people that included executive directors from CBOs we had worked with in the past, a mix of people from large and small nonprofits in the area, faculty colleagues, graduate students, representatives from governmental agencies, and representatives from funding agencies. We held a meeting with the ad hoc committee members to obtain feedback from the group regarding the mission of our center, the services we would offer, and the viability of our plan. In addition, this meeting allowed us to begin to spread the word about the existence of our center.

Based on the ad hoc meeting, we decided to target smaller nonprofit organizations because of their need for the types of services that we could provide, and the fact that they would benefit most from the reduced fee structure associated with the center. Next, we tailored our list of services to include those most relevant for small CBOs. We simplified the presentation of our original list of services to include general descriptions of program evaluation, program development, staff training and development, and management of organizational change and development. We presented our center as providing a broad and general range of services. If we had decided to target larger organizations, we would have specialized in one particular area. It is not feasible to provide a broad array of services to a large organization because of the increased number of people, divisions, and locations associated with such organizations, and the propensity of decision makers in those organizations to hire specialists for particular projects.

We were fortunate in that we were already working on a few projects that we brought into the center. As for attracting new projects, we created brochures that detailed our mission, and explained in general terms the services that we provided and how those services could enhance the effectiveness of organizations (see Appendix 11-1). We used these brochures to spread the word regarding the center via face-to-face encounters and a few mailings. In addition, we created a Web site for our center. However, more often than not, potential clients heard about our center through word-of-mouth. Executive directors and program managers tend to rely more heavily on word-of-mouth as a means of identifying consultants rather than mailings or searching the Web. Our brochures and Web site were more useful as sources of information after initial contact was made with prospective clients. Given the increasing use and accessibility of the Internet, future consultation centers and independent consultants with limited funds may find greater benefit from allocating more resources to a Web site rather than brochures.

Soon we discovered there was additional work available for the center, and for the next 5 years, we worked on a variety of projects with approximately 7 different CBOs, most of whom we have worked with on multiple projects. Since the inception of the center, approximately 22 students have worked on various projects. The amount of time that faculty have invested in these projects has varied considerably depending on the nature of the project. Projects with new clients or novel projects tend to demand more faculty time compared to repeat business or cyclical projects that have become routine over time. Faculty time on these projects has ranged from 5 to 30 hours per week. These projects have afforded students and faculty the opportunity to work in diverse community settings with a wide range of interesting people who are passionate about the work they do in their communities.

THE EFFECTS OF PASSION ARE PARADOXICAL

Across the board, one of the most salient characteristics of small CBOs has been the passion of the people who do the work in these agencies. It makes sense that people who would choose to work in these types of organizations would likely be motivated by the cause associated with the agency, or by the opportunity to make a positive difference in the community being served. For example, we have worked on multiple repeated projects with agencies that serve people living with HIV/AIDS, runaway youth, and people living with chronic hepatitis C. A relatively large percentage of people in these organizations have gravitated to these respective causes because they have been touched by it directly, or through someone close to them. And, if initially a person takes a job in one of these organizations for other reasons, the passion of their coworkers is often contagious.

Passion can be contagious for consultants, too, particularly if it is a cause that the consultant feels strongly about. Performing work that is meaningful and satisfying should not be underestimated, nor should the exhilaration one experiences in consulting with people who have passion for their work. In our experience, working on consulting projects with members of an agency whose staff is passionate about the project has been an extremely productive and satisfying experience. However, from a consultant's point of view, agency passion can seem to have paradoxical effects on the work that they do as it can facilitate projects and fuel organizational growth, but can also result in heightened conflict, resistance to change, and program evaluation apprehension. Thus, passion can be very beneficial, but clearly has a challenging side, as well.

When staff weigh the costs and benefits of participating in a new activity such as a program evaluation, if it is perceived as diverting time and resources away from "their cause," a consultant can experience a great deal of resistance to, and animosity toward, the evaluation. For example, in at least two agencies, resistance to program evaluation data collection stemmed from the additional work it required on the part of staff and/or volunteers, thereby "diverting" attention away from their work with clients. There is also a parallel issue that can occur when a consultant is working with an agency to evaluate an existing program that people are passionate about and believe is working—that is, they may be skeptical of evaluation findings to the contrary. In extreme cases, they may only select consultants for evaluation activities who will support their program and mission. As a consultant, it can be important to consider whether this is likely to be the case, and to develop a shared understanding of the importance and usefulness of evaluation for the agency and programs that are being evaluated. Considering scenarios regarding potential negative findings can be important in beginning stages. It helps to develop clear mutual expectations regarding the nature and purpose of the evaluation, and how it can be of use to the CBO.

The passion of people working in small CBOs often fuels program and agency growth because staff want to reach out and make their services available to more people, or to provide additional services to those in need. This inevitably leads to expansion as more staff and volunteers are needed to provide services and manage additional programs. As an agency grows, there are changes in job duties, amount of client contact, quality of interaction with coworkers, and the nature of supervision. Often, the organizational structure changes as agency programs and the work needed to complete and maintain them becomes more differentiated. As these changes occur, there is a greater need for coordination and integration within the organization that often lags behind the growth. Ironically, the very passion that fuels rapid growth can show its challenging side by resisting the organizational changes occurring within the agency, thus exacerbating the role that ambiguity, stress, and conflict can play as a part of the growth process.

We have found these passion-fueled "growing pains" to be a common occurrence in CBOs, and an important phenomenon for consultants to understand because when growth occurs, it creates organizational issues that require expertise in that area. It is at the point when these volatile issues reach a crescendo that an executive director may decide to bring in a consultant. Another scenario could be that a consultant may be working on a program evaluation in an organization, and realize that the potential effectiveness of the program is in jeopardy due to organizational issues that must be addressed. Understanding how passion can fuel growth cycles, while at the same time promote resistance to the organizational change that is associated with such growth, has been a key learning concept associated with our consulting work. Understanding and appropriately addressing the seemingly paradoxical issues associated with passion and growth can facilitate building a foundation for a long-term partnership. In the next section, the preparation that can lead to surfacing and working through issues, including those related to the paradox of passion, are discussed.

PREPARATION BUILDS THE FOUNDATION FOR ENTERING INTO A PARTNERSHIP

When beginning a partnership with a small CBO, we have found it to be particularly important to make time to lay the foundation for working together. Small CBOs can be complex in terms of the programs they offer and the varied communities they serve. In addition, as we have previously mentioned, the level of passion that exists in these organizations can run high. Thus, in preparation for partnering with a CBO, it is important to gain an understanding of the culture and history of the CBO, the community being served, the people being served, and the people working in the CBO. There is no substitute for spending time in the CBO and the community to learn about the strengths of the individuals, the organization, and that particular community. In addition, this is an opportunity to observe behavioral instances reflecting struggles and conflicts that may thwart a project. It is also important to begin developing rapport and trust with the people (all constituencies) whom you as a consultant must ultimately depend upon to carry out the project.

The nature of the consulting partnership with small CBOs may be quite different compared to those developed with larger organizations. First, small agencies tend to serve a particular community or segment of the community, though that is not always the case. To the extent they do serve and identify with a particular community, the norms and values of that community may be reflected in those of the agency. Therefore, the consultant may not only be perceived as an external agent to the organization, but to the larger community as well, resulting in a larger gap that must be bridged in order to gain trust and build rapport. If a consultant is perceived as an outsider, some staff may be less cooperative at first until the consultant has demonstrated a commitment to the community and agency. Also the consultant may be "tested" in different ways by staff members to see if he or she is truly dedicated to the community or the population. This may occur during casual conversations at the agency, while having lunch, or even more directly during project team or staff meetings.

Having previous consulting experience with other agencies in that community, or similar communities, can be beneficial in terms of establishing common ground. Reaching out to people in the organization and the community through involvement, or at least presence, in activities sponsored by the agency can be a means of showing interest, building trust, and gaining a better understanding of the agency and the context in which it functions. We have attended health fairs, fundraising events, support groups, community outreach, cultural celebrations, and other activities sponsored by agencies with which we have worked. Attending these functions has provided useful assessment data for the projects, while also demonstrating our willingness to get to know the staff and the community, and understand the programs associated with the organization. For example, an organization that we were beginning to work with was having a large fundraising dinner and award ceremony. Two of our student consultants volunteered to help with the event by setting up and checking coats. The volunteer work that they did afforded them the opportunity to see how the team from the CBO worked together, the nature of the fundraiser, and what it was like to participate in an event as a volunteer. The people from the CBO appreciated the consultants' willingness to help, as well as their interest in the event and the work that they did.

Also, with some organizations there may be a particular philosophy or approach to social issues that is important to be aware of. For example, if working with a substance use organization, they may have a harm reduction philosophy where they do not encourage clients to abstain from substance use, but instead encourage safer practices. Conversely, another agency may adhere to a substance use abstinence philosophy, whereby clients are discouraged from any use of substances. It is critical for the consultant to be aware of and fully understand the agency's particular philosophy and approach to service provisions very early on in the relationship, in order to provide the most beneficial services. In addition, some consultants may have value conflicts with a particular agency's philosophy and/or service delivery approach that may negatively impact their ability to provide unbiased services. In these situations, the consultant will need to make some difficult decisions about the appropriateness of either initiating or continuing his or her involvement with the agency.

Understanding the past experience a CBO has had with external consultants and researchers can be critical. Bad experiences with consultants can leave a lasting impression on the people in an organization, and can spill over into new projects with new consultants. In our experience, it has been surprising that a relatively high percentage of the people with which we have worked have reported negative experiences with consultants and researchers at one time or another. A common theme of these reports has been that consultants, and particularly researchers, come into the organization and "get what they want," and leave without much lasting benefit to the CBO. Through an understanding of this history, one may avoid pitfalls and gauge the extent to which expectations regarding past projects were mutual and realistic.

Developing a clear set of expectations and ground rules regarding the project is critical, but sensitivity is required when creating a mutual understanding. Many processes in these organizations are done through informal means, and overemphasizing a "legalistic" type of relationship can be off-putting to people if the reasons for clarifying expectations and ground rules are not explained to them in terms that make sense from their perspective. The key is the collaborative process that leads to the contract and ground rules. We are not suggesting that consultants neglect to explicitly state them in written form, but rather allow enough time and dialogue with the client to ensure they understand the value of a contract, and ground rules for both the agency and consultant.

NURTURING A PARTNERSHIP IS A BALANCING ACT

Once a project is underway, formative feedback loops regarding how the project is progressing and people's reactions to the project are a means for identifying potential problems and issues before serious conflicts or problems arise. Such problems, if left unchecked, may threaten the acceptance and ultimately the maintenance of the change brought about by the project. Formative feedback may take the form of data that are collected at numerous points during a project that provide information about the extent to which the project is proceeding on schedule, is on track, and is meeting expectations. Data can be collected through individual meetings, group meetings, survey data, or other means, if appropriate.

It is suggested that formative feedback be collected after key decisions are made, and each phase of the project is completed, to ensure the project is moving forward appropriately and meeting the expectations of those involved. For example, formative feedback played an important role in a long-term consulting project with an agency that provided services for people living with HIV/AIDS. We charted the progress of the project to ensure that our objectives were being met within our proposed time line, and after each piece of the project was completed, group meetings were held to assess whether or not mutual expectations were being upheld. We also assessed the process involved in completing the project so that changes could be made at that point. Meetings were more frequent at the beginning of the project in order to become accustomed to working together, and to correct any misunderstandings regarding the project. We also celebrated completing each step of the project by taking time to acknowledge our successes, and to emphasize the progress being made and the role that each successive accomplishment played in meeting our larger goal.

We found that making the completion of steps in the project more salient can result in participants viewing the project as more relevant and tangible to them. Too often, the end point of a long-term project seems far off and obscure. Building in time to celebrate each successful step, and linking each of these smaller successes to the long-term project end point, can boost morale and create a sense of ownership in the project. Finally, post project follow-up is important in the form of a more complete overall program evaluation, and also in terms of post-implementation support.

On the other side of the coin lies the concern regarding the client becoming overly dependent on the consultant. One of the mutual goals inherent in our consulting partnerships has been to empower clients to manage the systems that we have worked with them to develop. People in small CBOs are often very competent and appreciate the opportunity to learn new skills and improve their work processes if they perceive the value of making changes. While there may be some functions that consultants have unique expertise to perform, it has been our experience that people in client organizations acquire the knowledge and skills to support the systems we create, such as evaluation tools, employee attitude surveys, and performance management systems. In sum, building participation and training into a project in order to empower employees to operate and manage a new system may increase acceptance and maintenance of the change, and be appreciated by the people working in that organization. In the long run, it can be a very cost-effective strategy for the agency.

In our experience as consultants, it has been a difficult task to achieve a balance between immersing oneself in an agency in order to develop rapport and trust, while still clearly maintaining one's status as an external consultant. It can be especially difficult to maintain this balance if the agency has a mission that is aligned with the consultant's activist/advocacy work, which in our experience has frequently been the case. However, maintaining this balance is necessary because the consultant's role in the project may be unique in that it provides an external perspective on the project based on the consultant's training and expertise.

If a consultant actually becomes perceived as an internal agent, his or her external perspective may be compromised, resulting in a loss of that perspective to the client. Also, the consultant may increasingly find him- or herself embroiled in issues that are not relevant to the project, are time-consuming, and better handled by others (someone internal to the organization, another external consultant, or the board of directors, etc.). As consultants, we can find ourselves, at times, in the awkward position of having role demands that require an external perspective, but increasingly playing the role of someone internal to the organization. When we lose our "external status," it can result in a loss of effectiveness regarding the original purpose of the project. In summary, achieving the most effective level of involvement and role status as a consultant is a tenuous balance that must be achieved. The balance lies somewhere between being immersed enough in the organization to develop trust and rapport, but not to the extent that it detracts from performing the activities that the consultant has contracted to perform.

FUNDING SOURCES INFLUENCE THE CONSULTING RELATIONSHIP

A key feature that can differentiate working with small CBOs from working with larger organizations is the reliance of the smaller agencies on funding from governmental agencies and foundations. The vast majority of agencies that we have worked with have been dependent on some sort of external support. The dependence on outside support can exert large and meaningful effects on all aspects of organizational life within these CBOs. For many CBOs, their very existence depends on maintaining funding, as well as finding new sources of funding. Developing new programs, capacity building, and other organizational changes often depend on securing external funds. The number of staff that can be supported and the scope of their job duties are also significantly affected by funding. Availability of funds can influence job duties and the time staff has to participate in projects. These changes can be particularly difficult if a project requires a heavy investment in staff training, and due to funding changes, those people are no longer available for the project. The level of uncertainty regarding funding is often reflected in the sense of stability and predictability within the CBO.

A CBO's dependence on external funding affects how projects are funded and how consultants are paid. In our experience, consultant fees often need to be written into grant applications from the primary funding agency, or other foundations must be identified and grant applications submitted in order to support new projects. Furthermore, financial support is more readily available for certain types of projects, thereby affecting the viability of some projects over others. Knowledge of these streams of funding is critical for the consultant to understand because in order for a project to come to fruition, the consultant may need to partner with the agency to secure funding for various phases of the project.

The grant writing process can significantly add to the investment in a project by the consultant and client. This may take the form of identifying potential sources of funding for the project, contacting sources of funding, writing grant proposals and negotiating the terms of funding with the funding source. This investment of time may be divided into various parts between the consultant and the CBO, but still requires dedication and commitment from both parties.

Writing grants can also create a sense of uncertainty regarding the viability of a proposed project. This, in turn, may create challenges for recruiting students to work on consulting tasks since funding may not be secured until the very last moment. One way we have addressed this ambiguity is to divide projects into phases, and then seek funding for subsequent phases while prior phases are still being implemented. A final concern is the time frame between when the grant application is submitted, and when funds become available. Some city, state, or federal government grants and contracts, in particular, may have prolonged time periods between when the grant is due, when funding decisions are made, and when funds are actually dispersed to the agency. These delays can result in the consultant receiving payment after the project is completed. On the other hand, there are times when extra funding is made available at the end of a governmental fiscal year, so the agency may all of a sudden have a surplus of money that they have to spend quickly on new programs or evaluation activities. When attempting to write grants for subsequent funds, the CBO and consultant must consider the value of the project in question, and the likelihood of obtaining funding in a timely manner.

Funding for the vast majority of projects for which we have contracted services has usually been for a fixed amount that was contingent on the work to be completed. It is unusual for a consultant to work for a small CBO charging an hourly rate for an open period of time. The agencies that provide funding for the CBO want to know what the end product of the project will be, and the time frame within which it will be completed. Compared to consulting fees paid by large corporations or nonprofits, small CBOs pay less for consulting services, however, if funding is available, fees can be reasonable. Our fees have varied greatly because of the educational function of the center. Rates for consultants have ranged from course credit to $100/hour for more experienced consultants. At times a CBO also may have funding for a program where a specific amount of money is designated for program evaluation, for example, so the consultant will be asked what type of program evaluation can be done for that amount of money and within the specified time frame.

In summary, the introduction of third party funding can add additional resource investments and uncertainty into the process of contracting with CBOs. Therefore, the consultant and client need to assess both the importance of the project, and the viability of potential sources of funding for the project. The extent to which the client or consultant has had success in the past securing third party funding for projects increases the likelihood of future funding. On the other hand, third party funding is an additional resource that can bring important projects to fruition. For some CBOs, their board of directors can play a key role in setting priorities regarding new projects and identifying potential sources of funding for those projects.

BOARDS OF DIRECTORS ARE OMNIPRESENT

In larger organizations, for many projects, a consultant may not directly experience the influence of the board of directors. It is much more likely to happen when working with a small CBO. The board of directors of a CBO can exert a great deal of control and influence over the decisions made by the executive director and program directors. The executive director is hired by the board, and in effect, is accountable to the board for his or her actions. Consultants need to be aware of this relationship, and must understand how their project affects the relationship between the board and the management of the CBO.

An executive director of a CBO may undertake a change-related project for a variety of reasons, but often a central concern is the reaction of the board of directors to the activities or the eventual results from the intervention. Projects may be designed explicitly to identify a particular organizational need to present to the board, or to impress the board with the things that the organization does well. For example, a CBO may conduct an attitude survey, as much to impress the board with the high level of satisfaction of its employees and volunteers as to identify sources of dissatisfaction to use as the basis of action planning. From a management perspective, positive results are important in their own right, but just as importantly, could lead to greater support from their board for other initiatives and for management in general.

CBOs work closely with their boards of directors, because they ultimately have decision-making power over new programs and changes that may occur within the organization. Boards of directors also play a key role in the hiring and firing of executive directors and other personnel within a CBO. Members of the board are often chosen because of the expertise they possess, and the power and influence they have in the community. They often simultaneously hold positions on other boards, sometimes even for foundations that are potential sources of support for the agency. In some cases, it may be advantageous for the consultant to meet with the board, particularly if the consultant is in the role of the "outsider" and the people on the board are influential members of the community being served. In summary, if one is considering working as a consultant with a small agency, it is important to understand the role of the board of directors, and its relationships with and influences on the agency and its employees.

VOLUNTEERS ARE SOVEREIGN

Many small CBOs rely heavily on volunteers, which may affect the nature of consulting projects. For CBOs that are dependent on volunteer help, organizational policies and procedures are often designed to simultaneously serve their clients and maintain high levels of satisfaction among the volunteers. These dual goals may influence the types of activities that the agency is willing to undertake regarding program evaluation, action research, strategic planning, and other interventions. The importance of volunteer satisfaction is underscored when there is significant investment by the agency in the training of their volunteers.

Again, like employees in many CBOs, volunteers are there for the cause and/or the community being served, and may resent change or time-consuming activities that divert their attention away from the service they have volunteered to provide. As a result, agency administrators are often wary of involving volunteers in time-consuming consulting projects, and are sensitive to their complaints regarding involvement in activities associated with these projects. From the consultant's vantage point, it is important to spend the volunteers' time wisely, and to take steps at the beginning of a project to understand the volunteers' perspectives and provide detailed explanations of the project and its value both to the organization and the client base that is served. Without the support of the volunteers, a potentially great project may never get off the ground.

For example, we developed a process to evaluate the effectiveness of a hotline for runaway youth that consisted of a structured interview with the caller after the call had been completed. Highly trained volunteers handled the calls from runaway youth and/or their parents. The program director was concerned that there would be resistance from the volunteers to administer the evaluation interview, based on their past experience with evaluation. During the development of the evaluation interview, the consultants had a number of meetings with staff and volunteers to develop interview questions related to the tasks they performed when responding to calls on the hotline. Volunteers were very cooperative in this process, but indicated that they felt that it was awkward and at times inappropriate for them to make an abrupt transition from helping the caller who was in crisis to asking questions about how the volunteer performed as an agent of the hotline.

We introduced a plan where initially only paid staff would evaluate their calls using the new evaluation measure. After a period of time, when volunteers saw how the process worked and became more comfortable with it, the evaluation was expanded to include the calls responded to by volunteers. However, the procedure was modified so that after the volunteers resolved the purpose of the call, they then turned the caller over to a staff member to administer the structured evaluation interview. This change in procedure eliminated the awkward transition that had concerned the volunteers. The evaluation project ultimately provided important information for both the agency and its funding source, and did so in a manner that eliminated feelings of awkwardness and inappropriateness on the part of the volunteers.

PROJECT SCOPE IS EASY TO UNDERESTIMATE, AND IT EXPANDS

Determining the appropriate project scope is always a challenge when negotiating a consulting contract. In our experience, it can be even easier to underestimate the scope of a project with a small agency than with a large organization, since small agencies may have a surprising number of programs for their size. If you have not consulted with small CBOs before, the size of the organization may be misleading with regard to the amount of potential data they collect and the complexity of the programs they offer. When working with larger organizations, there is more likely an expectation of large data sets and multiple programs. With small CBOs, one needs to be more careful about making the assumption that a small agency is associated with a small number of programs and small client bases.

For example, a community-based agency providing services related to HIV/AIDS or chronic hepatitis C may offer programs related to awareness, prevention, testing, treatment referral, treatment, complementary therapies, and support groups. The volume of client contact, even for these small agencies, can be large, and often people in the agency do not realize how large their client base is since they are advocates trying to reach as many people as possible. Our center also conducted a program evaluation with a small grassroots agency where pre- and post-test data were collected as part of an evaluation of an HIV/AIDS prevention education program administered in several public schools. The program included approximately 10,000 participants, resulting in a large data set for an agency of that size.

In the context of program evaluation, one can reduce the probability of underestimating the size of a potential data set by clearly determining the requirements set by the funding agency from the onset of the program and evaluation. These requirements then serve as the minimum requirements for the evaluation. Next, it is important to determine the priorities of the CBO in relation to information it would like to collect. What is critical in terms of future decisions versus what might be useful or interesting? Is it worth the effort, and is it feasible to collect additional data? Also, a sequential data collection strategy where the process is periodically assessed can be used to identify ways to simplify and streamline the data collection process and the amount of data collected throughout the life of the evaluation.

In addition to the data issue, *scope-creep* can be a concern when working with small CBOs. Given the enthusiasm of the people in such organizations, and their capacity for fundraising, advocacy, and motivating volunteerism, there may be more of a tendency for the expansion of projects over time, resulting in the inclusion of additional activities not specified in the contract. Also, because of the significant services such organizations may offer, there may be a tendency on the part of the consultant to volunteer to take on additional responsibilities. The extent to which a consultant is willing to perform activities beyond the contract is a personal choice, but should be tempered with consideration about how it affects his or her ability to function in the role of an external consultant. At some point, a consultant can become so involved in other activities that there is not adequate time for the primary project, or other commitments may be jeopardized.

A further complication that we have experienced is the multidisciplinary nature of some of the consulting projects with which we have been involved. For example, when working with an agency providing services to people living with HIV/AIDS, we interact with people living with HIV, agency employees, volunteers from the community, community leaders, health care professionals, public health professionals, and representatives from funding agencies. This has led to difficulties in communication and decision making because of the differing agendas, terminology, and perspectives of the various stakeholders involved. Learning to communicate and present information to people coming from a wide variety of backgrounds and interests is a critical skill when working with many agencies. The upside of working with an agency with numerous stakeholders is that interesting projects develop, and opportunities for growth and development exist for participants in the project as well as the consultant because one has the opportunity to view and understand issues from different perspectives.

A COMPREHENSIVE FRAMEWORK LINKS CONSULTING, ADVOCACY, AND RESEARCH

Working in a consulting center in an academic environment affords the opportunity to integrate research and consulting work into a more comprehensive framework that involves advocacy, capacity building, action research, and field research. At its best, these activities are not distinct entities but rather different parts of the whole, where the parts are complementary and aimed at improving conditions in the community. If one is interested in using this type of approach to move into a new area of interest, it is very useful to develop contacts in the community, and begin building trust and rapport with representatives from the relevant constituencies. In this section, an example will be presented detailing the steps we took to begin conducting research and consulting with organizations providing services for people living with chronic hepatitis C virus (HCV).

In order to develop a deeper understanding of the HCV community, contact was made with the local chapter of the American Liver Foundation

(ALF) that resulted in the development of a research partnership. In order to spread the word about the project and recruit participants, we attended and/or presented information about our study at a number of events that the local ALF sponsored, including town hall meetings for people living with HCV, support groups for families and people living with HCV, and a conference for midwest HCV coordinators who are charged with integrating HCV programs with existing programs for people living with HIV/AIDS. Through attendance at the coordinators' meeting, we learned about the local HCV task force and advocacy group, and began to attend their meetings. In addition, informal exploratory interviews were conducted with patients being treated for HCV at a hepatology clinic within a large medical center in order to better understand patient concerns and attitudes regarding research and researchers.

Attendance at the HCV task force meetings led to contacts with representatives from numerous agencies providing services for people living with HCV and their families. Through involvement with the task force, we gained a deeper understanding of the issues people face and the constituencies represented in the HCV community, increasing our capacity to work as researchers/evaluators and consultants in this area. After about 8 months, a consulting opportunity arose where we were asked to participate in a community-based health education program. The program sponsors educational presentations for health care professionals working with people who have been living with or are at risk for HCV infection.

Currently, other possibilities for partnerships between our center and the task force agencies are under consideration, and look very promising. Thus, what began as an interest to learn more about a topic of concern in order to develop a program of research, ultimately led to the opportunity to share knowledge, build relationships, and provide consulting services in a new area.

REFLECTION AND PLANNING STREAMLINE FUTURE WORK

Our experience working with small CBOs has been both professionally and personally rewarding. The center we created has been operational for about 5 years, and recently, we have been evaluating what we have done in the past and planning for the future. A significant issue that we have dealt with over the years has been maintaining a balance regarding our workload. The feast-or-famine nature of consulting is a problem that all consultants must deal with, and we have not been an exception to that rule. Therefore, one question we have continued to struggle with is how we increase the impact of our center while maintaining our other commitments as academics and individuals. We have begun to consider streamlining the mission of our center to more closely align our research interests with the services provided through our consulting center. Given our interest in health-related issues, particularly those related to people living with HIV or HCV, we plan to move toward a more health-related mission for our center, and when possible, link research and consulting interests.

In addition, as a means of increasing the predictability of our work schedule, we have considered a heavier reliance on developing and presenting workshops rather than having the majority of our consulting services focusing on longer term projects at external sites. The workshops would be based on some common needs we have identified through consulting with CBOs over the years. There has been interest expressed from our clients for workshops related to program evaluation, program development, capacity building, grant writing, and managing organizational change. Our plan is to supplement our impressions with data collection in the form of a needs assessment to help guide the types of workshops that we may ultimately offer. Finally, engaging the services of more faculty/staff consultants and students is a means by which we can build our own capacity. One possibility we have considered, given the multidisciplinary nature of some of our projects, would be to include faculty/staff and students from areas beyond psychology as partners in developing and presenting the workshops.

Given the educational objectives of our center, it was important to reflect on the quality of the educational experience of the graduate students who have been involved in our projects. Toward that end, an evaluation was conducted based on qualitative interview methodology. The results revealed that the graduate students who have worked in our center have had excellent opportunities for professional training and development while serving worthy causes. Students reported that working with faculty as mentors on a team has been an excellent means for expanding their classroom experience to applied projects that make a difference. In addition to the application of technical competencies, students have indicated that through their involvement in center projects, they have exercised their ability to communicate orally with a wide range of people about a project, improved group presentation skills, and learned to develop professional relationships with clients. As compared to other consulting experiences, our students reported that working in our center led to more client contact, project ownership, autonomy, and the application of theoretical material.

Some of the challenges that students have experienced working in our consulting center were related to their time constraints. Some students found it difficult to schedule meetings with their project team and/or client because of class schedules and research commitments. For some projects, because student time was limited, project teams were large, which made communication and coordination of efforts more difficult than if the teams were small. However, in spite of these concerns, students found consulting in the center a valuable experience, and one that helped shape their future consulting work with small nonprofit CBOs and other organizations.

The experiences of one graduate student exemplify the aggregated findings of our evaluation. She reported that several excellent opportunities were made available through our center that provided the necessary training ground for her to develop her own individual professional competencies to the point where she is now managing a consulting contract on her own. While seeking an interdisciplinary master's degree and serving as the executive assistant to both center directors, constant involvement in center activities and interactions with both directors provided the student with countless hours of professional training and development. And while working on several projects related to HIV/AIDS, the student was able to interact with various CBOs, and receive priceless hours of one-on-one professional training. She took advantage of these "hands-on" experiences with the two co-directors, and was able to enrich her in-class, multidisciplinary coursework, and even earn funds to help defray some of her graduate tuition costs.

The training she received working in the center resulted in the classroom theory being transformed into action in the community. This community work led to the development of a niche for herself doing program evaluation, and to the formation of a network of potential partners with whom to collaborate on future community projects. Without a doubt, the hands-on experiences and countless hours of mentorship helped her define her own specialty, and solidify herself as an independent consultant.

In summary, our work has been well received in the community, and we have provided valuable professional experiences for our students. Consultation experiences in the center have added value over consultation experiences outside the university setting, which tend to be less theory driven, and not as strongly connected to the students' coursework. The insights and understanding that we have gleaned during the operation of our center have served us well, and we hope the reader finds them to be of value when working with small CBOs. We have enjoyed the challenges of working as consultants with small nonprofit organizations, as they have provided ample opportunities for professional and personal growth. It has been satisfying to be part of a center that has played a role in advancing the respective missions of the organizations with which we have worked. We have had the privilege to work with a wide variety of people in diverse community settings, which has been a rich and rewarding experience.

APPENDIX 11-1: Example Center Brochure

page 1

THE CENTER FOR COMMUNITY AND ORGANIZATION DEVELOPMENT

The Center for Community and Organizational Development

North Kenmore Street
Chicago, IL 60614
Phone (773) 555-5555
Fax (773) 555-5555

MISSION STATEMENT

To provide consulting and research services related to clinical, community, and organizational psychology to not-for-profit, community-based organizations that may not otherwise have access to such services

OVERVIEW OF SERVICES OFFERED

- The Center for Community and Organization Development (CCOD) provides not-for-profit service organizations with a wide array of consulting and research services.

- Our services are primarily based on DePaul University's expertise in clinical, community, and organizational psychology.

APPENDIX 11-1: Example Center Brochure

page 2

HOW CAN THE CCOD HELP YOUR ORGANIZATION?

EXHIBIT YOUR VALUE

- Since many community-based organizations often receive funding from government agencies and corporate donations, these organizations must prove that they effectively provide the desired services to their clients

- Most of these organizations tend to focus resources on their clients and do not have the expertise or bandwidth to conduct thorough self-evaluations in order to prove that they are adding value to their community

- The CCOD has the resources and expertise to conduct these evaluations and can help organizations prove that the services that they provide are indeed valuable to the community

PROGRAM DEVELOPMENT

- The CCOD can help community-based organizations in the strategic development of new programs to offer their communities

ORGANIZATIONAL DIAGNOSIS AND DEVELOPMENT

- Provide expertise to diagnose organizational problems, design and implement interventions, and evaluate the effectiveness of interventions

- Assist the leaders of organizations with the effective management of change

- Assess the effect of changes on the existing workforce

TRAINING PROGRAM DEVELOPMENT AND EVALUATION

- The continued success of organizations is often contingent upon providing training for their employees, yet many community-based organizations do not have the time and/or expertise to develop relevant training programs and to subsequently evaluate their effectiveness

- The CCOD has personnel who are able to apply the technology necessary to identify training needs and to implement and evaluate training programs

ATTEND TRAINING CONFERENCES AND WORKSHOPS

- DePaul University will sponsor a wide variety of workshops and conferences related to important areas of clinical, community, and organizational psychology, which you will be able to participate in as a client of the CCOD

HUMAN RESOURCES MANAGEMENT

- Ensure that your organization effectively manages its human resources function by implementing an HR system that includes job descriptions, information for making employment decisions, performance measurement, developmental feedback, compensation alignment, employee development, and career planning

- The CCOD has the ability to design and implement human resources systems

LEVERAGE THE CCOD'S RESEARCH CAPABILITIES

- Utilize the research capabilities of a major university in order to cost-effectively perform applied research

Capacity Building with Faith-Based and Community Organizations: Lessons Learned from the Compassion Kansas Initiative

Sarah Jolley, Scott Wituk, Tara Gregory, Maaskelah Thomas,
and Greg Meissen
Center for Community Support and Research,
Wichita State University

INTRODUCTION

Many faith-based and community organizations (FBCOs) provide support and services to those in need across the United States. Over the past decade, the United States government has started to more formally recognize the assistance of small FBCOs by initiating a variety of programs to strengthen and expand their organizational capacity to provide social services (for a review, see White House Faith-Based and Community Initiatives, 2006). Organizational capacities such as leadership, management, adaptability, and technical capacity have been identified as critical to the success of FBCOs and other nonprofits (Connolly & York, 2002).

FBCOs represent a potential market for consultants who are in a position to provide capacity building support. The purpose of the current chapter is to describe the following: 1) organizational capacity building, 2) working with small nonprofit organizations, 3) steps and strategies for consultants to assist FBCOs, 4) an example of a consulting project that uses an organizational capacity building strategy with FBCOs, and 5) lessons learned in providing capacity building support to FBCOs.

ORGANIZATIONAL CAPACITY BUILDING

Light (2004) conceptualizes capacity building as a process for changing "some aspect of an organization's existing environment, internal structure, leadership, and management systems, which, in turn, should improve employees' morale, expertise, productivity, efficiency, and so forth, which should strengthen an organization's capacity to do its work" (p. 46). The results of a 2001 survey of 1,140 nonprofit employees suggest that employees of nonprofits understand the importance of capacity building for organizational effectiveness. Nearly three-quarters of those responding agree that capacity building involving strategic planning improves organizational outcomes, appreciate the willingness of their organizations to adopt principles of management that are more business-like, and approve of the emphasis on building and sustaining collaborative efforts. Further, responses from a wide range of 318 nonprofits, with missions ranging from services to children and youth, to economic and community development and science, indicated that the majority of represented nonprofits do engage in some form of capacity building, and those that do give high marks to their efforts and the results.

We believe that the framework developed by Connolly and York (2002) is useful for understanding the organizational capacities of FBCOs. This framework categorizes activities essential to operating a nonprofit (whether faith-based or secular) into four core capacity areas: (1) technical, (2) management, (3) adaptive, and (4) leadership. Technical capacity includes an organization's ability to handle day-to-day operations, such as paying utility and rent bills, and managing financial records. Management capacity is described as an organization's ability to utilize its resources effectively and respond to issues as they arise. This includes activities such as creating job descriptions for new positions, revising bylaws, and recruiting members. Adaptive capacity is an organization's ability to monitor, assess, and respond to internal and external changes. Within FBCOs, adaptive capacity can include identifying long- and short-term organizational goals, and networking with businesses and other organizations in the community. Leadership capacity refers to the ability of organizational leaders (i.e., directors and board members) to identify and implement the steps necessary for the organization to achieve its mission. This often includes team building and board training. This organizational capacity framework provides a useful starting point for understanding the organizational capacities and challenges of operating nonprofits, including FBCOs.

WORKING WITH SMALL NONPROFIT ORGANIZATIONS

Smaller FBCOs stand to benefit a great deal from capacity building assistance, and change/impact can often be more easily measured with these organizations than with larger organizations. Also, it is possible to see a measurable amount of change in a relatively small period of time. As consultants who are interested in helping achieve organizational and individual change, such experiences can be very rewarding.

The smaller FBCOs we have worked with have tended to be very appreciative of the assistance we provided to them. Successful capacity building can help in creating positive word-of-mouth, and can also be a source of referrals for future contracts for a consultant. Positive word-of-mouth can lead to additional business and a well-respected reputation. Several local community foundations and larger nonprofits have approached our organization, the Center for Community Support & Research, based on our work with FBCOs.

Furthermore, working with small community-based organizations increases your presence in the community as a resource for community assistance and improvement. Foundations and other funders that become aware of your assistance, and the impact on the work of organizations they fund, may seek to utilize your services to assist other funded organizations as a means to increase the overall effectiveness of their investments.

STEPS AND STRATEGIES FOR CONSULTANTS WORKING WITH SMALL FBCOS

Securing Financial Support As a Consultant

As mentioned in earlier chapters of this book (e.g., Chapter 1, "Before You Begin," p. 8), there can be various financial challenges in working with small community nonprofits. While small FBCOs are often the organizations that most need capacity building assistance, they are also often the least likely to be able to afford to pay for this type of assistance. A consultant can secure financial support from a number of sources, including grants, contracts, foundations, and workshops, and each of these strategies is described briefly below.

Grants and Contracts

In the case of Compassion Kansas (an initiative described in more detail later in this chapter), the capacity building assistance was provided through a grant from the Administration for Children and Families' Compassion Capital Fund. The Compassion Capital Fund, administered by the Department of Health and Human Services' Administration for Children and Families, was created in 2002 and is a key component of the federal Faith-Based and Community Initiative. This initiative recognizes the ability of FBCOs to serve individuals and families in need. Key populations served by these organizations include the homeless, at-risk youth, elders in need, families in transition from welfare to work, those in need of intensive rehabilitation (e.g., addicts or prisoners), and/or those in need of marriage education and preparation services.

The Compassion Capital Fund administers three grant programs related to building the capacity of FBCOs: (1) the Targeted Capacity Building Program, (2) the Communities Empowering Youth Program, and (3) the Demonstration Program. Each of these Compassion Capital Fund programs seeks to increase the effectiveness of FBCOs by building their organizational capacity. Through the Compassion Capital Fund Demonstration Program, intermediary organizations receive grants to provide training, technical assistance, and sub-awards to a diverse range of FBCOs seeking to increase their ability to provide social services to those in need. Capacity building assistance activities are offered at no cost to these FBCOs, and focus on strategic planning, financial management, board development, fundraising, outcome measurement, and similar needs.

Independent consultants may be in a position to attain work through state and federal grants and contracts in a number of ways. First, consultants may subcontract for a specific scope of work or service in a larger grant. It is not uncommon for larger grants to have multiple subcontracts for consultants or other entities. In our work, we have used consultants specializing in legal issues facing nonprofits and grant development. Given that grants often span multiple years, even subcontracts can serve as a good source of financial support, and provide some financial stability to consultants. Many states and communities have professional grant writers' associations and nonprofit associations that consultants may want to join to gain awareness of opportunities, and build their skills and reputation in the field. Other consultants may be in a position to co-write or develop grant applications. While writing a grant requires an investment of time, the benefit of obtaining a grant can provide multiple years of funding support.

Local and National Foundations

Consultants will also find local community foundations to be an important resource when working with FBCOs. Community foundations often recognize the important work of the FBCOs in their communities and are repeatedly asked to support FBCOs directly and indirectly through capacity building. Therefore, a community foundation may be willing to support a consultant to build the capacity of a few local FBCOs each year. After becoming familiar with the mission and scope of a community foundation, a consultant may want to educate the foundation regarding the benefits of capacity building, and the range of services they can provide to improve the skills and practices in FBCOs. Such partnerships take time to develop and may require several attempts in finding the appropriate opportunity to offer consultation. Some local community foundations have "open grant proposals," whereby a consultant may be in a position to partner with several local FBCOs, and propose a capacity building initiative that would benefit the FBCO's services and support the work of the consultant.

National foundations, such as the United Way, represent another potential funding source for consultants to consider. United Way works to "create lasting positive changes in communities and people's lives" (United Way, 2007). This is consistent with the goals of many FBCOs, which also seek to make positive changes in their communities and in the lives of people living in their communities. As with community foundations, a local United Way may be willing to fund a consultant to work directly with FBCOs. Again, it is important to show how your work and the work of the FBCOs will contribute to the achievement of the mission of the United Way.

One potential challenge when having a third party (i.e., community foundation, the United Way) support the capacity building of FBCOs, or any organization, is that the organization benefiting from the capacity building assistance does not make a monetary investment in that assistance. The lack of financial investment may affect their perceived value of the assistance, as the FBCO will need to make a substantial time commitment, as well as be invested in the growth and change in order to expect any lasting effect. At times, it may be appropriate to request that the FBCO receiving assistance make a financial investment, even if it is a nominal amount, as it increases the perceived value of the work and not just the outcomes. This may also encourage the FBCO to budget for this type of assistance in the future.

Workshops

Another potential funding source can be generated from conducting workshops for a small nonprofit organization or a group of organizations. If you find that many FBCOs need the same type of capacity building assistance, and could benefit from work in a group setting, they may benefit from capacity building workshops. You can conduct workshops on a particular topic common to FBCOs, and charge a nominal fee for attendance, or ask a local community foundation or the United Way to underwrite such a workshop. This will allow you to assist multiple organizations, and increase the awareness of your consulting services in the community. Consistent with adult learning methodology, workshops also provide the opportunity to create "learning communities," where organizations can share their own best practices, including what has worked well for them, especially when participant organizations differ in their sophistication, stage of development, or level of knowledge regarding the operation of an organization. Communities of learning allow for mutual engagement and present the opportunity for individuals to reciprocally share what has worked in their own efforts at organizational development, as well as to talk about challenges, and receive feedback and innovative ideas from a community of peers (Wasco & Faraj, 2000; Wenger, 1998).

Strategies to Promote Effective Relationships with FBCOs

As a consultant working with FBCOs, you should be able to customize your assistance to meet the needs of the individual organization with which you are working. Different organizations will have different needs, and different organizations with the same needs may not respond in the same way to a given process. While FBCOs often have similar capacity building needs, the different structures and stage of development of these organizations may impact the way assistance is provided. Consultants will need to be flexible and use multiple strategies to achieve desired outcomes given these differences.

In consulting work with FBCOs, it will be especially important to focus on and celebrate "small wins," as looking at everything that needs to be accomplished can be overwhelming (Weick, 1984). Having all board members attend a retreat and commit to roles and responsibilities, in itself, will be cause for celebration. Helping the organization take one step at a time can help keep the individuals in the organization motivated and optimistic.

In any consulting work, it is good to have a document outlining the scope of work to be completed along with measurable goals/objectives and a realistic time line for when activities can be expected to be completed. In fact, it may be appropriate to develop a phased process that indicates what activities are most appropriate to accomplish before proceeding to other goals. For example, an organization may need to solidify or increase its board participation prior to attempting strategic planning. In any case, a written plan for development keeps both the consultant and the organization on the same page about who is responsible for what, and when various goals will likely be achieved. A Memorandum of Understanding (MOU; see Appendix 12-1 for an example) is a helpful tool, as it outlines the services to be provided and documents the scope of work. The MOU will help keep you, the organization, and the work focused and on track. If your relationship with an organization will be ongoing or long term, it will be necessary to revisit the MOU from time to time to check progress and make changes as needed.

Relationships with small FBCOs can sometimes become more personal than other professional consulting relationships. On occasion, these organizations may begin to see the consultant as part of their "family," an integral part of their organization rather than someone outside the organization. Setting appropriate boundaries will be key to a successful consulting relationship, and MOUs can help with setting boundaries. Another document that may help in setting boundaries and expectations is a Meeting Agreement Form (see Appendix 12-2 for an example). This form identifies who is responsible for what activities and when those activities will be accomplished. This will help participants avoid the diffusion of responsibility that can occur when many individuals are involved in a project. The Meeting Agreement Form will remind individuals of their commitments, and help keep everyone accountable for their various responsibilities.

The particular steps and strategies used, as well as the specific challenges faced, will be dependent upon the unique needs of the organization with which a consultant works; however, in the following section we provide a description of the elements and processes used in the Compassion Kansas project as an instructive example. The issues highlighted above were very much present in our experience with Compassion Kansas. We designed this project to maximize the opportunities and minimize the challenges inherent in capacity building consultation.

COMPASSION KANSAS: A STATEWIDE INITIATIVE TO BUILD THE CAPACITY OF FBCOS

The Center for Community Support & Research (CCSR), a part of Wichita State University's Community Psychology Doctoral Program, has been working in Kansas communities to strengthen individuals, communities, and organizations for 25 years. CCSR's staff helps communities, nonprofits, coalitions, faith-based organizations, self-help groups, and government entities. CCSR provides a number of services to individuals, organizations, and communities including, strategic planning, vision and mission development, grant writing, program evaluation, team building, collaboration, conflict resolution, outcome-based planning and monitoring, evaluation, self-help group referrals, resource materials for leadership development, and self-help group development and maintenance.

Building on our previous work in communities and with nonprofits, we applied for and were awarded a Demonstration Program grant, "Compassion Kansas," from the Administration for Children and Families' Compassion Capital Fund (described earlier in this chapter). The Demonstration Program was consistent with the CCSR's mission to strengthen Kansas through education, leadership development, facilitation, and research. The purpose of Compassion Kansas is to build and enhance the capacity of Kansas FBCOs to better serve Kansans in need. Eligible FBCOs must be small or medium (i.e., annual budgets under $500,000) social service agencies or groups in Kansas who serve or plan to serve the homeless, elders in need, at-risk youth, families in transition from welfare to work, those in need of intensive rehabilitation (e.g., addicts or prisoners), or organizations that provide marriage education and preparation service. For example, through Compassion Kansas, we have funded a youth technology center seeking to foster competence, confidence, and increased self-esteem in their teenage participants. Another funded organization, a home for pregnant teens, seeks to network with similar facilities, and access important resources across the state to help their clients better meet the challenges of teen pregnancy. Still another group, a community foundation, is working to revitalize a dying rural community through the preservation and maintenance of community assets. The objectives of Compassion Kansas include: (1) enhancing and expanding the knowledge base of Kansas FBCOs; (2) providing professional training, technical assistance, and sub-awards to Kansas FBCOs; (3) encouraging and facilitating replication of appropriate models and best practices with FBCOs; (4) assisting FBCOs in seeking additional funding sources to sustain their new successful practices; and (5) determining the extent to which Compassion Kansas achieves its intended outcomes.

As part of the initiative, staff from the CCSR assist FBCOs in increasing their effectiveness and enhancing their ability to provide social services through: (1) direct one-to-one capacity building assistance, and (2) small grant awards of up to $10,000 for organizational capacity needs (e.g., computers, filing systems). These capacity building approaches aid selected FBCOs in strategic planning, board development and management, collaboration, staff and volunteer management, outcome measurement, and other aspects related to developing and maintaining a healthy social service organization as described by the organizational capacity framework proposed by Connolly and York (2002).

Process of Capacity Building in Compassion Kansas

As a statewide capacity building initiative for FBCOs, our work through Compassion Kansas has provided a number of insights about the process of developing a working, consultant-type relationship with FBCOs. The Compassion Kansas process is outlined in more detail below, along with findings from the initiative, followed by insights from our experiences in providing capacity building assistance to FBCOs.

Request for Proposal Workshops to Solicit Applications for Capacity Building Awards

To contact Kansas FBCOs regarding Compassion Kansas and the availability of capacity building awards, we chose a multicomponent outreach approach to build a network of organizations that might be interested in the services we could provide. Our outreach strategies included:

- Direct mailings to FBCOs based on extensive and updated CCSR address databases
- E-mails to key stakeholders across Kansas who are in a position to forward the opportunity to others, including community foundations, the United Way, state government departments, chambers of commerce, and nonprofit and faith-based associations
- News releases to the major newspapers in Kansas
- Compassion Kansas Web site and e-mail distribution list
- CCSR's e-mail distribution newsletter
- Collaboration with a Compassion Kansas Advisory Committee, which had multiple outlets for dissemination, such as conferences and newsletters

Through these outreach approaches, approximately 250 people representing 150 FBCOs attended one of four regional RFP workshops held each year. In these workshops, we outlined the requirements of Compassion Kansas, the key components of organizational capacity building, and the specific Request For Proposals (RFP) form. The RFP form required the following information:

- An organizational profile, including staffing, mission, board, contact information, persons served, and current services
- The capacity building assistance needs of the FBCO

- Purpose of grant, including desired impact, expected outcomes, and planned activities
- A budget and narrative explaining how the money would be spent
- A signature page indicating their agreement to accept capacity building assistance from us if selected as an award recipient and to the terms in the "Guidance to Faith-Based and Community Organizations on Partnering with the Federal Government" (White House Faith-Based and Community Initiatives, 2006).

Selection of Compassion Kansas Awardees

As mentioned previously, the CCSR has provided a wide range of technical support and capacity building assistance to nonprofits, coalitions, and grassroots organizations throughout the state of Kansas over the past 25 years. For this reason, we chose to assemble an independent grant review committee (the Compassion Kansas Advisory Committee), with no knowledge of the applicants' prior work experience with the CCSR, to review applications and select award recipients; CCSR staff do not provide funding recommendations to the committee.

The Compassion Kansas Advisory Committee, comprised of 7 local grant makers and consultants in nonprofit development, reviewed and selected approximately 20 Compassion Kansas awardees each year. Each year, we received an average of 100 applications, and the review committee carefully studied each of the submitted applications that met the requirements of the RFP, and reached consensus regarding award selection. Consistent with the requirements of the Compassion Capital Fund, priority was given to FBCOs that had not historically received federal funding and had annual budgets of less than $500,000. Criteria for selection did not include consideration of the religious nature of the group, nor was there a requirement that participating organizations be recognized as tax exempt, as evidenced by having acquired 501(c)(3) status through the IRS.

Multicomponent Organizational Assessment

After the Compassion Kansas Advisory Committee selected the award recipients, two CCSR staff made initial contact with awardees to gather current organizational strengths, challenges, needs, and additional basic information about the organization.

Following the initial contact, awardees received a more thorough and objective Organizational Capacity Assessment Survey via e-mail or mail (see Appendix 12-3). The survey included an assessment of the various capacities of their organization, including adaptive capacity, leadership capacity, management capacity, and technical capacity. These capacity areas were consistent with the organizational capacity framework developed by Connolly and York (2002). The FBCOs were to complete the organizational capacity assessment survey within 2 weeks. While the majority of awardees were compliant with this request, we had a few organizations that failed to complete the organizational capacity assessment on time. We then began using the first award payment as an incentive to complete the assessment in a timely fashion; awardees would not receive the first installment of their award until they completed the organizational capacity assessment. This has resulted in nearly 100% compliance with our 2-week deadline.

Based on the results of the survey, we created an Organizational Capacity Assessment Profile (see Appendix 12-4) for each awardee that included details about the strengths and areas of the organization potentially needing capacity building assistance. CCSR staff and awardees then discussed specific types of capacity building assistance needed based on the profile. The organizational capacity assessment profiles served as a guide for the FBCOs and the CCSR staff as they developed specific activities and strategies to build the organization's capacity.

Memorandum of Understanding

Based on the organizational capacity assessment profiles, we developed Memorandums of Understanding (MOUs) for each Compassion Kansas awardee. More often than not, organization leaders presented a laundry list of needs and desires. The MOU development process involved negotiating with members of participating organizations (i.e., executive director, key board and/or staff members) to prioritize technical assistance needs, and together we determined what could realistically be accomplished in the 1-year grant cycle. In most cases, this was a simple process, involving an hour or two of discussion between one of our staff members and the relevant members of the awardee organization. Based on this discussion, we customized the MOUs to each awardee, outlining: (1) the goals for capacity building, (2) the assistance to be provided by the CCSR, and (3) the responsibilities of the awardee. A member of the awardee organization then signed the MOU, agreeing to the information outlined in the document. CCSR staff could then use the MOU as a direct tool to revisit on a regular basis with awardees to determine whether capacity building activities were meeting the goals identified in the MOU. MOUs served as an understanding of the needs to be addressed by CCSR's capacity building assistance.

Capacity Building Provided and Monitored

The first way in which awardees built their capacity was through their Compassion Kansas Capacity Building Grant Award (up to $10,000). These grant awards were directed at specific capacity building issues, but the primary way FBCOs were assisted was direct one-to-one capacity building assistance to each awardee for one year. CCSR staff visited each awardee multiple times over the year, working intensely with board members, staff, and volunteers on topics identified in the MOU. Our capacity building assistance included strategic planning, grant writing and review, public awareness, collaboration, 501(c)(3) application and guidelines, board development, policies/procedures, volunteer management, leadership development, and outcome measurement.

CCSR staff tracked their assistance by completing a Technical Assistance Form (see Appendix 12-5) that outlined the capacity building issues addressed during each consultation. We utilize this tool for other capacity building processes on other projects as well, as it provides a useful tool for measuring the assistance we provide, and tracking the outcomes of our work. The technical assistance form was also useful as a formative evaluation measure examining the extent to which CCSR staff were addressing the agreed upon capacity building topics identified through the MOU. This form may help you track the time you spend with each client, so that you can document hours for billing (if you charge hourly fees). Alternatively, if your fees are based on the project, this form can provide a log for your personal use to adjust your fees in the future, in the event that you over- or underestimated the amount of time you might spend on the project. The technical assistance form also allows you to identify the areas you are doing the most work and can help you reflect on topics for which you could conduct larger trainings.

In addition, awardees submitted quarterly program and fiscal reports. Completed quarterly reports had to be received before the second and third installments of funding were provided. Quarterly reporting offered yet another opportunity for our staff to build the organization's capacity in the area of fiscal management, grant management, and recordkeeping, and this was often included as part of the agreed upon technical assistance via the MOU. Finally, awardees were required to attend two capacity building assistance sessions hosted by the CCSR and involving the other awardees, though most actually attended more than two. These sessions provided additional contact with the awardees, and tracked progress on capacity building goals as identified in their MOUs.

If an awardee did not meet the necessary requirements, we developed a customized corrective action plan, working in conjunction with the awardee. If corrective actions were not taken by the awardee, they were ineligible to receive future funding. However, we used this challenge as yet another opportunity to work with the organization to build its capacity, often explaining that such reporting is always required of grant recipients, regardless of the funder, and the potential for future grant funding necessitated that they be able to develop the skills and discipline to file timely and accurate reports. Ultimately, corrective action almost always results in compliance, and only one of our funded organizations was ever defunded or disqualified.

LESSONS LEARNED

We have learned many lessons through our consultation work with faith-based and community organizations. We have highlighted some of the lessons we described in this chapter below as a review.

- Work with small FBCOs to expand your abilities and types of services.
- Provide an organizational assessment to understand the FBCO's strengths and weaknesses. Utilize multiple methods to gain the best understanding.
- If a third party underwrites the capacity building, consider requesting the FBCO provide a small financial investment to increase perceived value and participation.
- Celebrate small organizational capacity wins with FBCOs often.
- Be flexible and willing to utilize multiple capacity building strategies.
- Consider developing a Memorandum of Understanding (MOU) that documents the services to be provided.
- Create meeting agreements that specify who will do what by when.
- Recognize the unique contributions of small FBCOs in serving the community.

CONCLUSION

FBCOs help millions of the neediest Americans address challenges each year, and as the number of these organizations grows, many consultants will inevitably find themselves in contact with them. The majority of these FBCOs are small in size and find organizational capacity building helpful. Compassion Kansas provides an example of a statewide initiative in building the capacity of FBCOs, and allows for insights to be drawn for consultants assisting similar organizations. Consultation to FBCOs provides an opportunity to strengthen organizations to do what they do better, and well-equipped and knowledgeable consultants are often in the best position to provide assistance to them. Assistance to FBCOs can be beneficial to the consultant, as well as help maintain a strong ecology of nonprofits in the community.

APPENDIX 12-1: Memorandum of Understanding

Memorandum of Understanding
Organization A
January 1, 2010

Center for Community Support & Research Background

The vision of the Center for Community Support & Research (CCSR) is that all Kansans use their talents and experiences to create thriving communities. The mission is to strengthen Kansas through education, leadership development, facilitation, and research. As part of the CCSR's Compassion Kansas initiative, the following memorandum outlines the scope of work provided by the CCSR and its consultants for Organization A.

Proposed "End-in-Mind"

The end-in-mind of the proposed activities is to strengthen the organizational capacity of Organization A. After discussion with organizational leadership, it is agreed that the CCSR will prioritize assistance in these areas, targeting the following outcomes along with associated indicators:

Outcome 1: Organization A will increase the adaptive capacity of the organization to monitor and assess internal and external changes.

Indicator 1.1: Organization will engage in partnership arrangements with other organizations in the community/service area.
Indicator 1.2: Organization will begin collecting regular feedback from service recipients on their satisfaction with services.

Outcome 2: Organization A will increase the adaptive capacity of the organization to respond to internal and external changes and opportunities.

Indicator 2.1: Organization will create and adopt a written strategic plan.
Indicator 2.2: Organization will develop plans to put a budgeting process in place that ensures effective allocation of resources.
Indicator 2.3: Organization will develop plans for systems that will help manage the organization's finances more effectively.

Outcome 3: To increase the leadership capacity of the organization to create and sustain the vision, to inspire, model, prioritize, make decisions, provide direction, and innovate.

Outcome 3.1: Organization will create a plan or locate resources to help the executive director or other staff improve their leadership abilities.

Outcome 3.2: Organization will recruit board members with diverse experience.

Outcome 3.3: Organization will provide information to the board so they can better understand their responsibilities and create plans for improving their performance.

Outcome 3.4: Organization will begin keeping minutes and attendance at board meetings.

In summary, the Center for Community Support & Research will:

- Facilitate up to four (4) retreats/meetings of Organization A's board and other identified stakeholders that will include:
  - » Strategic and outcome-based planning and course correction
  - » Board/staff working relationships
  - » Collaboration with other organizations in the community
- Meet with Organization A's board, volunteers, and other identified stakeholders to determine progress, course correct, and celebrate successes related to strategic plan.
- Work with the board and identified partners in creating and implementing a set of board roles and responsibilities.
- Meet with Organization A's leadership in identifying key community stakeholders in the community and opportunities for collaboration.
- Identify projects within the organization that match local and/or federal funding opportunities.

Organization A will:

- Make its board and volunteers available for retreats/meetings
- Recruit all key stakeholders for events
- Host all retreats/meetings
- Provide all food and refreshments needed for meetings
- Provide appropriate facilities for all meetings
- Duplicate and mail correspondence related to meetings
- Be available for conference calls with CCSR to design and create the process

Project Time Line

CCSR assistance will begin in January 2010 and end in December 2010, unless outcomes are achieved sooner. More specifically, the following time line gives an overview of the activities between Organization A and the Center for Community Support & Research.

January 2010	· Complete organizational assessment to identify strengths and areas needing attention, and to help in the development of next year's strategic plan.
February	· Meet with Organization A's leadership to identify community stakeholders who may be in a position for collaboration.
Spring	· Facilitate retreats/meetings with Organization A's board, partners, and stakeholders to develop/implement a strategic plan.
June 26	· Attend the Strategic Communication Workshop at the Center for Community Support & Research.
August 16	· Attend the Volunteer Recruitment and Retention Workshop at the Center for Community Support & Research.
November 8	· Attend the Leadership Succession Planning Workshop at the Center for Community Support & Research.
October – December 2010	· Meet with Organization A's leadership to identify local and/or federal funding opportunities that match with project. Provide feedback as necessary. · Meet with Organization A's director, board, and volunteers to determine progress on strategic plan, course correct, and celebrate successes. · Provide formal organizational assessment to identify strengths and areas needing attention for additional course correction, and to help in the development of next year's strategic plan.

Note: All dates are based on availability of project partners. This time line may change if project partners are not available during any given time.

I have read the above Memorandum of Agreement and do hereby agree to the above agreements.

_____

Signature (an authorized signer for Organization A)

APPENDIX 12-2: Meeting Agreement Form

Meeting Agreement Form
Date & Time:
Location:
Attendees:

Meeting Objectives/Agenda & Summary

1. Agreements from previous meeting (see below)

2. Agenda item 1

3. Agenda item 2

4. Agenda item 3

Agreements From Previous Meeting		
Who	**What**	**By When**

Agreements From Current Meeting		

Next Meeting Agenda
Date & Time:
Location:

1. Agenda item 1

2. Agenda item 2

3. Agenda item 3

APPENDIX 12-3: Organizational Capacity Assessment Survey

Organization: _____   Name: _____

Role in Organization: _____

Please answer the following questions about your organization's ability to monitor, assess, and respond to changes (Adaptive).

Does your organization:	CIRCLE ONE		IF "YES" How Well?	1 = Not Well (Needs Improvement!)				Very Well = 6 (No Improvement Needed!)	
Collect feedback from service recipients on their satisfaction with services?	No	Yes	IF "YES" How Well?	1	2	3	4	5	6
Conduct activities to determine the needs of service recipients?	No	Yes	IF "YES" How Well?	1	2	3	4	5	6
Have strong partnerships with other organizations in the community/service area?	No	Yes	IF "YES" How Well?	1	2	3	4	5	6
Conduct activities (e.g., community mapping, surveys) to determine community needs?	No	Yes	IF "YES" How Well?	1	2	3	4	5	6
Have a written strategic plan (e.g., goals, strategies)?	No	Yes							
Have a budgeting process that ensures effective allocation of resources?	No	Yes	IF "YES" How Well?	1	2	3	4	5	6
Have a written fundraising/fund-development plan?	No	Yes							

Please answer the following questions about your organization's leaders to identify and implement steps to reach mission (Leadership).

Does your organization:	CIRCLE ONE		IF "YES" How Well?	1 = Not Well (Needs Improvement!)				Very Well = 6 (No Improvement Needed!)	
Know and understand your mission statement?	No	Yes	IF "YES" How Well?	1	2	3	4	5	6
Have a board that reviews progress on the strategic plan (e.g., goals, strategies)?	No	Yes	IF "YES" How Well?	1	2	3	4	5	6
Have a board that reviews the budget (with comparisons) at board meetings?	No	Yes	IF "YES" How Well?	1	2	3	4	5	6
Help the executive director or other staff improve their leadership abilities?	No	Yes	IF "YES" How Well?	1	2	3	4	5	6
Have board members with diverse experiences?	No	Yes							
Run effective board meetings (i.e., keeping minutes, attendance, commitments)?	No	Yes	IF "YES" How Well?	1	2	3	4	5	6
Have a written plan in case of leadership transition or turnover?	No	Yes							
Have a board and executive director with distinct roles and responsibilities?	No	Yes							
Have board members who fulfill their commitments and responsibilities?	No	Yes	IF "YES" How Well?	1	2	3	4	5	6

Please answer the following questions about your organization's ability to use resources effectively and respond to issues (Management).

Does your organization:	CIRCLE ONE	IF "YES" How Well?	1 = Not Well (Needs Improvement!)				Very Well = 6 (No Improvement Needed!)
Have 501(c)(3) status with the IRS?	No Yes						
Have written job descriptions for staff positions that describe roles and responsibilities?	No Yes	IF "YES" How Well?	1	2	3	4	5 6
Conduct annual performance reviews for staff?	No Yes	IF "YES" How Well?	1	2	3	4	5 6
Have an effective budgeting process ensuring allocation of resources?	No Yes	IF "YES" How Well?	1	2	3	4	5 6
Recruit volunteers?	No Yes	IF "YES" How Well?	1	2	3	4	5 6
Develop and manage volunteers?	No Yes	IF "YES" How Well?	1	2	3	4	5 6
Have written financial management procedures that provide checks and balances?	No Yes	IF "YES" How Well?	1	2	3	4	5 6

Please answer the following questions about your organization's ability to handle day-to-day operations (Technical).

Does your organization:	CIRCLE ONE		IF "YES" How Well?	1 = Not Well (Needs Improvement!)					Very Well = 6 (No Improvement Needed!)
Have the ability to use functioning computers?	No	Yes	IF "YES" How Well?	1	2	3	4	5	6
Use computer software to keep financial records?	No	Yes	IF "YES" How Well?	1	2	3	4	5	6
Keep records on the number of individuals or families enrolled/served through programs?	No	Yes	IF "YES" How Well?	1	2	3	4	5	6
Keep records on referral sources of service recipients (i.e., referred by another agency)?	No	Yes	IF "YES" How Well?	1	2	3	4	5	6
Use an electronic method of tracking?	No	Yes	IF "YES" How Well?	1	2	3	4	5	6
Keep records on service recipients' outcomes?	No	Yes	IF "YES" How Well?	1	2	3	4	5	6
Keep records on the types of services provided to individuals/families?	No	Yes	IF "YES" How Well?	1	2	3	4	5	6

Please answer the following questions about your organization's ability to offer social services and fundraising (Programs and Fundraising).

Does your organization:	CIRCLE ONE		IF "YES" How Well?	1 = Not Well (Needs Improvement!)				Very Well = 6 (No Improvement Needed!)	
Have plans to increase the number or scope of services offered to clients?	No	Yes	IF "YES" How Well?	1	2	3	4	5	6
Have plans to increase the number of clients served?	No	Yes	IF "YES" How Well?	1	2	3	4	5	6
Have plans to expand services to include a new group of service recipients or geographic area?	No	Yes	IF "YES" How Well?	1	2	3	4	5	6
Have plans to incorporate a new approach to services to improve quality/effectiveness?	No	Yes	IF "YES" How Well?	1	2	3	4	5	6
Have plans to strengthen the organization's ability to evaluate program effectiveness?	No	Yes	IF "YES" How Well?	1	2	3	4	5	6
Seek funding from new sources?	No	Yes	IF "YES" How Well?	1	2	3	4	5	6
Have funding from several different sources (i.e., donations, grants, government)?	No	Yes	IF "YES" How Well?	1	2	3	4	5	6
Regularly submit grant applications for funding?	No	Yes	IF "YES" How Well?	1	2	3	4	5	6

Thinking about all of the capacity building needs of your organization, please describe the top three (1 = Greatest Need).

1. _____

_____

_____

_____

2. _____

_____

_____

_____

3. _____

_____

_____

APPENDIX 12-4: Technical Assistance Form

Organization Name: _____ **Contact Type (Circle one):** In Person   Phone/E-mail

Your Name: _____ **Date of Contact:** _____ **Number of People:** _____

Amount of Time (to nearest ¼ hour): _____

Who was assisted (circle all that apply): Director   Other Staff   Board   Other Volunteers

Other: Explain _____

Brief Description: _____

_____

_____

Capacity Issues Addressed: Check all that were addressed during contact.

Adaptive Capacities	Leadership Capacities	Management Capacities
☐ Collect feedback about satisfaction of services	☐ Mission statement	☐ 501(c)(3) status with IRS
☐ Building partnerships with other organizations in community	☐ Director/staff leadership development	☐ Written job description for staff
	☐ Board with diverse experience	☐ Annual performance reviews for staff
☐ Community needs assessment	☐ Running effective board meetings	☐ Budgeting process that ensures appropriate resource allocation
☐ Strategic planning	☐ Transition planning	
☐ Budget process	☐ Director/board member roles and responsibilities	☐ Recruiting volunteers
☐ Fund-raising/development plan		☐ Developing/managing volunteers
	☐ Board members fulfilling commitments	☐ Management procedures that provide checks and balances

Technical Capacities	Programs & Fund Development	Other—Project Specific Items
☐ Ability to use functioning computers	☐ Plans to increase number of scope of services	
☐ Computer software to track financial transactions	☐ Plans to increase number of clients served	
☐ Records on # of persons served through programs	☐ Plans to expand to include new service recipients or area	
☐ Records on referral sources	☐ Development of new quality/effective services	
☐ Use electronic method of tracking	☐ Plans to strengthen organization's ability to evaluate program	
☐ Records on outcomes	☐ Seek new funding sources	
☐ Records on services provided to members	☐ Funding from multiple sources	

Next Steps:

Who	Who Else	What	By When

Improving Service Delivery and Effectiveness: Taking an Organizational Learning Approach to Consulting

Pennie G. Foster-Fishman, PhD, and J. Kevin Ford, PhD

INTRODUCTION

Consulting with nonprofit organizations is often about change; something in the client organization is not working effectively, and you—the consultant—are hired to help foster the needed changes. Maybe a program is not achieving the necessary outcomes, or a current strategic plan has become misaligned with community needs. Perhaps internal operations are filled with strife and inefficiency, or a new federal or state initiative requires a shift in service delivery philosophy or collaborative arrangements.

In our experiences as organizational consultants, we have found that we are more likely to succeed at addressing these concerns when we can incorporate into our consulting processes guiding frameworks that can both inform our work *and* provide insights for the targeted organizational employees and leaders. Theories and frameworks can provide explanations for why organizational challenges exist, and can help one identify which levers to target in a change effort. Theories can also help to explain why change can and cannot happen, as well as help guide the creation of healthy organizational systems. They can also help reduce blame within an organizational system because they provide an explanation that is larger than current employee behavior and personalities.

As organizational consultants, we rely often on our existing knowledge bank of organizational perspectives and change theories, and also seek additional frameworks to help us better understand and problem solve around a consulting assignment when needed. Certainly, we work to understand the local "theories in use" (Schon, 1983)—insiders' explanations for why problems exist or change are needed. However, we have found that it is the combination of emic (the knowledge of insiders such as employees) and etic (the knowledge of outsiders such as consultants) knowledge (e.g., Morris, Leung, Ames, & Lickel, 1999) that creates the most powerful tool for understanding an organizational system and identifying appropriate change activities.

In this chapter, we describe how we have used one theoretical perspective—organizational learning—in our work as consultants with one statewide disabilities organization. While we often draw upon a variety of theories in our consulting practice, including organizational culture theory, systems thinking, strategic management, organizational change and development theories, and diffusion of innovation theory, we have found organizational learning particularly useful in the nonprofit sector given its emphasis on building capacity for continuous improvement. In this chapter, we explore what it means to consult from an organizational learning perspective, and highlight the following issues:

- What is organizational learning, and why is it needed?
- How can consultants drive change through an organizational learning lens?
- What are key consulting tips when using an organizational learning framework?

WHAT IS ORGANIZATIONAL LEARNING?

The increased push for accountability and excellence that has emerged from funding agencies and community stakeholders has resulted in an active demand for reform in the nonprofit sector. As a result, many nonprofit organizations are looking for better ways to improve their service delivery and effectiveness, and consequently, for consultants who can help them solve their service delivery dilemmas and organizational effectiveness challenges. For example, consider a small nonprofit that provides after-school programming for low-income youth. For the past year, the agency has struggled to recruit youth for this program. The funding agency has become aware of this low enrollment, and has threatened to terminate the grant if participation does not increase. You have been hired to help the agency improve its effectiveness and recruit more youth.

We—the authors of this chapter—have received numerous requests like the one described above; requests from a variety of nonprofit organizations looking for someone to help them "get better," "get more effective," "figure out why things aren't working," or "become more strategic." In our experience, these requests often require an organization to reevaluate its current state and consider future possibilities. Usually, it requires organizations to adopt a continuous improvement orientation and a focus on organizational learning.

Organizational learning has been described in many different ways by many different people. Generally, organizational learning refers to a change in the organization's capacity for doing something new. This definition involves both learning and change. More specifically, organizational learning involves issues such as: (1) analyzing the gap between the organization's evolving vision/values/purpose and current organizational practice; (2) determining what changes are necessary to reduce this gap; (3) incorporating shared knowledge and skills of individuals, groups, and other organizations to approach the organization's evolving vision/values; and (4) returning to analyze the gap in order to continuously improve (Cutcher-Gershenfeld & Ford, 2005).

Unfortunately, given resource constraints and constant staff turnover, many nonprofits lack an efficient learning orientation (e.g., Miller & Shinn, 2005). For example, nonprofits often do not have the time or staff resources to engage in a full learning cycle: collect information, reflect on what they gathered, and act in response to this new knowledge. With the pressures to write new grants, implement new programs, and meet constituents' needs, the opportunities for such reflection are limited. Yet, organizations with stronger learning environments are more likely to be effective (Tannenbaum, 1997). A learning organization focuses on any activity that might help the individual, team, and organization to continuously improve and develop. Thus, the goal of continuous learning is to encourage everyone in the organization—leaders, employees, supervisors, and support staff—to become actively engaged in expanding their skills and improving organizational effectiveness. Learning becomes an everyday part of the job rather than being confined to formal training sessions in the classroom. Employees can learn skills from others in their work unit (cross training), teach other employees in their area of expertise, and learn from one another on a day-to-day basis. Thus, while learning and development are clearly rooted in individuals, organizations can attempt to create the context for a positive learning environment.

As an organizational consultant, an individual can bring this perspective of organizational learning to help organizations improve service delivery and overall organizational effectiveness. Becoming a learning organization is a complex and difficult process of change and development. It requires a firm *vision* as to where the organization needs to progress. Therefore, it is crucial that becoming a learning organization is an integral part of the organization's strategic plan and future vision.

A number of people have identified key attributes or components of becoming a learning organization. Overall, organizational learning occurs when:

- Members convey learning to one another and develop shared understandings (Rousseau, 1997).
- There is a capability to deploy knowledge and demonstrable skills in novel ways, and to deal with flexible combinations (Argyris & Schon, 1996).
- A group of people have woven an enhanced capacity to learn (Kapp, 1999).
- Individuals are working together across traditional organizational boundaries to solve problems and create innovative solutions (Senge, 2006).
- Members find opportunities to learn from whatever resource is available and convert individual information into organizational knowledge (Nonaka & Takeuchi, 1995).
- Teamwork, collaboration, creativity, and knowledge processes have a collective meaning and value (Confessore & Kops, 1998).
- There is an emphasis on training, problem solving, and innovation for all organizational members (Goldstein & Ford, 2002).

These statements provide a basis for understanding what is meant by a learning organization. Underlying these basic ideas is the fundamental notion that learning requires iterative cycles of data collection, knowledge sharing, and collective action (see Figure 13-1).

Data collection is often the first step in creating a learning organization. Data will let you know where your organization stands relative to where you want it to be. Data needs to be collected to form a baseline by which you can measure future change. It can come in many forms. Data can be collected through stakeholder surveys, employee suggestion systems, focus groups, informal conversations, benchmarking of other organizations or departments, task forces, and organization records. The method of data collection is less important than the reason for collecting the data. As a first step in this process, consultants need to work with organizations to identify the organization's vision for change or learning goals, and then

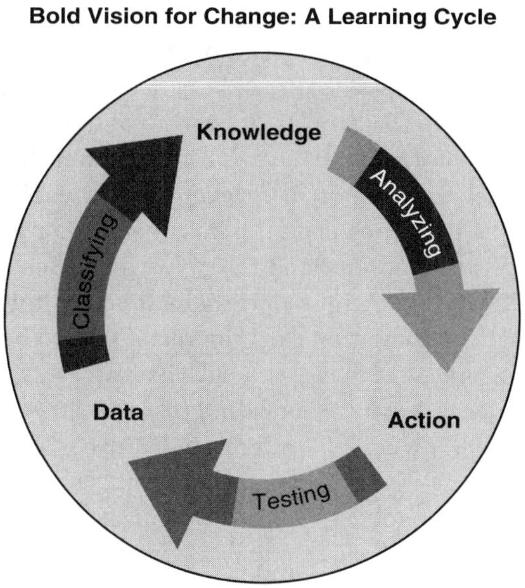

Bold Vision for Change: A Learning Cycle

Figure 13-1 The Organizational Learning Cycle

Source: Cutcher-Gershenfeld, J., & Ford, J. K. (2005). *Beyond disconnected learning: Bold visions and harsh realities of organizational learning.* Oxford: Oxford University Press. Reprinted with permission.

identify what kind of data will be relevant to these expectations. Once the needed data is identified, the organization can work on collecting relevant data and stop collecting any data that is not needed. For example, let's return to our example of an organization providing after-school programs for low-income youth. The organization has struggled with low youth participation in their programs, and has hired you to help the agency improve its effectiveness and recruit more youth. For this organization, a learning goal could become: "Understanding why youth are not participating in our programs." With this goal in mind, data that might be needed could include interview data from youth who are and are not participating in the program.

Linking learning goals to what data is really needed is a critical step in building a learning organization. Because nonprofits face numerous requests for information/data from funders, board members, other organizations, and clients, they often collect reams of information with the anticipation that it might be needed—someday. Until a request emerges for a specific fact or finding, the data often sit untouched in files or on shelves. Becoming a learning organization requires organizations to become mindful of why they collect information and how they intend to use it.

Although data is crucial to becoming a learning organization, it is useless until is it turned into knowledge. In order for data to be turned into shared knowledge, organizational members need to interpret and then agree on the meaning of the data. Tacit individual information or data is more likely to be transformed into shared organizational knowledge when organizational members engage in discovery processes where they, together, challenge existing assumptions, explore patterns and inconsistencies within the data, and cogenerate new meaning (e.g., Argyris & Schon, 1996; Swan & Scarbrough, 2001). Some argue that the best forum for creating such discovery is through the intentional development of learning communities or communities of practice where peers, such as coworkers, spend time together examining their current realities and relevant data to improve their practice (Wenger, 1999; Wenger, McDermott, & Snyder, 2002).

By engaging in these discovery processes, organizational members can reach agreement on the problems in their organization, as well as identify *barriers* and *drivers* to *organizational change*. Through this analysis, they can identify actions to take to reduce the gap between where the organization is and where members want it to be. Once action has been taken, it is important to evaluate whether or not the action was successful. In order to evaluate the results of the actions taken, organizational members must monitor and measure changes that occur. This involves gathering new data and comparing it to the old (baseline) data. This leads us right back to the "data" section of the learning cycle.

From a practical perspective, all organizational learning processes need to be driven by a set of guiding questions that are determined in collaboration with stakeholders within the targeted organization. These questions need to be identified at the beginning of the consulting arrangement, and then continually reexamined to make sure they are still meaningful and appropriate given the insights that have occurred. The case study below highlights an organizational learning approach to change, and the types of exercises used to gather data and foster discussions to facilitate organizational learning (e.g., creating ways for organizational members to generate information and develop shared understanding, and for creating innovative solutions).

HOW TO DRIVE CHANGE USING AN ORGANIZATIONAL LEARNING FRAME

Overview of Case: Disabilities Organization

The Disabilities Organization (DO) is a statewide agency that provides strategic direction and support to the disabilities movement in our state. The DO consists of a number of subgroups that include paid staff and volunteers (e.g., disability advocates, leaders from other disability agencies). Each subgroup has unique goals and objectives, and is responsible for carrying out an action plan that is derived from the overall strategic plan of the organization. This project was designed with the intent of creating an organizational learning environment within the larger organizational context. All of the agency's work groups had lost membership over the years due to a lack of momentum and focus. We responded to an RFP that requested consultants to work with the DO to improve its organizational effectiveness, particularly by enhancing the performance of these work groups. We received the contract and began our effort with the Respite Care Work Group because this group was facing a significant membership crisis and was eager to improve its efforts.

The overall goal of the Respite Care Work Group was to monitor implementation of respite care and other family support projects, and to provide a statewide forum for exchange of information among state agencies, advocacy groups, and parents on respite care and family support issues, as well as explore opportunities to expand awareness of family support services. For example, one potential role for this work group would be to assess the impact of health care proposals at the state level on families with children with disabilities.

We worked with the work group for approximately 1 year. During this time, we engaged organizational leaders and work group members in a series of activities that simultaneously promoted data collection, shared knowledge, and collective action. Below we describe eight steps that we took along with the exercises we used.

Step 1: Determine What the Organization Hopes to Achieve

Before data can be collected, you must work with your consulting client to establish learning goals for the consulting project. This includes engaging in conversations with organizational leaders and other organizational members to determine the current problem(s) or issues that generated the need for change. It is important to note that the problems that are initially identified by organizational stakeholders are not necessarily the problems that become the focus of the organizational learning process. Sometimes, through the inquiry process, a deeper set of issues or the root causes to presenting problems are identified. Whenever possible, consultants should attempt to elicit root causes, and make these issues the target for inquiry and change. We have found the process of exploring current organizational problems through the "Five Why's" exercise a very effective method of identifying root causes. In this exercise, consultants ask organizational members, "Why does this problem exist?" each time they describe a problem. When an explanation is provided, the consultant continues to ask this question, eventually identifying the underlying causes of the presenting problem.

We were called into the organization by the director. In initial discussions with key work group members, the primary concern presented was membership recruitment and retention. To better understand this issue, we spent approximately 2 months interviewing 45 key stakeholders who were familiar with the DO and the respite work group (e.g., key disability leaders in the state, current and former work group members). Interviews lasted approximately 1 hour. Then, through an exploration of this data with the director and work group members, we identified the underlying reasons for the membership problems by considering questions such as: What does this data tell us about the membership problem? Why is recruitment a problem? What issues need to be addressed before membership retention will improve? Through this process, we identified two core root causes for the presenting membership problem: 1) ineffective activities and plans predominated by reactive versus strategic thinking, and 2) few efforts to learn from previous failures and successes. We designed a consulting process that would tackle both of these issues by engaging work group members in a strategic planning process that would help them create a new vision, investigate key challenges, identify key goals for the work group, and develop a strategy for meeting those goals. Throughout all of these activities, we embedded an organizational learning orientation by having work group members consider data, develop integrated shared knowledge, and use this information to design actions and next steps. All of the forthcoming activities were designed to meet these goals. Overall, we spent approximately 6 months on Step 1.

Step 2: Building Team Readiness for Meeting Goals

Team effectiveness in meeting the goals of any change project depends on a number of factors. One useful team performance model contends that teams must move through a number of stages to create oneness of mind, and to move towards unity of action (Forrester & Drexler, 1999). Important steps in creating oneness of mind include orientation (Why are we here?), trust building, goal clarification to provide focus, and commitment or buy-in.

Step 2 of our project involved orienting and building trust when the work group began to meet. Many of the individuals in the work group had never worked together before. A key goal then of this step was to develop shared understandings of each other as a team before moving to creating a vision for the work group. In one exercise, we had the individuals in the work group answer the following questions in order to "discover the talent on the team."

1. What are the key skills, knowledge, and qualities that I bring to this team that are directly related to helping this work group meet its goals?
2. What are the key skills, knowledge, and qualities that I bring to this team that will help this group of individuals function well as a team?
3. What are the "hidden" skills, knowledge, and qualities that I have that I do not think everyone on this team knows about?

After the information was tabulated and presented to the group, the work group was asked to reflect on the implications of the "data" gathered about themselves:

1. What does the inventory tell us about this team?
2. How can the talent of this team be utilized in an optimal way?
3. What talents, knowledge bases, and qualities are we missing as a team, or need to be developed?

Based on this data, the work group had a greater appreciation of the talents on the team, as well as information to identify additional talents that were needed on the work group for it to be effective. Additional individuals who had those talents were then asked to join the team. This process took approximately 3 months.

Step 3: Creating a Vision of Opportunities

A critical step in mobilizing organizational members to change is the creation of a shared vision for what the organization can become. This vision becomes the background for all future learning activities and establishes the ideal state that is pursued. To be effective in this process, a vision must be created by all critical stakeholders. A variety of group processes exist for engaging stakeholders in vision creation (see Holman & Devane [1999] for a nice description of several processes). We are particularly fond of the Technology of Participation (ToP) process (developed by the Institute for Cultural Affairs) because it is designed to develop a realistic action plan from the visioning process, and promote stakeholder ownership for these plans. In addition, this process promotes a learning process throughout all phases.

In the ToP process, a vision is created by first challenging participants to imagine a future of success. In our process, work group members were asked:

Imagine that it's 5 years from now, and you have been contacted by Detroit News/Free Press. The Respite Work Group has just won an award for being the "Most Successful Collaborative" in Michigan. The newspaper wants to interview you to learn about the Respite Work Group's successes over the past few years. What do you want to say that the Work Group has accomplished? What story do you want to tell them? What do you want the Work Group to be known for?" Please describe your answers to these questions in the space below.

Individual responses then became the "data" that was explored, first by small groups, then by the large group. An example of the data included the following response from one participant:

As I look back on the last 5 years, the foremost contribution that led to our work group getting this award was the strides we made in designing and implementing a statewide, comprehensive service delivery system. Wherever a family goes in Michigan with their adult or child with developmental disabilities, they can find adequate supports to keep their family together.

Our work group has had 5 years of strong involvement and representation from a diverse group of people from families, community agencies, different cultures, political systems, and the general population. With state-of-the-art telecommunications, we have come together to develop common visions and values. Through achieving a common goal, we were able to partner with families and consumers, and between agencies to build teams and make resources available that meet a variety of different lifestyles and needs.

The end results of our efforts have been two outcomes. Several times each year, training is provided about services in Michigan. The first half of the day has been dedicated to presenting information and a resource kit to participants. This gives people an overview of the entire scope of services that may be available, shares resources, and avoids duplication. The second part of our day looks at what future needs may be surfacing and engaging in the process once again to look at solutions.

Overall, this exploration of the individual responses (data) culminated in the identification and prioritization of shared vision elements (shared knowledge). We spent 2 hours with the work group members facilitating this phase of the ToP process. Some examples of the shared vision elements that emerged included:

- People with disabilities and their caregivers are aware of existing resources and systems throughout Michigan.
- All counties have quality respite care services.

- A more comprehensive information sharing, one-stop shop information system exists (Web site, 1-800 number) for parents, caregivers, educators, consumers, and agency personnel to call for answers to questions or a need for help.
- A strong parent-to-parent support network exists statewide, connecting parents who have children with similar disorders.
- Stronger networks among mental health, FIA, community advocates, school representative, community agencies, churches, and parents exist, fostering the sharing of resources, a continuum of services, and little duplication.

Step 4: Understanding Conditions for Success

Critical to the successful pursuit of a vision is an understanding of the conditions needed to fully implement the identified vision elements. This often requires an identification of the various systems that intersect with each vision element, and examining how they can contribute to its success. Work group members formed analysis teams around each of the vision elements. Each team was responsible for researching and identifying conditions that needed to be put into place to ensure the realization of the vision elements. They were given 1 month to complete this task. While analysis teams were asked to work on their own to collect relevant data, we supported this process by offering our time outside of group sessions to meet with each team, and help them identify possible information sources. This "data" was then presented to the larger group for discussion and analysis. A final set of agreed upon conditions was generated during this discussion. Below is an example of one set of key conditions generated during this process.

Key Conditions Required for Creating Consistent Respite Care Services in All Counties

- Receptive local policy makers
- Clear service delivery guidelines for all advocates and service delivery providers to follow
- Strong advocacy from the work group to support these guidelines
- Accountability measures are in place to ensure that county officials are working towards the guidelines
- State agencies fund advocacy efforts at the county level (e.g., mileage reimbursement for attending meetings)
- Parents are knowledgeable advocates in the process and are familiar with how to work with county boards and other groups to influence outcomes

- All boards of directors in key agencies have members who are vested in supporting respite care

Step 5: Identifying Challenges/Barriers to Success

Steps 3 and 4 helped participants develop a shared, tangible image of their vision. When these two steps were completed, participants were excited and energized—they could "see the future" and were motivated to make it happen. The question remained, however, why this vision was not yet in place—what's in the way of this vision becoming a reality right now?

To answer that question, participants were asked, first individually, and then in small groups, to identify the obstacles, issues, or constraints that could prevent the vision from becoming a reality. Participants were directed that these should be specific, objective realities that are based on actual experience or firsthand knowledge. Participants were asked to identify at least one obstacle or barrier for each piece of the vision identified by the group. Once small groups identified a set of five to seven barriers that were shared by their group members, they were asked to present these to the larger group. Again, with an eye towards identifying root causes, the larger group used the data from all of the small groups to identify the underlying causes of the list of barriers. Overall, this process helped to generate a shared understanding of the problems the group must face together to realize its vision.

One quick note about the small and large group processes used in this method. Small groups can be formed intentionally (so they include a good representative mix of participants, for example), or they can form naturally during the process. In this consulting project, we let groups form naturally, though we often assign individuals to specific small groups when we are concerned about stakeholder mix in the groups. Different small groups were allowed to form for each step in this process. In general, most of the time during Step 5 was spent in small group processes because deeper conversations and insights are more likely to emerge in small groups (versus a larger group context).

Step 6: Developing Strategies to Overcome Obstacles and Meet Vision Elements

Using the root causes identified in Step 5, the group was then challenged to develop a collective understanding of possible innovative solutions for these problems. Specifically, work group members were asked: "*For each root cause identified by the group, please identify a general course of action which could be taken to overcome or circumvent this obstacle, and lead the group to its vision.*" In small groups, individuals brainstormed possible strategies for each root cause. Then, in the large group, suggested actions were assessed according to how <u>feasible</u> (*this is something we could do*), <u>desirable</u> (*this is something I want to do*), and <u>appropriate</u> (*this would help us achieve our vision*) they were. Actions that met all three criteria remained on the strategies list.

Step 7: Group Action Planning

Some consultants refer to Step 7 as when "the rubber hits the road." It can be relatively easy to get group members to envision a future and identify creative ways to achieve that new state (Steps 1–6). It is typically more challenging for group members to begin to assign and take on specific responsibilities to achieve these ends. Often, during this step, group members become concerned that the ideas generated could mean "just more work." If these concerns are not handled effectively during this step in the process, visioning processes lead to little change. Thus, it was critical that during this step we generated a shared understanding of action steps that needed to be taken, and <u>joint</u> responsibilities around expected outcomes. Toward that end, we again had the group consider issues of feasibility and desirability, continually asking them to determine, "*Who could do what by when?*" and if that request was truly feasible and likely to occur. As should be expected at this point in the process, some participants were concerned about their ability to take on additional responsibilities. As much as possible, we encouraged the group have an open dialogue about this tension. However, we also wanted to help the group move forward with its agenda. For this reason, we worked with the group to develop the norm that while every individual needed to sign up for at least one activity, group members should also keep each other aware of issues or challenges that emerge that might get in the way of them completing that task on time.

Step 8: Building an Active, Vibrant Membership

Voluntary groups—like this work group—are more likely to attract and retain an active membership base when the benefits of participation (e.g., having your purposive or social needs met) outweigh the costs (e.g., time commitment, affiliation risks). At the beginning of this consulting effort, this work group suffered from a significant benefit/cost imbalance. The work group had a terrible reputation statewide for "not achieving anything," and for "burning out" its few group members. Its work was viewed as reactive and almost aimless. It was not surprising, then, that group members were hard to attract or retain.

Given this history, it was critical to develop within the work group a shared understanding of how to sustain these new efforts over time. Through a critical dialogue process, the work group members identified two factors that were important to sustain: 1) the newly invigorated membership base; and 2) the learning process. Together, we identified two processes that would mutually support each element. First, we worked with group members to create a membership development and recruitment plan. This included examining questions such as:

- Who else should be involved?
- How can we broaden the membership base of this work group?
- How should these individuals and organizations be approached?
- How can members stay committed and motivated?

One strategy we used was to survey members to determine what they hoped to gain and learn through their participation in the work group, and embedding opportunities for these experiences into the work plan. We also identified new members to recruit who would be motivated to help carry out the new work group plans.

Second, we helped the group develop feedback processes to help track the progress of their effort, and determine what changes needed to be made to the plan. Critical to this process was the creation of a "Work Group Newsletter" that helped them share their plans and accomplishments with others across the state.

CONSULTING CHALLENGES

While our process with this work group was generally well received, we did experience some challenges along the way. Perhaps the largest challenge was the voluntary nature of the group. Many of the members were already overcommitted advocates or disability leaders in their paid positions. This put significant constraints on the number of meetings we could hold, and the expectations we could place upon group members. At times, we felt that we could have accomplished much more if more time had been available. Because these time constraints were real, we had to adjust our expectations—and those of the group members and organizational leaders—about what could be accomplished with the given resources.

Another significant challenge was the broader organizational context and its reputation within the state. As the analysis teams began to collect information regarding the conditions for success, they became even more aware of the negative stakeholder perceptions of the DO, and how some organizations were simply unwilling to partner with them. For some work group members, the increased awareness of these negative perceptions cemented their perspective that change was impossible. To address their concerns, we helped the work group identify their power and influence within this context, and what they could actually influence. In addition, as described above, we bounded the visioning process in ways that helped the group prioritize strategies that would be feasible and desirable.

AN UPDATE ON THE RESPITE WORK GROUP

We worked with the Respite Work Group approximately 5 years ago. Since then, other work groups with the DO have adopted this planning and learning framework. While the DO is still not as effective as it aims to be, its reputation has improved greatly across the state, and the Respite Work Group is considered one of the best working groups within the organization. For example, work group membership is up, and strategic actions are more common than reactive and defensive activities. In addition, an organization-wide data collection and feedback process has been implemented to help the DO and its work groups become more effective and responsive.

CONCLUSION: A CAUTIONARY TALE

Organizational change is difficult to create and sustain. As consultants, we have succeeded as much as we have failed, and unfortunately, that success ratio actually puts us ahead of many in the change business. We will not expound here on the many reasons why change efforts fail, but instead will provide the reader with some consulting tips that we have found useful when trying to create a learning system within an organization.

Consulting Tip 1: Always Think Systems, and Work to Change the Mindset of Team Members to Also Think Systems First

Systems thinking involves consideration of the interdependency, interconnectedness, and interrelatedness of parts within the organization that constitutes the whole. An organizational system can be characterized by a continuous cycle of input, transformation, output, and feedback, whereby one element of experience influences the next. As a consultant who is focused on a learning orientation, one must be ready to push work groups to find the interrelatedness and interconnections that are critical factors for success. In this way, work groups can better understand key leverage points for improving alignment across systems. In our example, improving connections of the work group with various systems that interface with persons with disabilities, was seen as a critical step in the process of meeting the overall goals of the work group.

Consulting Tip 2: Build Capacity for Active Participation in the Change Process

It is a widely held premise within the change field, those most affected by a change effort should be highly involved and empowered as the drivers of the change process. Employees and volunteers are more likely to support change if they have been involved as the architects of the initiative. For these reasons, when we were hired by the executive director of this agency, we emphasized the importance of having work group members become partners with us in this process. For example, in the proposed work plan we created, we explicitly stated that this change process would only be effective if those most affected by the change were engaged from the beginning in the "driver's seat." We also detailed specific steps in our plan, and how we would involve work group members throughout the process. Throughout the consulting project, we reminded the executive director of the need to be collaborative and, when necessary, suggested a more collaborative approach to the plans she put forth.

This focus on a participatory process allowed those individuals who would be most affected by the change process to determine the goals of the change effort and the change strategies they would implement. It also built their capacity to engage in learning processes in the future, as our process modeled for them how to collect data, transform it into shared knowledge, and create action steps from that process.

In a transformation process, a number of positive outcomes can arise from involving employees in resolving organizational issues and problems. These include increased trust and confidence between leaders/supervisors and employees, increased communication and information flow, more effective decision making, increased self-control, enhanced problem solving, and higher performance and quality goals. Of course, this process of employee empowerment is only effective when the larger system is able to support and allow employee control (Foster-Fishman & Keys, 1997). Thus, consultants also need to consider how organizational leaders will respond when other staff are given the opportunities to determine the processes and outcomes of a change effort.

Consulting Tip 3: Build Leadership Capabilities to Lead Change

Forrester and Drexler (1999) contend that highly effective teams move from oneness of mind to unity of action. The consultant can lead work groups through a series of exercises (as we have shown) to help build oneness of mind. A consultant can also facilitate the development of capabilities to generate unity of action. Nevertheless, ultimately it is up to the organizational members on the team to take on greater and greater responsibility to make change happen. Thus, generating commitment around goals must also include the discussion that making change happen requires individuals willing to step up to the plate, and take on leadership roles such as coordination of actions (e.g., setting up communication and integrative mechanisms), encouragement of efforts (e.g., promoting creativity and innovation, as well as dealing with failures), and maintaining the vitality of the project over time (e.g., focusing individuals on what has been achieved, what is needed to build on successes, and what can be learned so as not to reinvent the wheel). These roles (and others) require multiple leaders to emerge. The consultant needs to help the group identify what is needed to drive unity of action, and to push various group members to accept responsibility for driving certain parts of the change effort so that the burden does not fall on only one person. For example, we used the group action planning exercise to clearly identify what and how, as well as who needed to be involved to drive action.

CONCLUSION

Organizational learning is one of many frameworks consultants can adopt when working to improve the effectiveness of nonprofit organizations. As we have illustrated in this case example, organizational learning ideas can be embedded into other consulting processes (such as strategic planning, as described above). By doing so, we believe consultants will enhance the value and impact of their other change efforts by creating an organizational context that has the capacity to seek information, develop shared understandings, and use this new knowledge to pursue improved actions.

Chapter 14

Consulting in Public Policy

Jon Miles and Steven Howe

INTRODUCTION

If you are driven to use your skills to make the world better, consulting has several attractions, including a remarkable degree of control over the venue in which you work and the problems that you address. We work in the policy arena, which offers many opportunities to satisfy practical needs, even as you aim to be an agent of social change. Policy consulting appealed to the idealist in us, and it may appeal to you, too.

We focus primarily on *public* policy consulting in this chapter, but we also want to point out that there are other policy arenas in which consultants can champion their social goals. For example, there is a market for consultants who can help human resource departments devise new personnel policies for diversifying their management ranks or improving their benefits packages as a recruiting tool. While these public and private opportunities may differ in some ways, what they have in common is that they offer the possibility of influencing the process of making, implementing, or evaluating policies that aim to better society.

There are some features that distinguish consulting in public policy contexts from other types of consulting. The first part of this chapter describes some of the most salient features of being a public policy consultant, and the latter part of this chapter describes some of the lessons we have learned from our consulting experiences. We hope readers will find these lessons relevant in their policy work, as well as other types of consulting.

The first author is the Director of Searchlight Consulting, LLC, in Alexandria, VA. He consults on topics pertaining to child health and well-being for government agencies, advocacy groups, and research organizations, primarily in the context of federal policy. He was trained as a clinical psychologist with a child community focus, and worked on program development and evaluation at the Prevention Research Center at Arizona State University. Before establishing his consulting business, he served fellowships in the U.S. Department of Health and Human Services, where he worked on evaluating the Head Start program, and in the United States Senate, where he worked on child health and early education policy.

The second author has an academic appointment in a department of psychology, while also maintaining an independent practice through which he offers evaluation, policy research, and planning services to governments and nonprofits that aim to address problems associated with urban poverty. He worked for 13 years post-doctorate at the Institute for Policy Research at the University of Cincinnati as a statistical consultant, applied demographer, and program evaluator. Governmental and public clients who initially contacted him for research support often needed help making use of the analytic results, so it was a short step to asking him to participate on boards, task forces, or committees charged with allocation or public policy decisions. After moving into a more traditional academic appointment, it was natural for these clients to continue consulting with him, and from these contacts, his practice grew.

YOUR RESEARCH EXPERTISE IS RELEVANT TO THE POLICY WORLD

Perhaps the biggest barrier to doing policy work is the suspicion that what you do may not be relevant or important to policy makers. But almost any social scientist has been trained to use a powerful tool with the potential to inform public policy: research. Landmark decisions such as Brown versus Board of Education and Title IX were meaningfully influenced by social science research conducted outside of the pressures of the policy process. Similarly, the work of the Ohio Housing Research Group proceeded for several years in a policy-conscious fashion, but without respect to any initiated policy process. All of these researchers attempted, and succeeded, in bringing the fruits of their research to the attention of policy makers, although the relevant policy debate was already winding its way through the legislative or judicial process.

Sometimes, the social scientist's research skills are sought to conduct a study that will directly address a policy issue. For example, after a failed attempt to secure passage of a Medicaid Buy-in (MBI) program by the Ohio legislature, the Ohio Developmental Disabilities Council retained the second author specifically to research the implementation course of

Medicaid Buy-in programs in other states in order to inform legislators how likely it was that MBI expenses in Ohio would be as large as some legislators feared.

This example is probably more what the reader imagines policy research to be. But what is a better basis for public policy, well-established scientific conclusions from a long-standing program of research, or a single study done under time constraints with readily available data? Do not make the mistake of thinking that the best research for policy making is research that was conducted expressly as policy research. Your ongoing research, or even your in-depth knowledge of an established research literature, can have an important impact on public policy decisions, particularly when you couple that expertise with some other topics discussed in this chapter that pertain to using your knowledge effectively.

Consider the matter of transition to employment. We might distinguish among three kinds of policy relevant research: (a) basic research that can inform the policy process, (b) applied research that is designed to support or facilitate current policy, and (c) applied research that aims to influence future policy. Katherine Newman's (1999) work on low-wage employment in Harlem exemplifies basic research. It is impossible to read her anthropology of entry-level jobs in an urban setting and not gain a better understanding of the forces buffeting low-wage, entry-level workers, from which one might then begin entertaining a variety of policy ideas. That kind of research is very different from, say, research that low-income worker advocates might undertake to understand why more low-wage workers do not take advantage of the Earned Income Tax Credit, a policy designed explicitly to reward low-income households where one or more members is earning income relative to low-income households without members in the workforce. And different yet would be research that aims to provide evidence supporting why some new policy would be worth the cost of implementation. There is currently, for example, much interest in trying to demonstrate that universal health insurance might reduce barriers to and increase the appeal of low-wage employment.

Having substantive expertise based on a long-standing program of research is a distinct plus in the policy world, where your credentials as expert are far more important than in the scientific publishing world, with its policy of blind review. And while we do endeavor in what follows to teach you some lessons that might make you operate more nimbly in the policy world, you mustn't make the mistake of thinking that because you have not previously operated in that world, that the barriers to entry are insurmountable.

CONSULTATION IN POLICY SETTINGS

The Lay of the Land

People often refer to the *public policy world*. While this phrase is used frequently, it is also misleading. There is no unitary public policy world in which all the same rules apply. Instead, policy making happens in many different ways in many types of places. Legislatures (government lawmaking bodies) are influenced heavily by electoral politics, but also by a less visible set of lobbying practices. Government agencies must balance wishes of the legislative bodies that fund them, the political priorities of the elected officials that oversee them, and the needs of those they serve. Private organizations, such as foundations and the United Way, devise policies that are calibrated to governmental policies, but do not require the approval of a voting public. Furthermore, some public policy dictates exactly how massive flows of funding are directed (e.g., Medicaid policy), while other public policy is designed to create incentives for household-level economic decision making (e.g., the Earned Income Tax Credit), and these are but two examples.

Very little in our graduate school training had prepared us to understand how public policy processes work—how policies are formulated, implemented, and evaluated, and who plays what part when and where. Instead, we had to learn on the go while at the same time we were trying to be effective within a given setting. Learning while trying to influence the system was particularly challenging because some of the values we absorbed from academia were in direct contrast to the values in our new policy settings. For example, academic research is grounded in the scientific method, and testing incorrect hypotheses is viewed as an important incremental step toward enhancing knowledge. Elected policy makers, on the other hand, are rewarded for being right and defeated in elections for being wrong (Nelson, 2007). Learning about these differences was an important part of our informal education.

Unfortunately, many social scientists receive little or no training in the public policy process beyond introductory political science classes as undergraduates. Those who recognize their public policy interest while still in graduate school should take advantage of academic training available in a number of departments at most universities. We encourage those readers to seek out courses in economics, public administration, and government. Furthermore, many research universities now have interdisciplinary policy research centers, where one might arrange an internship, post-doc, or visiting appointment. Such institutions are often far more open to community-based collaborations than are traditional academic institutions. These opportunities can be a great added benefit when it comes time to start a consulting career.

The more fortunate among you may find yourself at an organization or institution where policy interventions are valued. Urban universities, for example, frequently value civic engagement. There are numerous ways in which policy relevant activities can be justified to department heads and deans as academically relevant. It can count as service, for example. Or your expertise may come to the attention of the college president as a result of his or her serving on a community task force concerned with public education, poverty, or regional development. It may also be the case that your department has academic interests in community engagement. You may be able to arrange an affiliation with a quasi-academic center charged with addressing a pressing community problem, such as obesity reduction, literacy, affordable housing, etc.

For those of you opting to work outside of academia now or in the future, we offer this chapter as a way to understand some important aspects of working in public policy settings. Instead of trying to lay out a detailed map of every public policy setting and what you need to know about it, we provide some important distinctions that help you start to make your own map. Our hope is that as you encounter a particular public policy issue or domain in your work, these distinctions can help you ask questions that effectively inform your approach.

Before we describe these distinctions, though, we want to offer a few thoughts about one of the most difficult stages of consulting—establishing yourself in the field. Many, if not most of you, will have to endure a difficult stage in which few people know about you and what you can offer them, and the bulk of your time will be spent trying to position yourself for work opportunities. While this stage will inevitably be challenging, we can offer a few pieces of advice that may be useful in helping you navigate through it.

Getting Started

Understanding the complexity of the policy world is important for deciding what niches are most appealing to you. But it is equally important when deciding where your skills and expertise are most marketable, because the entry ticket to these worlds tends to be expertise. If you are a researcher, you may have methodological expertise that will allow you a wide variety of entry points on a range of policy problems, but you will often need to demonstrate that expertise to gain entry.

If it isn't methodological research expertise you offer, then substantive expertise in a content area relevant to policy will often be the entry requirement. For example, expertise in child language acquisition will lead people to be interested in what you have to say about early childhood education policy issues. Alternatively, you may be able to provide a combination of scientific and policy expertise that makes you ideally suited for a particular clientele.

If you don't see a niche that fits your expertise, one option is to create a new niche for yourself. Aim to be unique. The second author was trained with expertise in program evaluation. But as evaluation has become required for many funded programs, the number and variety of people who do program evaluation has greatly increased. He was also fortunate to be trained in a program that had strong organization development components, so he acquired skills in group facilitation and strategic planning. And because of his statistical consulting and applied demographic analysis work, he was equipped to work with a variety of secondary data sources (e.g., the census, Current Population Survey). None of these skills is rare, but the combination of them is. So he markets himself under the rubric "evaluation, policy, planning."

Another option is to develop a reputation as someone who can bridge disparate groups. As more people recognize the need to connect policy decision making with scientific knowledge or other highly specialized information, there is a corresponding recognition of the need for people who can serve as communication bridges between the cultures and communities of policy makers and scientists or other experts. People, such as the first author, who augment their formal social science training with a working knowledge of public policy processes, structures, and/or settings, may find numerous opportunities to bridge those worlds, particularly if they are able to cultivate trusting relationships with policy makers as part of their experience in policy.

The hardest part of getting started in policy consulting is getting a toehold, or finding that first opportunity to demonstrate your particular expertise. One option is to identify a particular technical strength you offer and try to leverage it. For example, if you have training in organization development and group process, your initial marketing efforts might focus on your ability to pull together groups of stakeholders and conduct focus groups. A student of the second author developed a group process for developing logic models and marketed herself to nonprofits that she knew were being required by their funders to develop logic models. As another example, if you have expertise in working with demographic data, try to identify planners who need that expertise. Once you have established yourself as having one form of expertise in the eyes of people who can make decisions about hiring consultants, you will find yourself being consulted for other research, as well.

It is important to have a clear identity. People need to know to contact *you* when they need help related to (fill in your specialty here). We know fellow consultants who specialize in conflict resolution, demographic projections, diversity, disability services, evaluation, homelessness, mediation, Medicaid services, and change management. We do NOT recommend trying to sell yourself as a generalist. Try to develop a *unique selling proposition* (USP). Here is an example: "providing high-quality, custom research services to organizations who want to change." Taken seriously, this USP rules out a wide range of research services; it says, "don't call me for quick and dirty projects," "don't expect a cookie-cutter approach," and "don't call me if someone is requiring you to do research; only call me if there is some problem with your organization that prompts you to want to do business in a new way."

If you have substantive interest in such areas as health disparities, low-income housing, or disability services, adopt a snowball sampling approach to identifying key decision makers. The second author saw an article in a newspaper that suggested a city official had an incorrect understanding of some inner city population losses that were occurring on her watch. He corresponded with her and offered to meet with her to explain some key pieces of census data that supported his view. Needless to say, he emphasized how easy it was to misinterpret these data, and how widespread the misconceptions were. She had invited two or three of her staff to join the 45-minute meeting. Several weeks later, her office sole-sourced a demographic analysis project to the author.

Regardless of what techniques you use to establish yourself as a policy consultant, once you are established, you will need to meet the new challenges of navigating in the public policy context. That is when it will be helpful to understand some of the following distinctions, which can hopefully help you start to form your own road map.

GOVERNMENT SETTINGS

One of the first distinctions that helps organize the policy consulting landscape is to differentiate between government and non-government policy settings. Sometimes, you might work directly for a government body to help inform or shape a policy decision, and other times you might find opportunities with nongovernmental organizations that are looking to inform, shape, or even make policy decisions themselves. Either way, it is important to know something about how those bodies are structured and how they function.

While the complexity of governmental settings is daunting, there are three questions that can simplify the landscape and help match your interests to the opportunities different settings might provide.

1. What Level of Government Is Making the Decision?

Is it a federal body? State? County? City? Regional? International? Knowing the level of government you may be working with, and the constituency it serves, can have practical implications. For example, a federal government program is typically (but not always) designed to address the needs of a larger population, unlike a local government program. This often means that federal policy makers need to think broadly about regulations that can work in a wide variety of settings for many different groups, whereas local programs provide more opportunities to tailor policies to meet the needs of specific populations.

The level of the government may also influence the type of work a consultant might typically do. For a consultant specializing in research, for example, government levels that cover broad constituencies (international or federal) often take a less "hands-on" approach to research than local governments. While a local government policy consultation might involve local data collection or analysis, an international research project of the scope that a small consulting group might take on is more likely to consist of reviewing and synthesizing existing research. Thus, deciding what level of government to work with may depend on which type of research or other consulting activities fit your strengths.

An example of the contrast between levels of government consulting may be illustrative. The United States' Department of Housing and Urban Development (HUD) sets policy for how funds such as Community Development Block Grants (CDBG) can be used. CDBG is one of the major avenues by which federal tax revenues flow back to local communities for projects such as low-income housing, neighborhood renovation, and projects designed to promote quality of life. There are requirements for how the money is used that prevent cities, for example, from using all of the funds in high-income neighborhoods. Municipalities have to interpret those federal guidelines, set policy on local use, and solicit the services of partners (such as low-income advocacy groups or neighborhood development corporations) to actually put the funds to use. But all of these uses must be officially approved by the municipal legislators, and then sent to HUD for approval.

At the federal level, a consultant might be contracted to write a report that helps HUD design those guidelines. This could involve reviewing scientific literature that assesses community needs and effective interventions, looking at existing guidelines in related fields or in states that are known to be doing a particularly effective job, and synthesizing and summarizing those into policy recommendations.

At the state level, a consultant might help a state housing authority draft a document that helps local officials interpret the guidelines and determine their eligibility for funds.

At the local level, the consultant can play a critical role in helping local partners figure out what possibilities are in relation to the needs of that particular community, and which choices will arrive at the best results for all stakeholders. For example, one role that the second author played in creating a consolidated housing plan for the city of Cincinnati involved systematically pulling together data relevant to particular topics (e.g., segregation, low-income housing), and then facilitating meetings of stakeholders with concerns about a topic from which came policy and programming recommendations for inclusion in the larger plan.

2. Is the Government Entity an Executive, Legislative, or Judicial Body?

In addition to serving different functions, these bodies have meaningful differences in how they typically operate that may have important implications for a consultant. While it is always wise to understand the communication style and needs of a particular agency, body, or project rather than relying on broad generalizations, knowing certain typical characteristics of the different bodies can be a helpful starting point for gaining a more refined understanding.

One common distinction between executive and legislative branches is that the executive branch is usually made up of agencies and offices that are far more specialized than legislators have the time to be, so executive officials often have a greater depth of knowledge on a given topic. One implication of this difference that will be discussed in greater detail later in this chapter is that brevity is typically in greater demand when consulting for the legislative branch as opposed to the executive branch. For example, the first author has completed writing projects for both legislative audiences and executive branch audiences. While the background research for both was equally exhaustive, involving extensive literature reviews and interviews with experts, legislative policy briefs were typically around 4 pages long while executive agency reports on the same topic were often 20 pages or more.

Another distinction between the executive and legislative branches is that while it is quite common for a consultant to contract directly with an executive branch agency, a consultant will usually interact with a legislative body indirectly by consulting to a nongovernmental advocacy organization or some other group, rather than providing paid consulting for a legislator. Those hoping to do consulting work in order to inform and influence legislative policy making typically need to find nonlegislative entities to pay for their services.

It is also useful to understand that executive branch offices are often staffed with project officers whose primary function is not to carry out the agency's work themselves, but rather to award and oversee grants and contracts to private companies to carry it out on behalf of the government. This can create numerous opportunities for consultants, particularly larger and more established consulting groups, to find work. However, just gaining eligibility to compete for those grants and contracts is an exhausting process, and many larger consulting groups have full-time staff dedicated only to the process of competing for them. For those familiar with the research grant process, it is not dissimilar to the workload associated with obtaining research funding from the National Institutes of Health (NIH) or the National Science Foundation (NSF).

There is also a tension commonly faced by those working in the executive branch that is worthy of discussion. Most bureaucrats in executive branch agencies and offices must find a balance between being seen as impartially serving the needs of their constituents while simultaneously fulfilling a political agenda set by the city council, mayor, governor, or president. Bureaucrats seen as leaning too far in either direction are sure to face criticism from the slighted party. For example, a consultant assisting on a program evaluation within an agency might discover that the governor wants to eliminate the program, while the people served by it are heavily invested in having it continue. Clearly, this puts the agency employees in a precarious position. Consultants who are sensitive to that will find themselves valued for their ability to maintain a sense of impartiality, and choose written and spoken language carefully so as not to appear biased.

The judicial branch may place an even higher value on appearing unbiased than the executive branch. This is not surprising given the centrality of fairness and impartial judgment to the function of the judicial system. While the authors have less experience working with the judicial branch than other branches, to our knowledge, most consulting opportunities found within the judicial branch focus on improving the legal process in some way. So, there is a high demand for expertise about the legal system itself, and much lower need for expertise about particular social science content areas.

The second author's work with the Ohio adoption system can be used to illustrate working with the judicial branch to improve the judicial process. The Department of Job and Family Services implemented all programming for foster care and adoption in Ohio. The state was under heavy pressure from the federal government to increase the number of children who were adopted within 36 months from the time of their removal from the home. Without improvements in this rate, the state stood to see federal funding levels fall.

A key legal milestone in the process of adoption is that of terminating parental rights so the work of placing the child for adoption can proceed. Obviously, such a decision as the termination of parental rights is often difficult, and wishing to be as fair as possible to everyone, judges would routinely put the matter off, granting extensions for any reason, and granting longer extensions than might have been necessary. A system had evolved in which the termination phase consumed such a large proportion of the 36 months that it was often literally impossible to finalize an adoption in the time remaining. Once those judges understood that those delays were going to cost the state potentially millions of dollars that could be used for adoption and foster care, they became convinced that changes were needed. Interestingly, however, because judges operate with a large degree of autonomy, it was not enough to convince one overseeing administrator what needed to change. Instead, it was important to convince each individual judge.

There is a very different way a consultant can also become engaged in the judicial system, and this is to end up involved on one or the other side in civil actions brought by advocacy groups. Here, the greatest shock for the consultant/researcher will be to learn by experience how the adversarial litigation system works. You will not be responsible for forming a nuanced, balanced decision; rather you will be affiliated with a team of advocates charged with presenting the strongest possible case for one side in the litigation, and you will learn that opposing advocates are not responsible for evaluating the evidence you have to put forth, but for discrediting it.

The second author has testified, though only at the deposition stage, in a half-dozen civil actions brought by advocacy groups. He found the work exhausting and unfulfilling, even when his side won, and now he avoids such projects assiduously. Somewhere between these two activities—a consultant to the judiciary and a consultant to an advocacy organization in support of a civil action—there may be a third opportunity to contribute to the judicial process via amicus curia briefs. These briefs are often used to inform a court about an aspect of a case that might otherwise be overlooked, and they are submitted only when all parties agree that they are warranted. Although courts do not pay for these briefs, an organization that feels it is in its best interest to submit one may seek a consultant's help in preparing such a report. Alternatively, a consultant may feel that there is some other benefit to writing such a brief, such as building a connection with the organization submitting it. Nevertheless, while such opportunities may occur from time to time, using them as the basis for a consulting practice strikes us as a difficult challenge.

3. What Type of Decision-Making Process Is Going on in This Setting?

Within each branch of government and at every level of government, there are multiple processes going on at any given time. The role a consultant might play in each process can be quite different. For example, at the federal legislative level, congress divides much of their work into *authorization* or *appropriation* processes. Generally, the authorization process is where a program gets conceptualized, designed, and described, and a dollar figure gets attached that suggests how much *should* be spent to implement it. The appropriation process, which is overseen by different committees than those who did the authorizing, involves allocating actual funds each year to support that program. Sometimes, appropriators fund programs at higher levels than were authorized, and sometimes they don't fund them at all. There is more to understand about these processes, as well as the legislative process in general (such as the difference between a briefing, a hearing, and a markup session).

A consultant who steps into the authorization process might be asked to come up with ideas for a health program, or report on what is known about an education program idea. A consultant working in the appropriations process may be more likely to provide justification or persuasive arguments for why those programs should get more (or less) money. Success in the appropriations process is generally evaluated by the ability to secure funding, and some argue that it is based more on connections with hard-to-access appropriators than with strong factual or theoretical arguments. In contrast, success in the authorization process is often assessed by a combination of the quality of the programs/policies being authorized and the ability to get them approved, and while connections are still important, ability to provide high-quality, substantive input is also valued.

The federal legislative level can also be divided into processes another way. *Long-term policy formation* is a process that involves in-depth development of a policy priority of a particular member of congress. For this process, a consultant working for an advocacy group might be expected to provide detailed analysis over a long period of time, and there may even be multiple iterations of feedback and revision of policy recommendations or actual legislative language.

Short-term policy formation involves developing policy quickly in response to current events, such as Hurricane Katrina, or the recent economic downturn spurred by the housing bubble. Sometimes the response is needed within days; sometimes all you have is hours. In these instances, a consultant may need to draw on easily accessible information to provide timely analysis, and the information may be reported verbally or in a written form as brief as a paragraph, and no formal report may be required. This means there may be little or no opportunity for a feedback process. In order to add value to this process, the consultant would have to: (a) be available, (b) bring a pre-existing store of relevant expertise or knowledge to the task, and (c) have a pre-existing understanding of the capabilities and limitations of the relevant executive agencies. These criteria help to explain why former executive branch members are in high demand for this type of consulting.

Policy promotion occurs once a congressional office has completed the formation process and made up their minds about what course of action to take. In this process, a consultant may be expected to provide analysis about how to get the policy approved, rather than determine what it should include. While a consultant may be involved in any or all three of these processes, it is important for the consultant to have a clear understanding of which one he or she is involved with at any given time.

NONGOVERNMENT SETTINGS

As stated previously, there are many public policy consulting opportunities outside of government settings. These opportunities typically occur with one of two types of nongovernmental organizations (NGOs) that affect public policy directly. First, there are advocacy organizations that are dedicated to influencing government policy decisions. Examples include the Children's Defense Fund (CDF), the National Association of School Psychologists (NASP), the Center for Science in the Public Interest (CSPI), and the National Rifle Association (NRA). For these organizations, their primary, or maybe even sole, reason for existence is to advocate or campaign for policies that are consistent with the values they promote. This category primarily includes lobbyists and public-interest advocacy groups.

Second, the other NGOs with explicit public policy interests are classified as operation/implementation NGOs (Duke University Libraries, 2007;

Maslyukivska, 1999). They are organizations that provide programs, activities, or projects that have significant public impact. Examples include the United Way, Oxfam, Amnesty International, the Red Cross, Bread for the World, and Save the Children. Because their activities are so directly linked to the public interest, their policy decisions about how to spend money and how to operate are inherently public policy decisions.

Beyond the division into these two categories, it is difficult to organize how these groups differ structurally and functionally, and how that affects the services they might seek from a consultant. It is particularly challenging because there has been an exponential increase in the numbers of NGOs in the past 25–50 years or so, and an accompanying proliferation of different models by which they operate. Nevertheless, it is safe to say that both types of groups may seek a wide range of services from a consultant who can help them achieve their goals.

From our experience, consulting activities for an advocacy group can entail writing policy briefs for legislators, the media, and the public, representing the group's membership or leadership in various settings, keeping the group informed about policy issues, engaging members in activities that influence policy makers, gathering and maintaining data about membership expertise and policy-maker involvement on given issues, training members to communicate effectively with policy makers, and linking different organizations to each other. What may be apparent from this list is that while social science expertise can be an important asset, advocacy work places a particularly high priority on legislative expertise. While there are a number of ways to cultivate this expertise, spending time as a staff member for a legislator can be a valuable building block for a consulting career in the advocacy arena. Fortunately, there are fellowship opportunities at the federal level, and the number of social scientists currently working in congressional offices suggests there is more awareness of the value of having a social scientist on staff than ever before.

Other activities that could apply to both types of NGOs may include grant writing, data analysis, report writing, including policy briefs or research summaries, organizing and preparing briefings for policy makers, and speaking or providing training sessions to organization membership.

For example, the United Way of Greater Cincinnati wished to develop a Success by Six© program. They needed a consultant to identify stakeholders, who in turn could help identify opportunities for programming. The second author met extensively with United Way staff to identify stakeholders, and then facilitated several large meetings with stakeholders to bring their collective expertise to bear on the project. An exciting idea that one of the groups developed was that of shifting some of the responsibility for children from households that were economically stressed to some kind of larger community; that is, to create "success communities" in which any child might benefit from the kinds of support and stability that children in high-functioning families take for granted. Success communities might be church-based, school-based, or even block-based. The intervention was specifically designed to keep responsibility for the child with the consumer population, and not to create a "professional intervention" model, which might have had the unintended consequence of conveying to consumers that professionals regarded them as incapable of raising their children.

A second example comes from the Legal Aid Society of Greater Cincinnati, an advocate for expansion of the Medicaid program in Ohio to include coverage for children in families with incomes up to 150% of the poverty level. They needed a consultant to develop budget projections (i.e., estimate the cost of the expanded coverage). It is critically important to understand that efforts such as these involve large numbers of people, and that your role as a consultant, however important, is only one of many important roles. In this case, the idea for Medicaid expansion came to Ohio as a result of Legal Aid Society attorneys from Cincinnati attending a workshop sponsored by the DC-based Center on Budget and Policy Priorities. Together with like-minded lobbyists from a variety of statewide groups concerned with poverty, the attorneys began crafting a proposed bill for consideration in the Ohio legislature. Only after this process was well along did they contact the second author in hopes of securing some estimates of the number of people who would be affected by the proposed legislation. As it happened, the census data was current enough to be relevant. The consultant worked closely with staff in the Ohio Department of Job and Family Services to estimate program participation rates. Because the staff viewed the consultant's work as rigorous, they were willing to critique it and offer suggestions. The result was a budget impact analysis that the advocates for the new legislation were able to present to legislators as having been vetted by the state. The legislators initially balked at the expense of the proposed program, the lobbyists scaled the program back, the consultant provided new impact numbers, and the legislation was approved.

A third example comes from Washington, DC. A major national association had been approached by congressional offices looking for policy ideas in response to public events that highlighted problems that threaten child well-being. At the time, the national association was undergoing staffing transitions, so they decided to farm the project out to a consultant, and contacted the first author at Searchlight Consulting. The project entailed communicating with experts from within the association, conducting a literature review, synthesizing current knowledge around the child well-being topics, and making recommendations for potential legislation. Those recommendations, as well as much of the background information, were presented to the congressional offices for use as the basis of legislation in a future session.

SEVEN DISTINCTIONS BETWEEN ACADEME AND POLICY SETTINGS

While the above questions help one start to understand the layout of the policy making worlds, and the wide range of entry points for consultants, there are also some generalizations about policy settings that can be useful for potential consultants to think about. These traits tend to distinguish policy settings from other settings to a large degree, but they also tend to be in direct contrast with the culture of academia, a world with which many consultants will be much more familiar. As with all generalizations, it's important to remember that they don't apply in every case. When encountering a new potential consultation opportunity in a policy setting, it's probably better to think of these as generalities to consider as you assess the situation rather than as replacements for that assessment. With this disclaimer in mind, the following are seven characteristics of policy settings that we, and others, have found useful to know.

1. Time

First, the concept of time means something different in policy settings than it does in academia or, in some ways, any other setting. While government decision making can be a notoriously slow process (the federal executive branch's penchant for a slower pace and verbosity is widely recognized), the day-to-day activities of policy decision makers can also move at a breathtakingly fast pace, regardless of the policy-making setting. Additionally, policy-making processes are largely influenced by current events, so that something getting no attention one day might be priority number one the next day, bumping everything else into the background at least temporarily.

The legislative process is particularly volatile since it is subject to obscure rules and political gamesmanship that drive legislative agendas and voting schedules, as well as sudden media attention to given issues. It's not at all unusual for legislative staff members in Washington to make a call to an advocacy group, think tank, or other resource person that sounds like, "Hi, I need to know how many people would be affected by XX and I need to know it in the next 2 hours. Can you do that?" Responses that come back more than 2 hours later may be worthless. (We get asked these kinds of questions fairly frequently, and as long as the amount of work involved is brief, tend to write it off as nonchargeable activity or, more grandly, as client relations.) Less dramatically, but just as importantly, a commissioned policy study that was expected to yield results before the conclusion of a legislative session may be irrelevant if those results don't meet that deadline.

Funding agencies in the federal government, as well as in other levels of government and the private sector, often have rigid deadlines for the submission of reports. This is quite a contrast from much of academia, in which many deadlines are self-imposed, and even some fixed ones have some degree of flexibility. The Department of Housing and Urban Development (HUD), for example, will not release Community Development Block Grant funds, HOME Investment Partnership funds, or Emergency Shelter Grant (ESG) funds until a municipality submits a Consolidated Plan, and since many local programs/organizations are dependent upon the continuous flow of those dollars, a late policy report can cost people jobs in a way a late journal article cannot. Those uncomfortable with these kinds of pressures will want to think twice before taking on consulting projects with such high stakes.

The time pressures are not just for the production of reports. Harried bureaucrats may not initiate the contracting process in a timely fashion. This leads to a lot of sole-sourced contracts, and if there is a bidding process, the consultant is likely to find that the deadline for a proposal is extremely short. Our experience has been that the higher the level of the government, the more the proposal process comes to resemble what academicians are used to.

Furthermore, the political nature of legislative bodies typically rewards resolving issues quickly and with immediate benefit over thoroughness and long-term effectiveness. The need to get reelected requires legislators to prioritize keeping constituents happy in the short term. Similarly, the need to simultaneously address a wide range of issues means that legislators rarely have time to delve into an issue in great depth. This has implications for how a consultant should present information to legislators or their designees: effective verbal or written messages are short, background information is limited, and the focus is usually on conclusions or recommendations.

When working with policy audiences, the short turnaround times, short attention windows, and firm deadlines have two main implications. One is that conciseness is valued above depth and precision. Ideas need to be conveyed quickly, and that can pose a difficult challenge for consultants working on highly complex issues. The inevitable executive summary at the front of a policy report plays a fundamentally different role from that played by an abstract in a scientific article. Scientists use abstracts to decide whether or not to read the article. Sage consultants use executive summaries to make certain that key decision makers who do not have time to wade through a report: (a) get all the key ideas in the report, and (b) are never surprised by someone who has read the entire report. Because policy decision making often uses communication as a tool of persuasion rather than information, there are times that conciseness can even take priority over accuracy, and a consultant must find the line between maintaining scientific integrity and maintaining relevance.

The other implication of the tight time frames is that while written communication is still vital, verbal and face-to-face communication are valued more highly in policy settings. Phone calls, one-on-one meetings, presentations to small and large groups, and testimony at hearings and briefings are all central to the functioning of policy settings. Scientists working in the policy arena do need to learn that policy audiences do not "play fair" according to the rules of scientific review. The second author once tried to argue that the paltry federal sums available for low-income housing virtually dictated that city officials should use those funds in an attempt to stimulate private development dollars for low-income housing. Just spending them without regard to leverage opportunities would literally be a waste since more assisted units would decline in value than would be renovated or built in any given period of time. Several (but fortunately not a majority) legislators heard that as proof that accepting any spending federal funds for low-income housing was a waste of time. The clichéd reclusive scientist, writing prolifically but never being seen, and always expecting that his or her writings will be parsed objectively, is a fat target for policy advocates for contrasting views.

2. Communication Style

Second, while this is also true for other types of consulting, there are many communication differences between policy consulting and the academic world that are helpful to understand. Even the language style used in policy settings is quite different from that used within scientific communities. Policy makers often prefer broad, evocative, accessible language to technically precise verbiage. This can be a tall challenge for someone accustomed to writing for scientists.

Additionally, scientific articles emphasize the introduction/background and methodology sections, and are full of caveats about the limitations of the findings and the statistical probability that the findings are not due to chance. Often, policy makers already have some ambivalence about the role of science influencing the decision-making process, and that type of depth and ambiguity just adds to their negative perceptions. If there are all these doubts and limitations about the findings, then why are you wasting their time? They want to see the results and implications, not the background and methodology, and this affects how consultants need to organize reports, and limit descriptions of methodology and statistical information. Be concrete. Consider stating your conclusions up front, and then supporting them with concisely stated facts. Avoid statistically complex statements. Define terms in context. And then tell your reader why what you just explained to them is important.

3. Role of Science

The third distinguishing characteristic of policy settings has to do with this notion of policy makers' ambivalence about the role of science/empiricism in policy. Scientists often feel that if only the decision makers understood the empirical facts, then the correct policy decision, as viewed by the scientists, would follow. They are surprised to learn that many policy makers already know what option the empirical evidence supports, and still select a different option. One clear example is that the DARE program continued to be one of the most widely used school interventions long after the scientific evidence began to suggest it was ineffective, or even detrimental, in its attempt to reduce teen drug use (West & O'Neal, 2004).

Ultimately, policy decisions are based on more than evidence. Empirical arguments may be downplayed if someone is making an effective morals-based, values-based, or political argument. Therefore, if you go in thinking you "have the numbers," you may be shocked to discover that your intended audience doesn't think the numbers are relevant. One challenge for potential policy consultants is to understand and accept this fact without allowing it to loosen the scientific standards you are using to evaluate the evidence. Arguing too vehemently may lead to being viewed as a technocrat who should be ignored, while being too agreeable may require compromising scientific standards.

4. Politics

The fourth characteristic pertains to partisanship. In policy worlds, things are often viewed through partisan lenses, whether that be formal Democrat versus Republican partisanship, or more subtle distinctions, such as taking sides in a conflict over which agency should have jurisdiction over an issue. Consultants, simply by virtue of who they work for, can run the risk of being seen as partisan. Of course, you might make a calculated choice to ally yourself with a particular group or viewpoint, either because you feel it will actually help you professionally to be seen as partisan in some way, or because you have strong personal convictions that lead you to that choice. Nevertheless, such a choice may have unforeseen consequences, so it should not be undertaken lightly. Many consultants will tell you that guarding against being seen as partisan whenever possible is worthwhile. Although perhaps atypical, we know people who have been deemed "unreliable" due to modest political contributions.

5. Confidentiality

These final three characteristics of policy settings are somewhat more logistical in nature. The first of them pertains to the notion of confidentiality. While researchers typically place a high priority on sharing information, policy makers take great care to control the messages that come from their offices. Reports that you write may not become publicly shared, particularly if what you report is inconsistent in some way with the views of your client. In some instances, even the fact that you are working on a project may be confidential. This can pose a particular challenge when you are getting started as a consultant, and you want to be able to include the work you produce as part of your promotional materials and vita. The best time to clarify and negotiate the disclosure limits of your work is before you sign the contract.

6. Authorship

Even if your work is not deemed confidential, consultants are often a small part of a very big process. Policy reform generally has a lot of parents, and your role may be an exceedingly modest one, even if critical. Legislators, of course, want credit for new legislation, but even leaving them out of the equation, the advocacy efforts necessary to effect policy reform generally involve lots of people. If there are published reports to be released as a result of your work, authorship decisions can get quite complex. Some agencies will want the agency name attached to the report rather than the names of the authors. Others may want to attach your name to it as a way to distance themselves from a controversial publication.

Getting your name on some work can be positive, depending on your situation, because it can provide evidence of your work; however, for some types of consulting, such as advocacy work, it may be less important, particularly in relation to the value of personal connections. Regardless of how you feel about these matters, once again the time to discuss them is prior to signing a contract.

7. Billing

One final characteristic pertains to billing. Some government agencies have legal restrictions that dictate the payment of consultants/contractors. Daily rates or hourly rates may be presented to you as predetermined. In such cases, you may need to decide if those rates are acceptable and turn down the work if they are not acceptable. Sometimes, however, there are lesser-known mechanisms for achieving greater payment flexibility within an agency. For example, an agency with a low, fixed daily rate may have more flexibility to provide reimbursement for overhead costs or other expenses. As you become more knowledgeable about consulting in your particular areas, you may learn about some of these options, and consider them as an alternative to flatly rejecting the opportunity.

LESSONS LEARNED THAT MAY APPLY TO OTHER CONSULTING SETTINGS

Thus far, we have focused on helping potential public policy consultants understand more about what that work entails. In addition, though, we learned some valuable lessons from starting our consulting businesses that may have relevance for consultants in all settings. Some of these may seem commonsensical. In hindsight, many of them did to us, too. Nevertheless, we would have found it helpful to be reminded of these four points at different times along the way. Our hope is these tips will help readers learn from our mistakes.

Going to Meetings Is a Good Idea

Most consulting businesses need to market themselves to become known and attract work opportunities. The word *marketing,* to us, conjures images of Web sites, logos, and advertising, all of which can be vitally important. However, we found that marketing can also take a much simpler form. In public policy, there are many public meetings and forums that bring policy makers and advocates together. Often, they are promoted as educational briefings, releases of new study findings or reports, or chances for public comment on government policy changes. Each of these provides opportunities to be seen and identified with your consulting role. At one meeting of an Institute of Medicine panel, audience members were invited to comment on the issue of food marketing to children. One person who identified himself as a consultant rose to speak. His appearance, the content of what he said, and his presentation style all demonstrated that he had anticipated this opportunity, and prepared himself exceptionally well for it. After the comment time, panelists sought him out for further conversation. Not surprisingly, this person can now be seen on numerous national media outlets speaking on child health issues. His talent and his expertise are what drive his success, but his ability to use public meetings to be seen and heard likely hastened it.

Sometimes, setting up meetings can also lead to unexpected opportunities. The first author, for example, helped initiate a meeting that led to such an opportunity. During his fellowship in a senate office, he worked on legislation that generated a report from an executive branch agency, but at the time he left the senate, the report had not been completed. As an unaffiliated party, he continued to follow up with the executive branch officials to inquire about progress on the report and, in order to generate anticipation for the report, facilitated a meeting between those officials and some of the advocacy groups that would be interested in what the report had to say. The relationships formed from the ongoing contact with these parties eventually opened the door to a consulting project.

Think Like a Consultant

The earlier section of this chapter explains a lot about the cultures of different policy settings. However, there is also a consulting/contracting culture to comprehend. In this culture, the central idea is to always be on the lookout for work opportunities. While new consultants may hesitate to appear too mercenary, it is important not to appear indifferent instead. Contractors who expect consultants to be eagerly seeking work may interpret hesitation as lack of interest.

For example, shortly after starting his business, the first author was attending a planning session of academic and government experts who were shaping a major report for an executive branch agency. The contractor who was charged with writing the report knew the first author was a consultant, and asked him what kind of involvement he would like to have with the project as it moved forward. Unfortunately, the first author was still thinking like an academic rather than like a consultant. He replied that he was excited to be a part of the team of thinkers working to shape the report, and kept the conversation focused on the report content area.

The contractor seemed somewhat confused and surprised by that response. It didn't occur to the first author until later that this might have been an opening to secure paid work.

Business Plans

Business plans and purposeful marketing strategies, such as those discussed in Chapter 7, "Running Your Business," can be vitally important to cultivating success in consulting. However, that doesn't mean that this is the only way consulting businesses get started. The first author, for example, actually started his consulting business when conversations with a colleague led to an opportunity for a contract to do some collaborative work. While working on that contract, he began to feel the need to develop a thorough business plan and a marketing strategy. However, since his picture of what he wanted to do was still emerging, the prospect of developing such a plan seemed daunting and overwhelming.

Meanwhile, more work opportunities became available through other personal contacts, and quickly, he had two more projects. Soon, taking the time to develop his business plan began to interfere with his progress on the projects he had, so he set the planning aside for a time. Since then, a small but steady stream of contracts has continued to fill his time, and with each successive project his work and business concept have become more clearly defined. Admittedly, this is not a model that we would recommend for others to follow, but it may be helpful to remember that not every consulting business emerged the same way, and sometimes it may be okay to delay some of the organizing process, particularly if work is already being generated.

Identity

Even if you do not have a business plan, it is crucial that you are able to explain to people what you do, and what the limits of your expertise are. We mentioned earlier that you do not want to advertise yourself as being able to do it all, and that knowing what projects to say no to can be liberating. But it is worth repeating here in terms of building a practice, because you should have a tag line, or a very brief description of your services that people will remember and associate with you. You need to advertise in some capacity. It can be as subtle as a few key words on your business card, it can be a Web site, or it might even be a brochure. But, people have to know how to contact you, and why.

CONCLUSION

Building a career as a policy consultant has many similarities to building other kinds of careers to which you might aspire, such as a career as a researcher, or an academician. You must have some demonstrated area of expertise—something to sell—whether substantive or methodological. You must also develop familiarity with the settings in which policy consultants work. This includes making the right choices about which conferences, workshops, and public meetings to attend. Networking is critically important.

If you were an aspiring academic researcher, new to a faculty position, you would be well advised to meet with your department head, senior colleagues, IRB staff, research office staff, and the like. You would ask for advice and guidance, and in turn, expect that they would keep you in mind should opportunities arise. Do the same thing to become a policy consultant. Identify people with consultant expertise or with policy responsibilities. Meet with them. And finally, learn the norms of the systems to which you aspire to enter. When your proposals are rejected, ask for feedback or, better yet, ask to see the winning proposals. Observe other policy consultants at work. Study their reports, Web sites, and ways of interacting with client systems. Hopefully, you will find that the work is rewarding, and the financial payoffs can be, too.

APPENDIX 14-1: Example from a Policy Report from Howe and Green (2004)

Poverty

Conclusion

Poverty rates fell across the board with the economic expansion of the 1990s, a largely successful policy experiment involving welfare reform and reductions in teenage pregnancy. Poverty rates outside the city of Cincinnati were 5.5% in the Hamilton County suburbs and 7.8% in the surrounding counties. The city's poverty rate of 21.9% is more than double the CMSA rate.

Findings
  · Between 1990 and 2000, the number of people in poverty and the poverty rate fell for the population as a whole, for children, for working age adults, and for persons ages 65 and over in the CMSA as a whole, in Hamilton County as a whole, and in the city of Cincinnati (Table 14).
  · The number of people in poverty and the poverty rate were essentially unchanged in the Hamilton County suburbs, except for a small downtick in poverty for persons 65 and older (Table 14).
  · Poverty rates fell overall and for all age groups in the 12 counties surrounding Hamilton County, as did absolute numbers of people in poverty, except for a small increase in the number of working-age persons in poverty (Table 14).
  · Married-couple families in the CMSA had a poverty rate of 2.6% in 2000, compared to rates of 10.3% for male-headed families and 25.0% for female-headed families (Table 15).
  · With respect to each type of family, African Americans have higher rates of poverty than whites do. Thus, while the higher incidence of female-headed families in the African-American community goes some way in explaining the higher incidence of African-American poverty, it does not account entirely for the black-white difference in poverty. In Hamilton County in 2000, the poverty rate for African Americans was 23.2% and the poverty rate for whites was 6.4%.
  · The central city poverty rate in Cincinnati of 21.9% is high, but among nearby large metropolitan areas, it is better than the rates in Cleveland and Dayton, and essentially the same as the rate in Louisville (Table 16).

The U.S. Census Bureau defines poverty based on family income, adjusted for the number of family members, the number of related children, and the number of persons age 65 and over. Poverty is also determined for single person households and for non-relatives living with families. The poverty thresholds are updated annually for inflation. Based on the poverty thresholds for 2003, an individual living alone is in poverty if his or her income was less than $9,573. A married couple with two children was in poverty with an income of less than $18,660. A single mother with one child was in poverty with an income of less than $12,682.

Implications

In later sections of this report, we will define a concentration to exist when a geographic area has at least twice the percentage of a subpopulation as the region as a whole. By this standard, the entire city of Cincinnati represents a poverty concentration.

There are four broad approaches to poverty reduction. One approach is to reduce it through regional economic development (an expanding economy creates job opportunities). A second approach is to reduce it through community development (a vibrant community creates incentives for individuals to move toward self-sufficiency). A third approach is to deconcentrate poverty (separating individuals from the deleterious effects of pervasive poverty). A fourth approach is to promote individual and family development (teenage pregnancy reduction, education, parenting and employment services).

In other words, to reduce its concentration of poverty, the city of Cincinnati has to work to ensure that the regional economy will generate more low-wage jobs in accessible locations, or better coordinate community development investments that target poverty, or promote low-income housing outside of the city, or improve the delivery of advancement opportunities to its citizens, or some combination of these.

Source: Adapted from Howe, S.R. & Green, E. (2004). *Impediments to fair housing choice in Hamilton County, OH.* Steven R. Howe and Associates, LLC.

Chapter 15

Grant Writing for Consultants 101

Andrea Solarz

INTRODUCTION

I never planned to become a grant writer, and in many respects, I am an unlikely grant writer. Although trained in research (with a doctorate in community psychology), I am not based in a university setting, and I have not conducted research since graduate school (beyond a survey here or there). Nor do I have any direct experience working in community-based organizations. Nonetheless, grant writing has become my most important "bread and butter" skill as a consultant, and the great majority (I estimate over 80%) of the proposals I've written have been funded.

My first foray into grant writing was by happenstance—a colleague at an organization where I had previously been employed asked if I might have time to help him with writing a grant proposal. Although I didn't realize it at the time, our successful collaboration convinced me that I did not want to go back to a traditional job, and that I had marketable skills that would allow me to make a living as a consultant. Since that time, I've written more than 20 funding proposals. It's an activity that I have come to enjoy, both because it taps into a nice combination of my skill sets (e.g., my science writing skills, analytical skills, and project development skills), and because of the exhilaration—some might call it terror—that inevitably comes in those last hours before the final proposal has to be submitted to the funding agency.

In this chapter, I will discuss my approach to proposal writing, as well as some of the knowledge, skills, and experiences that are useful for being a successful grant proposal writer. These comments, of course, reflect my own experiences, which have been almost exclusively with national organizations. Although much of what I say can be generalized to working with smaller community-based organizations, national organizations tend to have access to more resources (including national networks of experts) than do local organizations, a factor that can increase their competitiveness for funding (of course, they are also more likely to be competing against other more resource-rich entities, which elevates the bar for their proposals being rated highly). I also note that this chapter will not address the technical aspects of writing a grant proposal (e.g., how to write goals and objectives, how to write an evaluation plan). There are plenty of resources out there that provide this information (some of which are listed in Appendix 15-1), and I encourage the reader to explore them.

THE PROCESS OF WRITING A GRANT PROPOSAL

There are many different ways to approach the grant writing process, but I would like to frame this discussion by briefly describing the process that I typically go through when I undertake writing a grant proposal. Of course, the process varies somewhat depending on the type of project, the funder (e.g., foundation or federal grant), the circumstances (e.g., time lines), and the personal characteristics of the client. However, there are certain steps and activities that I have found to be especially important.

Getting the Job

It goes without saying that you won't be writing any grant proposals as a consultant if you don't have a client who wants to hire you! My clients tell me that they feel much more comfortable engaging a known quantity for this important job; in other words, relationships matter. You will be much more likely to land grant writing jobs if you have a well-developed network of colleagues—also known as "potential clients"—who are knowledgeable about your skills, and see you as a good collaborator (this network need not be large, but it should include individuals in organizations who are either responsible for managing programs that are supported by outside funding, or who have the ability to identify and contract with outside grant writers). One of my clients, a director of a national organization, noted to me recently that in his previous experience with grant writers, he had found himself doing (or redoing) most of the work himself because the writer did not have strong writing skills, or was simply unable to understand the important concepts of the proposal. These kinds of grant writers are not likely to get repeat business.

I have been lucky in that I have generally been able to rely on having clients contact me with offers of work, and have not had to go out and actively market myself as a grant writer. In order to achieve this enviable status, "all" I've had to do is spend over 10 years working in policy settings in Washington, DC, developing my skills and nurturing a professional network of key colleagues who respect my skills and who feel that they can call upon me to work with them on grant writing projects. Then, over the last 10 years as a consultant, I further developed and strengthened those networks. Especially now that I have a proven track record as a proposal writer, colleagues come to me when they need my services. But, it took years to develop a reputation as someone on whom they can rely to produce good work. That isn't to say that you have to spend 20 years in the wings before you can be a successful grant writer, but you will be much more in demand if you have a demonstrated set of skills that people actually know about (e.g., because they have worked with you before, or because someone they trust has referred them to you).

Finalizing the Contract

My least favorite part of the process is setting up a work contract with a client, but as this is essential to getting paid, it is a necessary evil! And, of course, the contract protects *both* me and the client, so it is to the advantage of both to have a proper contract in place. Ideally, the contract is developed and signed before work begins. However, the pressing time line of some work projects demands that work begin even before both parties have signed the contract. There is a real risk in doing this, in that work arrangements can potentially fall through at any point, but to date I have not experienced problems (this is likely in part because I work primarily for national organizations that have more than sufficient resources for supporting my services, and that also have internal checks and balances that require project approval before I am brought onboard). Once I have established an ongoing relationship with a client, and there is a history of prompt payment, I am also more willing to proceed with work before the final contract is signed.

Sometimes the client organization has a standard contract format that they use, in which case they draft the contract; otherwise I can draft the contract or let the client know what elements need to be included in the contract that they draft. The contract typically includes a statement of work that specifies the rate of pay (whether an hourly rate or a lump sum), the total payment of the contract, and the payment schedule; the deliverables (e.g., products to be produced and services to be rendered); the time line;

and how the contract can be terminated by either party. There may also be a statement regarding authorship (i.e., whether the contractor's name will appear as an author on any products that directly result from work on the project), as well as ownership rights (as these projects are "works for hire," the client typically retains ownership of the products).

Determining how much to charge for writing a grant proposal depends on a variety of factors, such as the client's resources, the types of tasks involved in the project, and whether the project is long term or short term. For example, if I believe that a project is worthwhile, and that the mission of the client is an important one, I will usually work with whatever limited resources the organization has, even if the rate of pay is lower than what I usually charge. I will also charge a reduced rate for ongoing projects that assure me continued income for a period of time (grant proposals are, however, typically short-term projects, so would rarely receive this "discount"). Otherwise, I stick to my standard hourly rate that I charge, which is based on my experience and market factors.

Payment terms may be by the hour, a daily rate, or lump sum (i.e., the total amount to be paid for the project is set in advance, no matter how many hours it eventually takes to complete the project, whether more or fewer than originally estimated). If the project is more open-ended or it is difficult to determine the number of hours that will be needed to complete it, then I prefer to be paid by the hour instead of a lump sum to ensure that my time is fully compensated. For some projects, though, I prefer a lump sum payment simply because it relieves me of the burden of meticulously tracking and accounting for all of the time that I spend on the project. As I have gained more experience writing grant proposals, I have become better at estimating in advance the level of work required to complete the project, and thus, am better able to set a fair lump sum amount.

Whichever method of payment is used, if the scope of work extends beyond the original agreement (e.g., I am asked to do additional background research, or to write additional sections of the grant proposal), I will discuss the need for additional payment with the client. I have never stopped a job in the middle because the budget has run out, but I will keep the client apprised of the rate at which resources are being used, and either get assurances regarding additional payment for additional work, or renegotiate the level of work expected to maximize the use of the remaining resources.

Mapping Out the Idea

Once I have been engaged to write a grant proposal, I meet with the client (usually in person) to learn more about the project they are proposing. In some cases, they have already spent a significant amount of time articulating the project, and have a clear idea of what they want to do. More commonly, they have a general idea of the project that they want to do, but have not yet thought through the details. My preference is to become involved in the project early on so I can have input into the development of the idea. One reason for this is simply because I enjoy the process, but more importantly, it allows me to provide critical input by identifying strengths and weaknesses, as well as gaps in thinking. I have found that proposals where I am brought into the process later do not fare as well as those where I am brought in at an earlier stage, and can help the client more clearly articulate their goals, objectives, and project activities.

No matter where the client is in their development of the project, we engage in an ongoing process of thinking through the project in detail, including clarifying the goals. As we continue to work on the proposal, more and more details get filled in, with ideas sometimes being proposed and then rejected until we are satisfied that we have a well-articulated and viable plan that accomplishes the goals of the project. Sometimes mapping out the idea involves just me and the client, but in other cases, outside experts (e.g., university-based researchers with expertise in the project area) are also brought in to review the ideas critically, and contribute their own. In any case, no good proposal is developed without getting the input of others—whether from me, other colleagues at the client's workplace, or outside experts.

Understanding What the Funder Wants

Another important early step is to carefully review the guidance from the funder to determine what information they want to see in the proposal, and to be clear about practical matters such as how the document should be formatted and how long each section can be. If we are going to submit the proposal online, there may be additional procedures that have to be followed. Depending on who the funder is (e.g., a foundation or a federal funder), they may want something as simple as a three-page prospectus, or as complex as a highly detailed (and lengthy) proposal that articulates the project's theoretical rationale, its goals and objectives, all of the project activities, time lines, evaluation plan, measurement tools, and more. The more detailed and complex the call for proposals, the more important it is to carefully read it to make sure that we address all of the items in the grant proposal. Thus, an important early step is to create an outline of the proposal that reflects the guidance from the funder, including any reference to rating factors. This is not a time to be creative; we want to make it easy for the reviewers to see that we have addressed all of the items in the guidance. The penalty for not following directions can be severe, even preventing your proposal from entering the review process.

Although carefully reviewing the guidance is critical for understanding what the funder wants, it is also important to have a general understanding of the funder's mission, its history, and any contextual political issues that might affect what types of projects are funded, and even what kind of language one should use to describe projects to increase the likelihood that they will be funded. Awareness of some of these issues is something that you may be able to pick up after working in a particular area for years, but it's also important to get your client's take on them (your client will likely be more knowledgeable about these factors since they are immersed in them on a day-to-day basis). The project officer responsible for the call for proposals is also potentially a source of information, as are your colleagues who may work in the same or similar areas.

Writing the Proposal

At some point during this process, the actual writing begins (usually once there is some clarity about the goals and activities of the project). Based on the guidance provided by the funder, my client and I decide who will be responsible for writing which sections. At a minimum, I am usually responsible for writing the project narrative (e.g., describing the project and all of its activities). I also typically develop and write the evaluation plan and develop the time line, and sometimes also draft the budget. Responsibility for assembling supporting documentation (including securing letters from potential partners, obtaining project staff vitae, etc.) usually falls to the client, as does completing any required forms.

As I write the proposal, I often draw upon my general knowledge and background to fill in details, anticipating the activities and procedures that the client will need to accomplish to meet the goals of the project (I sometimes jokingly refer to this as "making stuff up," but in fact, it's based on my broad knowledge of program development in a wide range of areas, and on previous experience writing proposals). This might include, for example, articulating the steps for recruiting participants to a project, identifying information dissemination strategies, describing the steps involved in organizing a focus group, or clarifying the types of individuals to serve on a project steering committee, and what their responsibilities should be. Writing is usually a collaborative process as the client and I exchange and review drafts, and as we work to resolve questions as they come up.

Ideally, this process begins far in advance of the deadline—as soon as the call for proposals is issued—in order to allow plenty of time for thoughtful discussions, multiple drafts, and critical review by knowledgeable colleagues before the draft is finalized and submitted. I won't say that this never happens; I will only say that it has never happened to *me*. Even in cases where initial discussions begin several months in advance of the deadline, the bulk of the work always seems to be concentrated in the final few weeks—and then the final days and hours—before the deadline (sometimes even the final night before the deadline, as my client and I forego sleep to make final revisions together, and assemble the application packet; this is not, however, a tactic that I recommend).

IMPORTANT SKILLS, QUALITIES, AND AREAS OF KNOWLEDGE FOR THE GRANT WRITER

There is no single pathway to becoming a grant writer, and no standard résumé that assures success (in fact, anyone who has written a proposal can say that he/she is a grant writer). However, there are a number of skills, qualities, and areas of knowledge that can increase one's effectiveness as a grant writer. Some of these things can be taught, but others come from years of experience, or relate to the personal characteristics of the grant writer.

Start With a Good Idea

Needless to say, a bad idea (e.g., one that is not feasible with the given resources, is not likely to be acceptable to the population it is targeting, or that the client does not have the technical skills or capacity to execute) is unlikely to be funded, no matter how well crafted the grant proposal is (or how pretty the cover). On the other hand, it's very possible for a great idea to be scored poorly because the grant proposal does not articulate it well (one reason why having a skilled grant writer is so important).

Sometimes a client may have a good idea that he or she just hasn't thought through enough; in this case, it's important to be able to recognize the kernel of a promising program, and work with the client to develop it into something fundable. However, some ideas are just not yet "ready for prime time." It may be an ill-conceived idea, the client may not understand the complexities of completing the process, or they may not have the skills or resources needed to make the project successful. As a grant writer, it's important to be able to critically assess ideas, and to say "no" to the potential client if the project truly doesn't seem viable. If you see "fatal flaws" in a client's proposed ideas, articulating those in a straightforward and professional manner can both help the client see that it would not be beneficial to move forward, and help them to focus on more productive ideas.

Have a Broad Knowledge Base

Although it's not necessary to have a deep knowledge of all topics for which you might be engaged to write a grant proposal, it's important to have general substantive expertise that you can draw upon. This might include, for example, knowledge about communities, organizational systems, mental health issues, evaluation, and the like. It also includes having a strong basic understanding of scientific methods, and how programs are developed. There are many grant writers out there who are essentially technicians; they know what the parts of a proposal are and how to put a proposal together, and they are competent at doing that. However, having substantive knowledge enables you to understand the proposed project more deeply, to critically analyze its strengths and weaknesses, and to help your client shape and strengthen their project. In other words, you can become a vital partner in developing the proposal in a way that someone without that reservoir of knowledge cannot.

The grant proposals that I've written address topics as varied as violence prevention, education policy, adolescent health, HIV/AIDS-related technical assistance for community-based organizations, mentoring for early career researchers, education research, and mental health services for gay, lesbian, and bisexual adolescents in schools. Although I did not necessarily come to each of those projects with specific knowledge about the underlying issues, I had lots of general knowledge that I was able to bring to the process of writing the proposal. Sometimes I will identify and read additional background material as part of developing the rationale for a proposal, but I find that I am usually able to rely on whatever material the client provides me (e.g., research articles, previous work by the client that includes a literature review). Frankly, it is more cost effective for the client to produce this information than it is for me to generate it by doing a traditional literature review myself.

Be a Good Critical Thinker

Perhaps the skill that most contributes to my being a good grant writer is an ability to think critically (i.e., to rationally and logically review, synthesize, analyze, and evaluate information). Critical thinking skills are essential for carefully analyzing a proposed project, evaluating its strengths and weaknesses, and identifying gaps in how it is conceptualized, and how the proposed activities address the project goals. Has the client carefully thought though each step of the project, or are there gaps? Does the theoretical basis make sense? Does the proposal clearly take the reader from point A to point Z, covering needed steps in between? Can a reader who is unfamiliar with the project clearly understand what is being planned from reading the proposal? Does the proposal respond effectively to the funder's guidance? These are the kinds of questions that one must ask when crafting a strong proposal.

Be a Good Communicator

Obviously, strong writing skills are important in grant writing. One must be able to clearly and concisely convey complex information in a well-organized and logical way that is appropriate for the target audience. However, there are other communications skills that are also very important. For example, it is critical that the grant writer and client be able to communicate effectively with each other. If the client has trouble communicating their interests and plans, then the grant writer must draw upon his or her communication skills to help the client articulate the proposed project. During the process of writing the proposal, the grant writer must be clear about what the expectations are both for the client and for the writer. Sometimes this requires that the grant writer be clear and assertive about what is needed from the client (e.g., critical information, brainstorming time, supporting documents for the proposal, information about the client's resources for doing the project), while not antagonizing the collaboration. At times, the grant writer must also work with a variety of project partners and collaborators in the process of developing the proposal. This can require an ability to interact comfortably with individuals from a variety of backgrounds (e.g., community agency representatives, federal officials, scientific experts).

Be a Good Collaborator

Writing a grant proposal is a collaboration between the client and the writer. When I work with a client to write a proposal, I consider us to be members of the same team who are focused on a common goal. Although it is certainly possible for a grant writer to craft a proposal after reviewing a stack of resources provided by a client, this is not how I like to work, and it is not an effective strategy for developing the strongest proposal. Writing a proposal is an ongoing process of give and take; both the grant writer and the client must rely on each other to do their part. Being a good collaborator involves being honest about the project and what is needed to make it successful, maintaining open lines of communication, and following through on what has been promised.

Stay Calm

Writing a grant proposal can be an intense, sometimes frantic process. It is not for the faint of heart. Even with the most careful planning, it is not unusual for the last days before the proposal is due to be fraught with anxious moments and short-term crises. If you are easily rattled or have a difficult time handling stress, grant writing is not a good match for you. Being able to see an anxious client through the process without getting overwhelmed can make the difference between a proposal that is "almost" ready to send in at deadline, and one that is truly ready to go. More than once, I have found myself spending an "all-nighter" with my client, making last minute changes to finalize a proposal; at these high-stress times, it is essential to be able to focus clearly and calmly on any critical issues so they can quickly be resolved satisfactorily before the proposal is submitted (e.g., assuring that the internal logic of the proposal is consistent, that the proposal addresses all of the requirements in the call for applications, that it meets the formatting requirements, that all submission forms have been completed).

CONCLUDING THOUGHTS

As a consultant, I very much enjoy collaborating with a client to write a grant proposal. I especially value the creative process of helping the client think through ideas and articulate them so they can be communicated clearly to a potential funder. Not only does this give me the pleasure of seeing the project ideas emerge, it provides me with an opportunity to tap into both technical and cognitive skills that I enjoy using, and to expand my knowledge base into new substantive areas. If I've done my job especially well, there is also the great satisfaction that comes in learning that a proposal I've worked on has been funded, and that my contributions have made a difference in helping to bring an important project to life.

APPENDIX 15-1: Resources for Grant Writing

The following resources provide a starting place for picking up strategies for writing grant proposals. These represent just the tip of the iceberg; many additional resources (some better than others) can easily be found on the Internet.

The Community Toolbox

The Community Toolbox (http://ctb.ku.edu/en/) was developed as a free resource to help build the capacities of community leaders to bring about change to improve their communities. The toolbox includes a very helpful section on writing a proposal for funding, as well as links to other useful sites. It also includes resources that are useful for grant writing, such as information on evaluation and on developing programs.

The Foundation Center

The Foundation Center (http://foundationcenter.org/) provides a wealth of information about the foundation world. In addition to an extensive database of foundations and their funding interests that can be accessed through their Web site for a modest fee, the Foundation Center holds classes around the country on proposal writing and publishes useful written resources.

Federal Resources

There is extensive information online about negotiating the complexities of writing federal grant proposals. The National Institutes of Health (NIH) Office of Extramural Research maintains a Web site (http://grants.nih.gov/grants/oer.htm) with a vast amount of information on applying for NIH grants; a good place to start is the section on writing a grant application. Another helpful resource for writing proposals to the NIH, *All About Grants Tutorials*, can be found on the Web site of the National Institute of Allergy and Infectious Diseases (http://www.niaid.nih.gov/ncn/grants/).

Project Officers

The project officers, who are listed on calls for proposals, can be very helpful resources. Although they cannot explicitly tell you how to write your proposal (or give you information that gives you an advantage over other submitters), they can help you better understand the guidance, and also help you decide if your proposed project fits under the funding announcement, or if it might be more appropriate to submit under another funding mechanism.

Your Colleagues

A very helpful tool for learning how to write a strong proposal is simply seeing good examples of funded proposals. There are some examples of these online, of course, but your colleagues can also be good resources for this information. One can learn a lot by talking with successful grant writers about what has worked best for them.

Chapter 16

The Path to Independent Consulting

Dawn Hanson Smart

My first steps on the path to consulting were in graduate school, where like many students, I took on small contracts. A literature review. Library research. Analysis of a survey. Thesis editing. Some of the work came from other students. Some from professors. Some from nonprofit organizations I'd worked with in the past. I had a fairly strong experiential background already, so felt fairly confident in taking on the work by myself. I had worked in direct service with individuals and families, created resource guides, developed training curricula, facilitated workshops and support groups, and managed the data tracking and reporting for a nonprofit organization. Each of these tasks provided experience that I could use on the consulting projects. I also was efficient, able to provide quick turnaround, and with no overhead to speak of, able to minimize the cost for clients. This was a plus, bringing clients back for subsequent projects. I never took on more than one or two small projects and found I liked the diversity of tasks and topics that this provided.

The consulting work also dovetailed nicely with my graduate studies, which included coursework in planning, program evaluation, research, and statistical analysis. I often would use consulting projects as examples in class discussion or in the papers I wrote. I graduated from the University of Washington with a masters in science in health education. Although I've never pursued a career as a health educator, the background provided an excellent foundation in planning, research, and evaluation. I also received a minor in business administration, which served me well in terms of managing the business-side of my consulting practice.

When I went to work as assistant director for a small nonprofit after graduating, I had less time for these kinds of projects and there were fewer opportunities given my move to another community. In time, however, relationships with individuals and organizations through my work at a United Way in the Midwest and some of my volunteer work generated the occasional small project. Again, they were short-term contracts usually lasting no more than a month, such as facilitating a staff or board retreat, conducting focus groups, and writing a nonprofit's annual report. Although offers for more involved and longer-term projects occasionally came my way, I found it difficult to manage them while holding a full-time job. I stuck with contracts I could handle in a few evenings or on a weekend.

Not only did the work bring in additional income, but it expanded my skill set, giving me the confidence to take on tasks with which I was less familiar. This required some "just in time learning" on occasion, but I found I liked the challenge and enjoyed the ongoing education the projects provided. For example, one project required client observation, which I'd not done before. Another project entailed a two-day retreat, which meant planning for and facilitating a more varied set of group activities than I had previously used. The work also cemented my decision about a planning and evaluation career and confirmed my sense that I was not destined for management or supervisory positions, preferring hands-on work with clients.

A move back West gave me my first chance to try independent consulting. I made arrangements to bring a couple of projects along with me, synthesizing a few boxes of data into a coherent community needs assessment and designing a grantee evaluation approach for my previous employer. Although the content of the work was satisfying, I discovered that toiling alone in my tiny home office (spare bedroom) was lonely and limiting, not just because there was no one to talk to, but because there were no colleagues to bounce ideas around or puzzle through a knotty problem. More difficult still was finding new clients in a new community.

It quickly became clear that it would take considerable time to build a sustainable practice, and it would take more time than I had savings. So, back to a full-time planning and evaluation job I went. Having a resume with both employment and consulting experience likely helped me land a job in local government. According to my new employer, the breadth of my experience and the variety of skills gained from consulting gave me a competitive edge over other candidates for the position. It proved to be a fantastic opportunity—mentally stimulating and hugely challenging. Our office was a focal point of human services policy and planning for the region. The level of effort this job required, however, left no time or energy for outside consulting work. It would be another five years before I re-entered that world. But the contacts I made in this position served me well when I went back to consulting.

Another change to a new employer gave me the chance to take the next steps on the consulting path. Although the new position was full time, it did not require the overtime or level of effort the previous one had demanded. I again had the time, and the mental energy, to take on consulting projects. The contacts I'd made provided the work. I created a marketing packet, basically a nice-looking letter and list of past projects, to let people know I was available, provide examples of the types of projects I had worked on, and give them a description of the tasks I could help them with. I sent it to individuals I had worked with and soon had a number of contracts, small pieces of work but enough to keep me busy. But it was back to that sense of isolation when working solo on projects. It became clearer than ever that "independent" consulting was not where I wanted to be or to go in the future. That, and the fact that a good friend had started her own consulting firm.

So for a few years, I took on one project at a time with my friend, allowing me to balance consulting with a full-time job. As the firm began to count on my knowledge and experience, however, I found myself overbooked and overworked. Some of the new projects also involved travel out of state, requiring time off from my job and some negotiation with my employer. In the end, my employer and I agreed that I could move to a three-quarter–time position, allowing me to maintain the safety net of a salaried position and full benefits while taking on more consulting work. Over the next few years, this shifted to half-time employment and half-time consulting. There were times when I worked many hours a week to handle this combination, and occasionally, the balance between the job and the consulting was out of whack. It seemed to even out over the course of any given year, so neither my employer nor my friend was displeased, and mostly, this period was fun and generally manageable.

I pondered the possibility of working full time for my friend's firm, but had the perception that a consulting business was an uncertain enterprise. As I was the primary wage-earner in my family at this point, that raised anxieties. I also was cautious about working full time with her, not wanting to jeopardize our friendship in any way. Over time, and through conversations with my friend, both of these concerns disappeared. The fact that the firm had been in business for 18 years, making a profit for most of those years, was important, and my friend reassured me that we could maintain the friendship as well as do business together. It was an economic downturn, however, that precipitated my eventual move to a full-time consulting position. My employer was facing major budget cutbacks and almost half of my 18-person unit was on the layoff list. Making the move was easier for me than for many of my peers who did not have a ready-made path to follow. I had built enough credibility and enough of my own client base to make the transition into the consulting firm a smooth one.

It's been six years since I joined Clegg & Associates. Six fun, prosperous, interesting years, for me and for the firm. We work in health, housing, and human services with nonprofit organizations and their funders. That's where our hearts are—we feel we're contributing to the communities we work with, making a difference in people's lives. I think my circuitous path in independent consulting gives me something unique to offer my clients. My work for different nonprofits, government, and philanthropic organizations gives me a multifaceted perspective—I've been on different sides of the table and understand the agendas, issues, and constraints each group faces. The work was generally the same in these organizations, but the context and culture varied. Working for government can give you a sense of the big picture and what drives public sector planning and policy decisions, the choices they're faced with, and the trade-offs and compromises they make. Working in the philanthropic world lets you see another approach to planning and decision making, with different philosophical underpinnings and criteria for allocations and project selection. The cultures and value systems across philanthropic organizations are as varied as can be imagined, but all of them strive to fulfill a vision for some greater good. It is this vision that often keeps staff and volunteers engaged and invested in the effort. Working for nonprofits is also about following a vision, but nonprofit work provides a clearer understanding of the realities of the community and the organization's clients. It also helps you see what it takes to pull together a program, staff it, implement it, troubleshoot and problem solve, and keep the program on budget. Each of these environments gave me a different perspective on the health and human service field, serving me well as a consultant who works in all of these venues.

Looking back I see a number of lessons along my path into consulting. The first is knowing yourself and the type of work for which you're best suited. My initial sense that the diversity of tasks and topics I would encounter in consulting would be a good fit with my nature was wholly on target. The choice about what to pursue and what to avoid almost always exists. My generally short attention span and my efficient work style make me a good candidate for multiple, short-term projects rather than long term ones. My early recognition that working alone was not the best venue also helped me seek a situation that gave me the collegiality I wanted and needed. I came to appreciate the benefits of working in a small firm rather than a larger setting. There are five staff in our firm and we generally have between 15 to 20 projects of varying sizes at any one time. In this kind of firm you perform a variety of functions as it is often the case that "all hands are needed" when we take on large projects. I enjoy that aspect of the work. The small staff size also means there must be real teamwork, something we value and pay close attention to. We need people who can design a project approach, do research, facilitate small group discussions, organize information, and write clearly and succinctly. But mostly we seek people who can work well with others. A small consulting office cannot function without this. The teamwork and versatility required also make a small firm the kind of place where people can grow professionally. We're always looking for opportunities that allow less experienced staff to take on additional responsibilities with coaching from a more senior member of the team.

A second lesson is the importance of a firm sense of ethics and an awareness of potential problems that may arise if a person is employed and doing consulting "on the side." When are conflicts of interest an issue if a consulting project comes to you through contacts made through your place of employment? What are the rules and the boundaries related to bringing a consulting task into the office, like taking a client phone call or sending or receiving a fax or email? How do you negotiate when project deadlines conflict with work requirements? I faced all of these, and fortunately, had a good internal compass as well as reasonable and patient employers and wise colleagues to guide me. In some of the places I was employed, personnel handbooks laid out policies or regulations to address my questions about these kinds of issues, but that was not always the case. Talking with my supervisors and colleagues, however, gave me the confidence that I was handling the situation appropriately.

A third lesson is recognizing when things aren't working. This is particularly important when you are trying to balance employment and consulting. Being clear about my limitations when deciding what projects to take on and which I should avoid because of their size, travel requirements, or short deadlines helped me manage, but that lesson was learned only after some stressful mistakes. There were times when I was overwhelmed and not doing as good a job as I should have in either my consulting or my employed position. My tendency to put down my head and slog through it did not always work. Asking for help, negotiating an extension, and finding ways to be kind to myself did.

The last lesson is to take a risk when you can. With the freedom of consulting work comes some uncertainty. There are times when you can live with that uncertainty and times when it feels too scary for any number of reasons. Acknowledging the reality of your situation will make it easier to distinguish between the two. My reality meant I needed to ease into full-time consulting rather than jump in at the beginning. But now, I can't imagine any other life.

References

American Marketing Association (2008). *Definition of marketing*. Retrieved May 20, 2008, from http://www.marketingpower.com/AboutAMA/Pages/DefinitionofMarketing.aspx

Argyris, C., & Schon, D. A. (1996). *Organizational learning*. Reading, MA: Addison-Wesley.

Barrow, C., Barrow, P., & Brown, R. (2008). *The business plan workbook: The definitive guide to researching, writing up and presenting a winning plan* (6th ed.). London: Kogan Page Ltd.

Bassi, L. J., & Van Buren, M. E. (1998). The 1998 ASTD State of the Industry Report. *Training and Development, 52,* 21–43.

Bellman, G. M. (1990). *The consultant's calling: Bringing who you are to what you do*. San Francisco: Jossey-Bass Publishers.

Bermont, H. (1997). *How to become a successful consultant in your own field* (3rd ed.). Roseville, CA: Prima Publishing.

Biech, E. (1998). *The business of consulting: The basics and beyond*. San Francisco: Jossey-Bass Publishers.

Biech, E. (2001). *The consultant's quick start guide: An action plan for your first year in business*. San Francisco: Jossey-Bass Publishers.

Block, P. (2000). *Flawless consulting* (2nd ed.). San Francisco: Jossey-Bass Publishers.

Catalano, R. F., Berglund, M. L., Ryan, J. A. M., Lonczak, H. S., & Hawkins, J. D. (1999). *Positive youth development in the United States. Research findings on evaluations of the positive youth development programs*. Retrieved November 21, 2002, from http://aspe.hhs.gov/hsp/PositiveYouthDev99/index.htm

Confessore, S. J., & Kops, W. J. (1998). Self-directed learning and the learning organization: Examining the connection between the individual and the learning environment. *Human Resource Development Quarterly, 9*, 365–375.

Connolly, P. M. (2005). *Navigating the organizational lifecycle.* Washington, DC: BoardSource.

Connolly, P. M. & York, P. J. (2002). Evaluating capacity-building efforts for nonprofit organizations. *OD Practitioner, 34*, 33–39.

Cutcher-Gersenfeld, J., & Ford, J. K. (2005). *Valuable disconnects in organizational learning systems.* New York: Oxford University Press.

Dyche, J. (2001). *The CRM Handbook: A Business Guide to Customer Relationship Management.* London: Addison-Wesley.

Edwards, S., & Edwards, P. (1996). *Secrets of self-employment: Surviving and thriving on the ups and downs of being your own boss.* New York: Penguin Putnum, Inc.

Elias, S., & Stim, R. (2007). *Trademark: Legal care for your business and product name* (8th ed.). Berkeley, CA: Nolo.

Epstein, J. L. (1994). From theory to practice: School and family partnerships lead to school improvement and student success. In C. Fagnano & B. Werber (Eds). *School, Family, and Community Interactions: A View from the Firing Lines.* Boulder, CO: Westview Press.

Forrester, R., & Drexler, A. (1999). A model of team based organization performance. *Academy of Management Executive, 13*, 36–50.

Foster-Fishman, P. G., & Keys, C. B. (1997). The person/environment dynamics of employee empowerment: An organizational culture analysis. *American Journal of Community Psychology, 25*(3), 345–370.

Freeland, J. G. (2002). *The ultimate CRM handbook: Strategies and concepts for building enduring customer loyalty and profitability.* New York: McGraw Hill.

Goldstein, I. L., & Ford, J. K. (2002). *Training in organizations: Needs assessment, development, and evaluation* (4th ed.). Belmont, CA: Wadsworth Group.

Greenbaum, T. L. (1990). *The consultant's manual: A complete guide to building a successful consulting practice.* New York: John Wiley & Sons, Inc.

Holman, P., & Devane, T. (1999). *The change handbook: Group methods for shaping the future.* San Francisco, CA: Burrett-Koehler Publishers.

Howe, S. R., & Green, E. (2004). Impediments to fair housing choice in Hamilton County, OH. Steven R. Howe and Associates, LLC.

International Institute for Sustainable Development (2008). *Participatory research for sustainable livelihoods: A guide for field projects on adaptive strate-*

gies. Retrieved July 17, 2008, from http://www.iisd.org/casl/caslguide/participatoryapproach.htm

Institute for Cultural Affairs (2007). *Technology in participation.* Retrieved December 20, 2007, from http://www.ica-usa.org

Kapp, K. M. (1999). Transforming your manufacturing organization into a learning organization. *Hospital Material Management Quarterly, 20,* 46–54.

Kishel, G. F., & Kishel, P. G. (1996). *How to start and run a successful consulting business.* New York: John Wiley & Sons, Inc.

Laurence, B. K. (2007). *Form a nonprofit.* Retrieved June 13, 2007, from: http://nolo.com/siteIncludes/printerfriendly.cfm/objectID/D47E4 D16-DE98-4DFD-835B4046E181EFD2/catID/CE94A6B3-EFB6-40 36-8498D5414328FD73/111/262/CHK/

Laurence, B. K. (2007). *Forming an LLC in Illinois.* Retrieved June 20, 2008, from: http://nolo.com/article.cfm/ObjectID/CE86696A-84 E6-4B5F-AC3B3B967996B4D1/catID/BAAE1B67-F54A-41 B4-91943A51F56C3F79/111/182/245/ART/

Lewin, K. (1958). *Group decision and social change.* New York: Holt, Rinehart and Winston.

Light, P. C. (2004). *Sustaining nonprofit performance.* Washington, DC: Brookings Institute.

Loza, J. (2004). Business-community partnerships: The case for community organization capacity building. *Journal of Business Ethics, 53,* 297–311.

Lukas, C. A. (1998). *Consulting with nonprofits: A practitioner's guide—The art, craft, and business of helping nonprofit organizations and community groups get the results they want.* St. Paul, MN: Amherst H. Wilder Foundation.

Mancuso, A. (2008). *Form a New York LLC.* Retrieved July 20, 2008, from: http://nolo.com/article.cfm/ObjectID/E83DE9A2-1A2E-47D5-9D3E FBE7983BD0C8/catID/BAAE1B67-F54A-41B4-91943A5 1F56C3F79/111/182/245/ART/

Miller, R. L., & Shinn, M. (2005). Learning from communities: Overcoming difficulties in dissemination of prevention and promotion efforts. *American Journal of Community Psychology, 35*(3/4), 169–183.

Morris, M. W., Leung, K., Ames, D., & Lickel, B. (1999). Views from inside and outside: Integrating emic and etic insights about culture and justice judgment. *The Academy of Management Review, 2*(4), 781–797.

Nelson, S. D. (2007). The contrasting cultures of science and policy-making. *AAAS Leadership Seminar in Science and Technology Policy,* Washington, DC.

Newman, K. (1999). *No shame in my game: The working poor in the inner city.* Russell Sage.

Nonaka, I., & Takeuchi, H. (1995). *The knowledge creating company.* Oxford: Oxford University Press.

North Central Regional Educational Laboratory (1996). *Critical issue: Creating the school climate and structures to support parent and family involvement.* Retrieved November 21, 2002, from http://www.ncrel.org/sdrs/areas/issues/envrnmnt/famncomm/

Patton, M. Q. (2008). *Utilization-focused evaluation* (4th ed.). Thousand Oaks, CA: Sage Publications.

Patton, M. Q. (2001). *Qualitative research and evaluation methods* (3rd ed.). Thousand Oaks, CA: Sage Publications.

Rousseau, D. M. (1997). Organizational behavior in the new organizational era. *Annual Review of Psychology, 48,* 515–546.

Scales, P. C. (2002). Ask a researcher: Are developmental assets related to school success? *Assets Magazine.* Retrieved November 21, 2002, from http://www.search-institute.org/assetmag/autumn02/askresearcher.html

Schein, E. (1988), *Process consultation, vol. 1: Its role in organizational development.* Reading MA: Addison-Wesley.

Schon, D. A. (1983). *The reflective practitioner: How professionals think in action.* New York: Basic Books.

Senge, P. M. (2006). *The fifth discipline* (2nd ed.). New York: Doubleday.

Staggs S., & Shewe, P. (October, 2004). *Laying the groundwork for successful consulting collaborations.* Symposium presented at the Annual Midwest Ecological Community Psychology Conference, Saugatuck, Michigan.

Swan, J., & Scarbrough, H. (2001). Knowledge management: Concepts and controversies. *Journal of Management Studies, 38*(7), 913–921.

Tannenbaum, S. I. (1997). Enhancing continuous learning: Diagnostic findings from multiple companies. *Human Resource Management, 36,* 437–452.

Torbert, W. R., & Cook-Greuter, S. R. (2004). *Action inquiry: The secret of timely and transforming leadership.* San Francisco: Berret Koehler Publishers, Inc.

Wasco, M., & Faraj, S. (2000). "If what one does": Why people participate and help others in electronic communities of practice. *Journal of Strategic Information Systems, 9,* 155–173.

Weick, K. E. (1984). Small wins: Redefining the scale of social problems. *American Psychologist, 39,* 40–49.

Weiss, A. (2004). *Getting started in consulting* (2nd ed.). Hoboken, NJ: John Wiley & Sons.

Weltman, B. (2000). *The complete idiot's guide to starting a home-based business* (2nd ed.). Indianapolis, IN: Alpha Books.

Wenger, E. (1998). *Communities of practice: Learning, meaning and identity.* Cambridge, UK, New York: Cambridge University Press.

Wenger, E. (1998). Communities of practice: Learning as a social system. *The Systems Thinker, 9*(5).

Wenger, E., McDermott, R., & Snyder, W. (2002). *Cultivating communities of practice: A guide to managing knowledge.* Boston: Harvard Business School Press.

West, S. L., & O'Neal, K. K. (2004). Project DARE outcome effectiveness revisited. *American Journal of Public Health, 94*(6), 1027–1029.

White House Faith-Based and Community Initiatives. (2006). *Guidance to faith-based and community organizations on partnering with the federal government.* Retrieved October 20, 2006, from http://www.whitehouse.gov/government/fbci/guidance_document_01-06.pdf

Index